The Generation of Rage in Kashmir

The Generation of Rage in Kashmir

DAVID DEVADAS

OXFORD
UNIVERSITY PRESS

OXFORD
UNIVERSITY PRESS

Oxford University Press is a department of the University of Oxford.
It furthers the University's objective of excellence in research, scholarship,
and education by publishing worldwide. Oxford is a registered trademark of
Oxford University Press in the UK and in certain other countries.

Published in India by
Oxford University Press
2/11 Ground Floor, Ansari Road, Daryaganj, New Delhi 110 002, India

ISBN-13 (print edition): 978-0-19-947799-9
ISBN-10 (print edition): 0-19-947799-X

ISBN-13 (eBook): 978-0-19-909578-0
ISBN-10 (eBook): 0-19-909578-7

Typeset in Arno Pro 10.5/15
by Tranistics Data Technologies, New Delhi 110 044
Printed in India by Replika Press Pvt. Ltd

This book is dedicated to the ideals of Mahatma Gandhi, and the hope that truth shall prevail. *Satyameva Jayate!*

Contents

Acknowledgements   ix
Introduction   xiii

1. Endings and Beginnings   1
2. Mass Rage   20
3. Caged Childhood   38
4. Varied Opinions   59
5. Radical Shift   78
6. Disillusionment with Politics   95
7. Law Subverted   113
8. Conflict Economy   137
9. Smoke and Mirrors   160
10. Hateful Polarization   179
11. Misplaced Responses   200

Index   217
About the Author   225

Acknowledgements

This book was enabled by all the students, principals, and teachers of the various colleges and schools across the Valley who shared their time, experiences, and insights with me and my fellow researchers. These included, among others, the Government Degree College in Uri, Government Degree College in Baramulla, Government Degree College in Kupwara, Government College for Women in Baramulla, Government Degree College in Bemina, Islamia College of Science and Commerce in Srinagar, Government College for Women in Nawakadal, Srinagar's Amar Singh College, Srinagar's Gandhi Memorial College, Government Degree College in Beerwah, Government Degree College and the Government Women's Degree College in Anantnag, Government Degree College and the Government Degree College for Women in Pulwama, Degree College in Shopian, Baramulla Public School, Hanfiya High School Islamiya in Baramulla, Baramulla's Saint Joseph's School, Government Higher Secondary School in Safapora, MPML Higher Secondary School in Srinagar, SSM School Paraypora in Srinagar, Chinar Valley School in Srinagar, Nawakadal Higher Secondary School in Srinagar, the Hista High School Anantnag, the Government Degree College for Boys, Anantnag, Merryland Educational Institute in Newa, Dolphin School Pulwama, Good Shephard School in Pulwama, the Islamiya Hanfiya Institute in Anantnag, Army Goodwill School in Aishmuqam, Army Goodwill School in Shopian, and the Sarfaraz B.Ed. College in Hyderpora.

I am grateful to Mr N.N. Vohra, the Governor of Jammu and Kashmir, for chairing the lecture I gave at Nehru Memorial Museum and Library (NMML) on 5 March 2011, where I first made several of the points which I have expanded in this book. His generous acceptance of the invitation, and his gesture of coming to Delhi solely to attend, were most encouraging. I am deeply grateful to the fellows of the NMML for their warm encouragement and support, and to the director, Professor Mridula Mukherjee, and all the wonderful staff, especially Mrs Aruna Tandon, for organizing that lecture and supporting me through my fellowship there.

I turned to this book immediately after that fellowship ended. In just a few months from May 2011, I had finished an extensive survey across the Valley and the first draft. Some material had already accumulated from my visits to schools and colleges the previous summer. I travelled north from Srinagar to Manasbal in the middle of June 2010. I am grateful to the students, principal, faculty, and staff of the Government High School at Manasbal for the enlightening insights I gained in discussions with them. During the trip, young Jehangir drove me down to Baramulla and on this trip he gave me important insights into the lives of young Kashmiris.

I am grateful to my friend and former colleague, Dr Jaleel Ahsan Zargar, Principal Mushtaq Wani, and other faculty of the Government Degree College, Baramulla, for facilitating my interactions with a very large number of students there. My interactions at that College began informally. Several students joined Jaleel and me for tea at the canteen.

A first-year student who walked into the canteen while we were chatting interrupted to ask my reason for being there. Since I did not see the need to interrupt the conversation, I ignored him after a perfunctory response. He sat down to listen and, as we were walking through the grounds from the canteen after tea, asked if I would like to stay at his home while I was in Baramulla. (Kashmir's amazing hospitality cannot be adequately described.) I thanked him, and turned away but, suddenly curious, I turned to ask where he stayed. When he said that he stayed in Old Town Baramulla, I accepted his invitation.

My friend Jaleel said he had already made arrangements for my stay. He emphasized the point, no doubt worried. It was the third week of June 2010, and stone-pelting was in full swing. But the student said I was welcome, and so I went. That evening, he and I walked up the length of the town on the right side of the river, and then down again, talking to young men and boys.

That began a close association. I am grateful to that student, the dynamic, open-minded, and courageous young Touseef Raina for having hosted me, and assisting my research. His parents and brothers have adopted me into their family since 2012. Living with yet another Kashmiri family, this one with both urban and rural roots, added a further layer to the rich learning experiences I had had with three other Kashmiri families of very different sorts from 1994 to 2002. I thank Touseef's relatives, and his neighbours too, including Peerzada Waqar, Inshan, and Waqar Khan, the talented singer, for their warm support.

A large number of public-spirited young Kashmiris helped me to conduct a survey in mid-2011. My heartfelt thanks to Hilal, Waheed, Tariq, Suhail, Zamin, Mudasir, Arafat, Khanday, and all the many others who joined me to conduct this survey in different corners of the Valley, and for giving others in the research team large-hearted hospitality when we were near their homes.

I thank Khalid Shah, Nazar-ul Islam, and other young Kashmiri friends who looked over parts of the manuscript for their advice and inputs. I am deeply grateful to them, and to my sister Fareeda, Raja Muneeb, Rayan Naqash, Tanveer Hussain Khan, Shah Irshad-ul Qadri, Najmu Saqib, Basharat Bhat, Anzar Raina, the talented rap artist, and the many other young Kashmiris who have been amazingly supportive.

I would like to thank Arshid Bhat, who has a PhD in linguistics from IIT Delhi after having studied at IIT Kanpur, for helping me to draft the questionnaire we used for the survey.

I am grateful to my friend Riyaz Punjabi for his insights on trends among young Kashmiris, and to his successor as Vice-Chancellor of

Kashmir University, Talat Ahmed, for his encouraging and efficient facilitation of the survey. I am also grateful to the students with whom I interacted and who I had the privilege of serving at Islamic University of Science and Technology (IUST). In particular, I thank those who treated me like family.

I thank Dr George Mathew and his colleagues at the Institute for Social Sciences. The library and facilities of the Institute have been valuable. I am deeply grateful for the hospitality of so many of my friends, including Sandeep Sunder, Naveena, Pawan and Adhiraj Sawhney, Vipul Mudgal and Sunrita Sen, Varun Tripathi, Dipankar Sengupta, Sucheta Mahajan and Bodh Prakash, Sushil Razdan, and Rakesh Batabyal and Mahalakshmi. I am also grateful to the owners and staff of the centrally located Golden Rose Houseboat and the New Majestic Houseboat on the scenic Nagin, to Feroz and the owners of the Zahoor guest house at Manasbal, and Hussain and his wonderful cousins at deApple hotel.

Most of all, I thank Rajiv Goswami, without whose constant assistance and unfailing logistical support I would never be able to manage a life which constantly keeps me on the move in uncertain circumstances.

The beginning of this collaboration with Oxford University Press (OUP) lay in a fleeting meeting at the European Conference on South Asian Studies at the University of Zurich in 2014: a hand raised in greeting and a simple 'I want your next book' to express interest in my work. I am glad it happened. It was a pleasure to take forward that quick proposal from OUP. I was surprised to find that, of the two manuscripts on which I was working, they were interested in this one; I had thought the Press focused on far more theoretical academic work.

It has been a pleasure to work with the entire team at OUP. I deeply appreciate the consideration and cooperation they have given me. The commissioning team has been superbly responsive, the editorial and design teams have worked magic, and the Marketing team has done impressive preparatory work. My sincere thanks to each of them, and their colleagues!

Introduction

It was a warm July morning. Sunshine streamed over Srinagar city through a mild haze, but the sun was not as sharp as it sometimes can be in the mountains. Srinagar, the centre (and capital) of the Kashmir Valley, is at about 6,000 feet above sea level. At the centre of a relatively flat and very fertile valley, the city contains more than a million people. The Dal Lake to the east of the city is lined by gorgeously carved houseboats and is flanked on the other side by the picturesque Zabarwan range. It draws sightseers from far and near. That summer too large numbers of tourists were in Srinagar. To most of them, Kashmir seemed like a beautiful, serene place.

I was out that morning with a research assistant and a visiting scholar. We did not focus on the beauties of the place. In my grey Maruti Suzuki Wagon R, we turned off the arterial Maulana Azad Road towards the old city of Srinagar—Downtown, as most residents of the city call it. We drove down Nallemar, the broadest street in Downtown. Nallemar winds along the course of what used to be a canal through the city. It is lined with concrete shops and a few old brick-and-wood houses, some of the latter deserted. On either side are the narrow, bustling lanes of Downtown, densely packed with shops and houses.

Not always bustling, to be sure. For, there could be a clampdown, or a shutdown—curfew or a hartal in the local parlance. Over a couple of decades of driving down Nallemar, daily in certain periods around the turn of the millennium, I had got used to keeping an eye peeled for trouble ahead. One might spot boys hurling stones at passing vehicles, to enforce a hartal. There could be policemen wielding long, thick batons at protesting boys, and at anyone else caught in the melee. There could be tear gas, or bullets from the guns of police or paramilitary forces. In fact, there were periods when one would routinely ask before taking that route: '*Haalaat chhu theeak?*' (Are conditions okay?).

We turned right at the Rajouri Kadal crossing, then left, away from the Jamia mosque, towards the Islamia College of Science and Commerce. That is the largest college in Downtown Srinagar and I was going there to ask students about their experiences, and their aspirations for their state. For my earlier book, I had spoken to large numbers of those who had led Kashmir's freedom movement, including the senior-most leaders of the Hurriyat Conference and many who had taken up arms as militants. After the agitations of 2008 and 2010, when stone-pelting crowds of young boys took to the streets with riotous rage, I had realized that interviewing so-called leaders had limited value now. Kashmir had a very large proportion of young people. Substantially more than half the population had been born in a time of violence. By the second decade of the twenty-first century, young Kashmiris had taken up the leadership of their resistance struggle.

So, that July of 2011, we travelled across the length and breadth of the Valley to survey and interact with thousands of young Kashmiris. Most students were very happy to fill our questionnaire. In fact, at the Bemina Degree College to the west of the city, some students who passed the rooms in which other students were filling our questionnaire asked what was going on and requested to be allowed to join. At the women's college at Nawa Kadal, even deeper in the folds of Downtown than the Islamia College, some students were waiting for me at the gate when I left their college. Thank you, they said, with great fervour. Nonplussed, I asked why they were thanking me. They said it was the first time anyone had asked them what they thought or want. 'Nobody asks us.'

At Islamia College, on the morning I went there, the atmosphere was raucous. Hundreds of students were packed into the large conference hall with me. As elsewhere, I had asked the teachers not to join us. There did not seem to be any windows and, under the white artificial glow, we might have been on a different planet from the sunlit beauty of the Valley outside. The cavernous hall was full and overflowing. Hundreds of students stood closely packed behind those who sat around the conference table. Some of them spoke loudly, simultaneously. Others raised slogans. Soon, the place was echoing with ringing cries for freedom.

My two companions disappeared, frightened by what appeared to be a riot. One of them was a Kashmiri student from another college. The other was a scholar from the US. Both decided that discretion was the better part of valour, at least for the visitor. The Kashmiri student soon returned, having left our visitor with a group of friendly students who interacted more calmly with him for the rest of the morning.

Their slipping out of that room was not surprising—so high-pitched was the rage that filled it. In fact, some of the college teachers came to rescue me from what sounded like an aggressive mob. I told them I was alright and that they should leave me with the students. I took a microphone and managed to calm them down, then suggested that those that wanted to talk to me should come out into a college garden. Those who wanted, and could find places to sit around the conference table, could fill the questionnaire. Leaving my Kashmiri student assistant in the conference hall with the questionnaires, I went out into the garden. Like a Pied Piper, I was followed by more than a hundred students.

We sat there in a large deep circle, and talked. Rather, they talked, animatedly, and I listened. I remained at Islamia College till late that afternoon. For, later, those most intensely interested in the discussion spoke to me in smaller groups. At that stage, some of the boys showed me torture marks, and told me what they had experienced—their reasons for the riotous rage I had witnessed in that conference hall. A few days earlier, boys at the Baramulla Public School too had shown me torture marks after filling my questionnaire. They were but schoolboys. Their skin looked delicate and soft; those welts and burn marks incongruous and shocking.

Those Baramulla boys were quiet as they took me into an empty classroom to tell me what had happened to them and to show me their scars. Filling the questionnaire at desks in their own classroom earlier, they had looked sedate, properly turned out in their uniforms of white shirts, grey trousers, and striped ties. If they had not spoken to me separately, it would have been difficult to make out what ugly torture they had suffered. Some normally liberal Indians with whom I have shared this experience have reacted with dismissive disbelief, as if I was sharing malign propaganda. I am not. It is what I witnessed. It is important to explore the nuanced truth beneath neat uniforms. Even at Islamia College, it was only when I had listened to the raucous yelling and then to the large numbers who gathered around me in the garden that small knots of young men told me what they had suffered, and showed the scars on their bodies. One has to look way past the placid beauty of the Dal Lake to understand what ordinary people have experienced. The apparently humdrum 'normality' of everyday life can be deceptive.

Many students and others expressed deep resentment at being frisked, at being humiliated, sometimes abused, manhandled or molested. Very often, those feelings were seamlessly mixed up with grief. I recalled my shock while chatting with a Kashmiri friend around 2002. He had taken me to his ancestral village a couple of years earlier. There I had met his eldest uncle, who was in his nineties at the time. This uncle was revered as a seer, a spiritually evolved Sufi Pir. He had sat propped up in bed, surrounded by people who had come to seek his blessings. When I asked about him a couple of years later, my friend said his uncle had died the previous winter. He had fallen ill after a midwinter journey. In a matter-of-fact tone, as if it was normal, he explained that, during that journey, his nonagenarian uncle had to walk some distance along with everyone else in his vehicle to be frisked at a security checkpoint. This was routine. Soldiers often did not bend the rule for the aged, the sick, or even for pregnant women; they all had to pass through those checkpoints. That nonagenarian spiritual seer had fallen ill and died after walking through snow in freezing air.

PERSONAL EXPERIENCE

I remembered my own trauma at facing a gun. I had realized the meaning of the word speechless that day in 1994 while driving back to Srinagar down the highway from Baramulla. Not far from the city, a man in a black salwar-kameez had leapt out of the bushes beside the road. He stood on the road, pointing a large black pistol straight at my face. I was sitting in the front passenger seat. Instead of stopping the car, the taxi driver slammed the accelerator. The man in black could either have fired or leapt off the road—or both. He leapt off the road. I wanted to yell, then speak, but could not utter a sound for many minutes. The taxi driver explained that the gunman was most likely a mercenary working with the armed forces, and that he probably wanted to loot whatever we had.

That summer, the same taxi driver drove me to Hajin, the nerve centre of such mercenaries, but stopped the taxi some distance from the village. He refused to go any farther. I walked the rest of the way and asked my way to Kuka Parray's house. He was the leader of the biggest group of mercenaries. His house and the area around it bristled with rifles, held up openly, but he insisted that his men were in hiding from the forces. How come you brandish your weapons so openly, I asked, when there is a police post and a military camp at the edges of your village? We sneak past them, he replied with a shrug.

I remembered the heart-stopping fear of driving to hospital one night in 1999. I was editing Kashmir's largest English language newspaper that night, when one of the staff had an epileptic fit around midnight. We quickly shoved a rubber slipper into his foaming mouth and carried him to my car. The hospital was only a couple of kilometres away, but that awful night was an obstacle race of barricades, gun-barrels, checks, and searchlights. It was the night of 14 August, the eve of India's Independence Day, and security was at its annual peak.

That was the sort of pall of fear that had enveloped people in Kashmir for years, the environment in which these students had grown up. People across India knew little of what life had been like for them. Everyone in Kashmir did know, and often presumed that everyone else did. Given the wide disparity in what different kinds of people believed, there could be little understanding, leave alone dialogue, or movement towards accommodation.

EXPERIENCES OF IMPUNITY

I remembered listening to Parveena Ahangar, the founder of Kashmir's Association of Parents of Disappeared Persons. A woman of immense grit, she never gave up the struggle to discover what happened to her son after he was taken away for questioning by soldiers in August 1990. He was a teenager at the time. It was generally acknowledged that her son had had nothing to do with militancy. Apparently, he had been mistakenly 'picked up'. When this mother's pleas at the desks of various officers, officials, and politicians achieved nothing, she began to demonstrate in public. Gradually, other parents and relatives of disappeared persons joined her. They demonstrate regularly in the centre of uptown Srinagar. I sat in her office with a common friend one day as Parveena related the traumatic travails she had undergone with friends and foes. She broke down, wailing as if her lungs would burst. 'I only want to know what happened to my son', she cried. 'Either let me know where he is, or show me where his body is buried.'

In September 2011, I was beaten in a police station. When I complained, the police officers inquiring into the complaint told me with feline calm that I was the one accused of having broken the law that day. The Station House Officer at whose police station I was assaulted told me with chutzpah: 'You don't know how much power your home ministry has given me.' And yet, when the assault became a public scandal, senior officers at the Home Ministry in New Delhi were concerned and sympathetic. The Home Minister asked the state government for a report on what had happened, but the state government simply did not respond.

While being beaten, I was threatened: I would be framed as a terrorist. 'Where is your gun', my assailants demanded. I could have been killed, and my body buried as that of a terrorist. If they claimed it was the body of a Pakistani militant, as they would, they would have got a substantial cash reward in the bargain. All this happened because I got out of my car when security men with a VIP convoy hit my car with a long, thick baton, apparently for not giving them way fast enough. We were all stuck in a traffic jam at peak hour in Srinagar. I could do nothing, since the convoy had honked and beaten its way ahead by the time I emerged from the car. But my failing to accept their gangster manner was my ticket to torture. That was the norm. The impunity of the police grated as much as the despotic misuse of the police, and of their own authority, by those in power.

Bruised, beaten, confused, and in shock, I could not understand why I was being assaulted, or what to do. Although I had visited Kashmir as a journalist for twenty-three years, had lived there for months at a time, and had moved there to work at a university four years ago, I still naively believed that the system worked the way it was established on paper. Even after I was beaten and threatened in that police station, I believed that justice would be done. I was convinced that what was right would happen. But when I was threatened with false cases by a police officer who spoke almost as if he sympathized with me, his voice as smooth as silk, I realized that I and other ordinary people in Kashmir were living in a nightmare world, like Alice in Wonderland. The rule of law was a chimera. The misuse of authority could make the institutions of the state the most potent threats to a citizen's rights, his liberty, even his life.

The young people I met during my survey and through the years I spent researching this book had lived in, and survived, this surreal, ever-threatening world from the time they were born. It was a world in which might was right, power dictated what the record would show—the record that would suppress and replace the truth. It was a world of power and manipulation in which bulletproof glass blinded those who ruled to the reality of life for those beyond the pale. It was a world in which many of those who wielded power did not care at all whether those who did not have power and influence lived or died, had security or dignity.

Given this reality, it is in fact amazing that so many young people were still positive about the possibility of moving on with hope. On the other hand, it was not surprising that their main concern in 2011 was the rule of law and a regime of rights for all.

It was during that summer of 2010, the summer of stone-pelting, that I realized I had to write. I lived in Kashmir already, to research another book. Sitting alone in my study before my laptop, I would hear raucous processions chanting slogans even late at night. And I saw the wide gulf in the discourses that shaped public opinion—within Kashmir on the one hand, and outside on the other. I realized that summer that that gulf could push Kashmir to another horrible round of militancy. It did—within a couple of years. The cynical, career-obsessed, desk-bound figures in power ignored it for another couple of years—until it became impossible to ignore.

This book describes why and how angst rose from peaceable calm to enraged rejection between 2007 and 2017. It describes the lived experience of young Kashmiris born and raised in a time of violence. Two-thirds of the 2017 population of the Kashmir Valley was born after militancy began in 1988. They have lived with death, destruction, and the overwhelming apparatus of counterinsurgency.

This attempt to tell the story of the violence experienced by young people stems from a conviction that the way towards a more peaceful future lies in discussing what shaped the rage of young Kashmiris, and the ways in which their experience of counterinsurgency shaped their choices. Not all of them chose to respond with violence. A large number have chosen to make money, find jobs, and accumulate the wherewithal of personal security. A few have chosen to take up arms in a new round of militancy. Some want to work towards peace. Very many are filled with disillusionment, anguish, and rage.

1

Endings and Beginnings

The year 2007 was a year of endings and beginnings in Kashmir. It is easy to identify a few of those endings and beginnings as events on a calendar. But there were others that slipped in unnoticed, like someone joining or leaving a crowd mesmerized by a circus. Some were more like tapering trends, almost disappearing like water from a saucer on a hot, dry day. The most important of such unnoticed endings was the end of Kashmir's militancy—which some prefer to see as a freedom struggle and others as insurgency. It had begun in 1988, when no one thought that by the end of the 1990s it would make Kashmir known as 'the most dangerous place on Earth'.[1] That round of militancy petered out around 2007 for various reasons, to which we shall come back later.

To be sure, a few Kashmiri boys, and some from Pakistan, still kept their fight going. Official statistics tell a story of relentless terrorism, but most people who actually lived in the villages and hamlets of Kashmir were convinced that militancy was more or less over by 2007. Most people within the Valley believed that barely a couple of dozen militants were actually active by then, and most of those were confined to four pockets: Lolab, Shopian, Tral, and Kokernag. Official versions of the situation must of course be taken seriously, but perceptions among grass-roots people in situations of conflict too matter. In fact, perceptions matter a lot, for perceptions shape responses, sentiments, and aspirations—aspirations that could range from an often ill-defined 'azadi' (freedom) to 'integration' of one sort or another, for accommodation and fraternity, or for renewed violence and revenge.

By 2007, even the militants who remained active had realized that they were fighting a losing battle—but they continued for the glories that their death in battle might bring them in another world. Others quietly surrendered; in most cases, the forces presented their sequestration as capture. Hardly any new ones had joined militancy since the beginning of the decade and, by the middle of the decade, far fewer Kashmiris than before were willing to shelter militants in their homes. Indeed, in the couple of years leading up to 2007, more and more Kashmiris who spotted militants in their villages or forests reported them to the police or armed forces.

Officials did not accept the perception that militancy had ended. Most people in India and beyond continued to believe that Kashmir was 'terrorist-infested'—making it seem like a bag of rice with worms in it. But within Kashmir, many common people had not only become more acutely aware of militancy dying, there was also a sense of having given up the fight against being absorbed into India. That was the sort of ending, or fading, which took place in the unpredictable, dark corners of the mind.

In the crevasses of the mind, a disquieting feeling slipped in around that time—a sense of illegitimacy about the army's continued presence in Kashmir. Many in Kashmir already despised the army after it had arrived by the hundreds of thousands in 1994. At that stage, however, there had been a general understanding that the Indian state had dispatched the army—indeed, all those military, paramilitary, police, and mercenary forces that many Kashmiris generically called 'army'—to fight militancy. This was accepted, however unhappily, as the natural reaction of a state apparatus faced with violent insurgency—bombs, grenades, guns. Since many ordinary people on the ground felt that 'militancy' was over, the continued presence of the armed forces—with suspicion, abuse, and force as their established stocks-in-trade—grated.

Frustration with the slowing down of the 'peace process' between India and Pakistan added to that sense of defeat about the insurgency. The peace process began when Atal Behari Vajpayee, one of India's finest prime ministers ever, announced during a surprise visit to Srinagar his willingness to send a diplomat to Pakistan immediately if Pakistan was willing to negotiate.[2] That was on 18 April 2003. By January 2004, the two countries, along with all other SAARC nations,[3] agreed to have free trade in two years, open borders by 2008, and to resolve their disputes.

It had seemed like a dazzling breakthrough towards peace and regional cooperation. In fact, a major cause for militancy to have wound down was that Pakistan had turned off the supply of arms, training, and other support since 2004. By 2007, however, the peace negotiations had unravelled. Some said an agreement over Kashmir was almost in place. Like those other beginnings and endings that slipped in or out that year unmarked, the fact that the peace process had stalled was not immediately apparent at first, but the opportunity for India to make peace with a dictator who headed Pakistan's army as well as its government was lost.

The assassination of Benazir Bhutto as 2007 was drawing to a close may have been the obvious marker of disillusionment, but it had already become clear that a very large number of Kashmiris did not want Kashmir to merge with Pakistan. They would still lustily cheer Pakistan's cricket team, but that was more an anti-India and Muslim solidarity gesture. Pakistan, which had seemed like their natural home to the generation of Kashmiris that matured between 1965 and 1990,[4] had become far less attractive to the generation that had grown up thereafter.

A new trend in self-perception began to seep into young minds around 2007. Kashmiris learnt to talk of themselves as a nation: a Muslim nation, an occupied nation. In a determined attempt to bracket

Kashmir with Palestine, they began to use words such as occupation, colonization, and resistance to describe their situation. There was a vigorous attempt to project this discourse internationally. Ironically, concerted efforts to validate this narrative began just when prospects for peace between India and Pakistan seemed bright. Subcontinental peace would have unsettled the India versus Pakistan, Hindu versus Muslim paradigms in which world powers to the West and the East had slotted South Asia. These paradigms had ensured that the two countries could not together resist the global balance of power since 1947. The peace process came to naught quite soon, but the new narrative continued to be pushed vigorously, particularly from 2008. From that year on, more and more young Kashmiris wanted to be journalists, writers, and academics, committed to pushing this narrative. They were trained and encouraged to promote the discourse of colonization and victimhood.

NEW GENERATION

Perhaps the most important of the beginnings that slipped in unnoticed was the new generation of Kashmiris that came of age around that year. Over the past few years, many boys and even more girls of this generation had become deeply cynical, even contemptuous, of their elders who had taken up arms. They saw militancy as futile and secessionist leaders as self-serving hypocrites.

Many of these boys dreamed of careers in modelling, acting, or singing in Mumbai, or in software engineering in Bangalore. For a while, around the middle of that decade, some of these young Kashmiris had been so willing to consider themselves Indian that they would occasionally support an Indian cricket team even against Pakistan. Sitting in front of televisions in the comfort of their homes, they would get into intense arguments with siblings and cousins during such a match.

There was another, far more important aspect of the generation of 2007: they had grown up amid mayhem and terrible violence. There were large numbers of fearless boys with pride and passion, a deadly combination. Unlike their elders, they would not cower in front of security forces. They would answer back, question authority. During the summer of 2007, Srinagar was agog with talk of how a Kashmiri had stopped his vehicle when a security vehicle bumped into it on the road, pulled the uniformed driver down, and made him hand over money for repairs. Until a decade earlier, in the mid-1990s, a Kashmiri vehicle would have scuttled to the edge of the road, even into a ditch, if its driver saw an army vehicle approaching far down the road. For, if he did not get out of that army vehicle's way, he risked being beaten up and his car being damaged.

TRANSFORMED POLICE

If 2007 was the year a generation that had been raised in a time of violence came of age, it was also the time when officers who had been in the state's police force only in that time of violence had taken up positions of commanding authority.

Javid Mukhdoomi, a sage and sensitive officer, had been the Inspector-General of Police in charge of Kashmir until the previous year. An officer steeped in the Kashmiri ethos, Mukhdoomi noted that the talk and body language of the police had changed during the long years of militancy. For example, an officer might say something like 'bump him off' about a militant or an anti-state activist. According to him, the police's focus on law and order had been disturbed during those terrible years, and it never returned. In 2005, Mukhdoomi went to the chief minister, Mufti Mohammad Sayeed,[5] to recommend steps to revive traditional policing.[6] Mufti did not remain chief minister after December 2005 and Mukhdoomi too retired soon after.

That some officers had got used to a 'bump him off' culture became explicitly obvious the year after Mukhdoomi retired, when a senior police officer was arrested for having signed papers claiming that the persons who policemen had killed were Pakistani militants.[7] As it turned out, those men had nothing to do with militancy. The officer who signed got into trouble apparently because he took at face value what his juniors told him—and claimed rewards that the Indian government gave for killing foreign militants.[8]

These two trends—a fearless, aspirational generation and a bump-them-off police attitude—which came of age in that quiet slip-in-slip-out year clashed head to head in 2008, and again in 2010. The new generation of youth pelted stones and barricaded roads, and the police and paramilitary forces responded with tear gas shells and bullets. In 2010, they kept responding with firing, day after terrible day, despite orders, pleading, and cajoling. The police, as Mukhdoomi said, had forgotten the basics of policing as crowd control. There were those in the force who had got used to killing at will, he adds.[9] Sometimes, they killed for rewards. At other times, calculations that were more devious could have lurked behind these killings. We will come back to this later in the book.

Either way, the result was that some of the actions of the armed forces enraged a new generation of Kashmiri youth, and reignited the conflict. This when, as I noted at the outset, youth had largely given up the desire to fight by 2007, and were looking for ways to settle down in peace. Peace, of course, would have meant a return to accountability, to working with—and within—normal laws, an end to special powers including those over life and death, and an end to the vast conflict economy. It would also have put a stop to the rewards, medals, promotions, special funds, extra staff, pay and perquisites, huge budgets—and opportunities for the corrupt to siphon them off. The fact that corruption had almost become a norm made it a particularly sinister reason why peace remained elusive.

TURNING POINT   *Page 7.*

High on what Kashmiri leader Syed Ali Shah Geelani called 'the arrogance of power', the politicians, officials, and other bosses of the Indian state did not notice these changes. The way many of those in authority saw it, the forces' behaviour towards people was much better than in the 1990s, when they routinely beat up drivers who did not veer out of their way on public roads well in time—and did much, much worse.

It was true that the forces now generally behaved better. For that new generation of youth, though, this sort of comparative improvement was not good enough. The fact is that some of the Indian forces continued to mistreat, humiliate, and (although this was relatively rare) arbitrarily kill Kashmiris. In fact, an important marker of the previous year had been the killing of Ghulam Mohammad Sheikh, a student in Srinagar. The boy was returning home from Amar Singh College, one of the best in Kashmir, when men of the paramilitary Central Reserve Police Force (CRPF) boarded the bus to check identity papers. They dragged him off the bus and shot him on the road. According to eyewitness accounts, the boy had protested to the CRPF that another group of security men up the road had just checked the passengers' identities.

This took place a few metres from one of Kashmir's most important trisections, at the head of Maulana Azad Road. Down that road is J&K Bank's headquarters, with the Polo Ground on the left, and a golf course and then the Nedou's and Broadway hotels on the right. Farther down, to the left, is Lal Chowk. Then, across the flyover,[10] are the High Court and the Secretariat. Another arm of that trisection passes the prestigious Burn Hall School and the chief justice's mansion before going on past the Cantonment to the highway to Delhi. The third arm of that trisection goes to the Dal Lake. It was the hub of Srinagar, often jammed with traffic. Kashmiris were naturally horrified that the CRPF men killed a college student in the open, in broad daylight, on this stretch. And most people believed that they killed him merely because he had the gumption to complain about the passengers' identities being checked twice within a few minutes. No greater fault than that was convincingly established, although the propaganda machine cranked at the time.

The logic behind the propaganda machine of counterinsurgency forces was that image is more important than reality. The image that concerned them was how the ones who they thought of as 'nationalists', generally people outside Kashmir, perceived them. Since there were almost no militant guns to confront them any more, some of these forces bothered even less about Kashmiri opinion than they had in the past. Most Indians beyond Kashmir, however, were not interested. What mattered at that particularly delicate juncture of beginnings and endings was the forces' image among Kashmiris of the generation that came of age around 2007. For, as they calibrated Kashmir's priorities afresh, the image of India in their minds hinged on their impression of counterinsurgency forces, and the impunity they enjoyed.

Photographs of that young student's body, spread-eagled against a wall in the touristy Dalgate area, were splashed across the front pages of Srinagar's local newspapers for days, but there was little media coverage in Delhi or elsewhere in India. Some brief reports quoted the CRPF 'top brass' claiming that the boy had been about to throw a grenade. Later in this book, we shall look into why Kashmiris were cynical about forces' versions of 'encounter' deaths during those couple of years. People tended to make their own enquiries before they made up their minds about whether a person killed in an encounter had actually been a militant. If he was, they often shouted pro-freedom and Islamic slogans at the funeral procession but did not organize protest demonstrations.

The day after the CRPF killed that student at Dalgate, many people in Srinagar were incensed. The boy's college mates marched out of their college gate to protest. The CRPF men beat them back into the campus. Students and teachers said the soldiers bolted a classroom from inside and assaulted students with batons, punches, and kicks for around fifteen minutes. They assaulted teachers and, according to students, even the principal in her office. Nobody in Delhi or elsewhere seemed to have noticed the atrocious event.[11]

It is difficult to precisely mark the beginning of a trend, but that particular killing might have been the turning point—the point at which Kashmiris stopped accepting the impunity with which some of the Indian forces had treated locals for years. It was not the first time Kashmiris had disbelieved the forces' version of an 'encounter' death, but this killing had happened in broad daylight, in uptown Srinagar. The victim was a student of an elite college. Not only had the boy been executed, most Kashmiris believed that he was killed only for having had the temerity to talk back. To most local people, it demonstrated the extent to which forces that were supposedly there to fight militants had taken as their task to keep the entire Kashmiri people tightly leashed—and treated murder as a legitimate method to achieve this. Some even believed that the deep, dark purpose of some of those who coordinated those forces was to keep the conflict alive. It jolted Kashmiris at a time when they were just getting used to a relatively normal life, staying out till after dusk, feeling less claustrophobic.

The easing of tensions and the hope for a better future that the previous couple of years had brought had increased Kashmiris' boldness, their resistance to humiliation and terror. Many teenagers particularly resented harassment by crude soldiers from the Indian plains. Not only had they been too young to become used to cowering during the 1990s, they had been immunized to tactics that had terrorized their parents. Even a demand to see an identity card—which every Kashmiri had to carry if they did not want to be detained, tortured, or perhaps killed—was now treated as an indignity. Most men had, at some point, been abused, slapped, or kicked on their way, after a soldier had looked at their card. Or they had watched a father or an uncle being slapped, or ordered to do squats while holding his ears, or made to stand on his hands with his feet propped against a wall on a public road, while neighbours and relatives passed by. Humiliation was one of the keys to control.

After suicide attacks became common at the turn of the century, soldiers had taken to blocking roads outside their camps soon after dusk—even if the road was a highway. A civilian trying to drive by would have to get out of his car with hands high in the air, slowly approach the barricade, and shout to the invisible soldiers in a bunker at the gate. A soldier would most likely question him about why he was out late and where he lived, and make him lift his *pheran* coat to show that there were no hidden weapons. Then, if the soldier in the bunker was satisfied, he might allow the Kashmiri to move the boulders, logs, and barbed wires that formed the barricade, drive across, then stop and return to replace the barrier.[12] For the armed forces, this was minimal harassment compared with the 1990s. Kashmiris who clearly remembered the repression of the 1990s also thought of it as much reduced trouble and humiliation. But to young Kashmiris with little or no memory of the 1990s, but an assertive new sense of self worth, it was intolerable.

THE STATE'S BLINDNESS

Various arms of the Indian state were blind to these changes. Cunning manipulators among them pretended blindness. Most others, steeped in cussed cynicism, were actually unaware. Their blindness was fourfold: first, they were even blind to the fact that the 1988 insurgency had ended; two, they were blind to the fact that they were dealing now with a changed generation of Kashmiris; three, they were blind to the desire of the generation of 2007 to settle down to peace and economic opportunities; and four, they were blind to this generation's fearlessness and insistence on dignity. When this blindness resulted in a new militancy by the middle of the next decade, they remained blind to the fact that they had missed the wood for the trees. Nor did they realize that their cynicism had allowed a golden opportunity to slip by. The teenagers of 2017 did not want peace and economic opportunities the way young people had in 2007. A new generation, shaped by different influences, experiences, and aspirations, had become teenagers by then.

The Indian state blithely treated the new insurgency as a continuation of the previous one. It was not. The crying irony is that, when the generation of 2007 demonstrated fearless rage on the streets in 2008 and again in 2010, the propagandists of the Indian state had already tried to project it as another sort of insurgency. Instead of responding after the 2008 agitations by winding down the apparatus of counterinsurgency, they created another category of insurgents against the state: 'stone-pelters' was now a category of criminals. In both 2008 and 2010, there were various obvious causes for rage, but it also had a lot to do with the failure to acknowledge that the insurgency that had begun in 1988 had tapered off. It had much to do with the continued, humiliating militarization of Kashmir.

When Kashmiri anger erupted again in 2010, Pakistan was evidently back in play, fanning the flames, but the killing of innocents was the tinder that lit the fire. Three specific incidents of killing by armed forces of five young men who had nothing to do with militancy sparked off rage. Kashmiris pelted stones against the police and paramilitary forces, even in some areas where there had never been much local militancy. Repressive action by those police forces, in which bullets and tear gas shells killed more than a hundred young men, stoked fury throughout that summer. Rage and repression had become a vicious cycle, with each firing incident provoking fresh ire. It was obvious that the firing had to stop if the cycle was to be broken. Yet, it continued. It was barely explicable— unless one turned to conspiracy theories. Orders to fire at demonstrators' legs, and not to fire to kill, were not followed either. Most shots hit heads or chests. Some eyewitnesses alleged that tear gas canisters were at times lethally shot from point-blank range.

Tragically, propagandist attempts to project the agitations of 2008 as having been organized by Pakistan became a self-fulfilling prophecy. Encouraged by the anger among Kashmiri youth that had become obvious, at least some sections of the ISI gradually began to restore support to insurgency in Kashmir. By 2016, that support was more intensive than it had been for a decade and a half. One might even use the word enveloping rather than intensive. For, as it had around 1990, Pakistan seemed once again to have taken over Kashmir's freedom movement by 2016.

The ISI's support had been tempered, and made far more secretive, after India massed its army on its border with Pakistan at the end of 2001. After the peace process got going in earnest from 2004, Pakistan brought down its support to Kashmir's militancy to a minimal level. Western diplomats[13] held that two assassination attempts during December 2003 had convinced Pakistan President General Parvez Musharraf that his army had created a Frankensteinian monster. But that policy of squeezing support to militancy appeared to have quietly changed after 2008. The new government could not control the ISI nearly as effectively as could a military dictator like General Musharraf, who remained the Chief of Army Staff until near the end of his time as head of state.

Pakistan had always sought to exploit unrest in Kashmir in its attempt to loosen India's hold over the region. Always in the past, the combination of two factors had caused insurgency in Kashmir: disenchantment with the government and dissatisfaction with the economic and social situation, on the one hand, and political, diplomatic, and material support from Pakistan on the other. A key element in this support had been training, planning, and the supply of arms by the Pakistan Army. The local anger that became apparent in 2008, and more intensely so in 2010, spurred Pakistan to restore its policy of support for militancy.

India's policymakers did not seem to grasp the fact that the converse was also true about those two factors: either of them was inadequate without the other. Just as insurgencies in Kashmir had depended vitally on Pakistani support, Pakistan could not keep an insurgency going in Kashmir without the people's support. For a few years after 2004, both factors had been at low ebb. It was the best opportunity for the Government of India to have weaned over the Kashmiri people at large. The first thing it needed to do in order to achieve that was to have ratcheted down the apparatus of counterinsurgency—for most Kashmiris perceived it as a regime of harassment and humiliation. According to narratives common among many ordinary Kashmiris, the most corrupt, venal, and cynical elements of that apparatus resorted to killing, maiming, blackmail, and extortion. The very visible presence of that apparatus made those narratives very real in the minds of even those who had not experienced those things, including those who had grown up after the most intense period of militancy and counterinsurgency. Around 2007, they perceived a clear mismatch between the level of militancy and the size of the counterinsurgency apparatus. After 2007, the narratives they heard built anger and vengefulness in a generation that was often too young to remember.

POLITICAL PUSILLANIMITY

To be sure, the apparatus of humiliation was dismantled to some extent after the 2010 stone-pelting. First thing every Thursday morning, India's home minister, P. Chidambaram, would chair a meeting in his office. He would go over detailed lists of specific locations in Kashmir, demanding to know whether the CRPF had dismantled a particular bunker or vacated a specific hotel. It demonstrated two things. One, handling Kashmir sensitively required political will, and India was ill-served by those who preceded and succeeded Chidambaram. Two, the officials who should have reviewed the need for bunkers or the occupation of hotels (often since 1990) had not. Inertia ruled, for they had been trained to guard against anything going wrong, to make sure their two or three years in a particular office passed without any of their decisions being questioned by their bosses or the media. And India had become such a security state since Indira Gandhi's assassination that the reflex tendency in government was to add more security, not reduce it. The fact that security could oppress and alienate citizens, generating processes that decreased national security, was ignored in the secure corridors of power.

What Chidambaram did after the 2010 uprising was well worth doing. Coming after that explosion of rage, it was, however, too little, too late. Mufti Mohammad Sayeed, who had been chief minister from 2002 to 2005, was the only prominent Kashmiri leader who publicly said in the winter of 2006–07 that it was time to begin to demilitarize Kashmir. He was soon silenced by shrill voices across India that described him as anti-national and in league with militants. No Kashmiri leader dared to make the point thereafter, during that crucial period when the ground became fertile for a new militancy—and the wheel turned full circle, gradually making any demand for a reduction in the counterinsurgency apparatus counterproductive.

CYBER TELEPHONY

Another change was taking place unnoticed around 2007, one that would soon transform the dynamic of people's power in different parts of the world, not least Kashmir. This was the spread of mobile phones, internet connectivity, and social networking sites such as Facebook. The generation of fearless Kashmiri youth that was just coming to adulthood had grown up around such electronic gadgets. Amid curfews and general insecurity outside their homes, they had had nothing to do after dusk through their childhoods but to speak to friends on the phone. They grabbed the cell phones that had belatedly become available to them.

Having severely limited the number of mobile phone connections when these were first introduced (only about a thousand mobile numbers were initially allowed in 2002, exclusively through the state-owned telephone company), the government allowed a private mobile phone service[14] in 2004. More than 70,000 new connections were sold between September and December that year. Around 2007, the number crossed a million, as more private operators offered services. Phone usage increased exponentially when mobile services switched in 2009 to charging per second rather than per minute. Data services jumped with

3G connectivity in March 2010. Its impact would be astounding during the uprising later that year.

What the Kashmiri youth accessed through these devices shaped their minds. Cynicism regarding America's 'War on Terror' had increased by 2007. More people were convinced about the falsity of the motives declared by President Bush and his team before the United States (US) had invaded Iraq in 2003. Muslims worldwide were convinced that the US was trying to take further control of the oil and other resources of Muslim countries in the Gulf and elsewhere. Many Kashmiri Muslims saw the Indian government's moves to increase economic, military, and strategic closeness to the US and Israel as proof that it was part of a global anti-Muslim axis. Over the next few years, this became a major subject of conversation on the internet, mobile phones, and bulk SMSs in Kashmir.

These communication networks also spread ideas about religion, ideas propagated by fundamentalist groups such as Tablighi Jamaat and Ahle-Hadith. For the most part, these groups had nothing overtly to do with politics. However, almost subconsciously, their teachings promoted the idea that Kashmir's was a Muslim community; and that the particular set of teachings of that school or sect was the only right way to be a true Muslim—or, in fact, to live life. Over the next couple of years, these groups began to make a far greater impact in Kashmir than they had ever done before. Both these groups rejected syncretistic practices among Kashmiri Muslims, such as asking divine favours at the graves of mystics, or respecting certain trees as sacred.

Ironically, it was hi-tech equipment such as mobile- and satellite-based tracking, surveillance, and imaging that had allowed the Indian army to break the back of militancy in Kashmir by 2007. The tacticians who congratulated themselves on this did not seem to realize that this technology was a double-edged sword. The relatively low-tech facilities of phone calls, messaging, and social media allowed hundreds of thousands of young Kashmiris to communicate, plan, strategize, and mobilize after 2007.

After 2007, these three processes—connectivity, global Islamic consciousness, and fundamentalist ideologies—combined to generate a new perception about the situation of Kashmir and its people. For, it happened in tandem with the orchestrated projection of Kashmiri colonization, exploitation, and oppression that had emerged in that year of quiet beginnings and endings. This view of their reality was projected vigorously through the media, academics, books, films, and the meeting point of all of these, the internet. More and more young men[15] began to see the militarization of Kashmir as part of a global pattern of oppression of Muslim communities.

These perceptions had very little to do with the India–Pakistan dispute over Kashmir that dated back to 1947. Young Kashmiris who grew up around this time focused only fuzzily on events to which historians, politicians, and war and peace strategists gave importance—events that took place in 1948 or 1953 or 1987 or 1989. Their perceptions were formed by their own experiences, combined with the narratives they received, more than by what had gone before. In their minds, history was telescoped, so that the soldiers and bunkers they saw at every corner became physical proof of 'Indian occupation' since 1947. This they saw in exclusivist Hindu–Muslim terms more than had been common before 2007.

Geography too played a part. Kashmiris lived mainly in the bowl of the Kashmir Valley, less than 5 per cent of the area of the entire state called Jammu and Kashmir, which the Dogra rulers of Jammu had put together in the middle of the nineteenth century.[16] Tensions that emerged between legislators from the Jammu region and those from the Kashmir region within the coalition government that ruled the state from 2002 to 2008 plugged into the Kashmiri perception of a Muslim nation facing Hindu antagonists. These political tensions were perceived as proof of a primal Hindu–Muslim conflict. A sometimes abusively vicious mistrust of the other erupted into the open after 2007.

GEOPOLITICAL FACTORS

Events and trends, manipulations and insensitivities, inefficiencies and greed led quite quickly after 2007 to the emergence of a new militancy in Kashmir, one that threatened to be more lethal than the previous one. Between 2008 and 2010, the two factors that had always been vital for militancy in Kashmir came back into play. Kashmiri youth were angry, frustrated, and vengeful. And Pakistan became ready to support another round of militancy.

If Pakistan saw opportunity in Kashmiris' fresh mood of belligerence, its calculations must surely also have been positively influenced by the geopolitical scenario. In the second half of that decade, two factors would have influenced Pakistan's objectives regarding Kashmir. One was how it should choose between its two mentors, the US and China. It was easy to choose the latter. China was the rising power while the US seemed to be on the decline, economically and militarily. Moreover, the US was wooing India, while China at times treated India belligerently. The other issue that Pakistan's ISI had to figure out was how safe it could feel with regard to Afghanistan. That was another easy call. By around 2007, it was clear that the US was looking for a face-saving way out of Afghanistan.

For Pakistan, the answers to those overarching geopolitical questions that would determine the history of the twenty-first century were simple. As a first step for China to dominate the resources of Central and West Asia, Pakistan would help China to increase influence in Afghanistan. After the trend established by the US Congressional elections at the end of 2006, strategic analysts around the world could guess that the US would ease itself out of Afghanistan after a Democrat won in 2008. That would be when Pakistan would want another insurgency in Kashmir—perhaps even something like a civil war, or even a war.

2008 was also the year of the Beijing Olympics. Soon after that prestigious event ended successfully, China made it clear that it considered that the state of Jammu and Kashmir was disputed. It started issuing visas to citizens of the state on pieces of paper stapled to their Indian passports. And Chinese troops periodically intruded into India-controlled parts of the state across a border over which there had never been a formal agreement.

If things did move towards a war-like situation, the generation of young Kashmiris that had come of age since 2007 would be a crucial factor in determining the balance of power, not only between India and Pakistan but between India and China. In 1947—and more so in 1965—ordinary Kashmiri people were India's bulwark against 'infiltrators' sent by Pakistan to lead the Kashmiri people to become Pakistanis. Boys who could, given their attitudes around 2007, have been India's best defence once more had instead become its most furious enemies by 2017, in just a decade.

NOTES

1. Described so by Bill Clinton in 2000; Clinton was the US president at that time.
2. 'PM extends "hand of friendship" to Pakistan', *The Hindu*, http://www.thehindu.com/2003/04/19/stories/2003041905500100.htm, accessed on 27 March 2017.
3. SAARC stands for South Asian Association for Regional Cooperation and includes Afghanistan, Bangladesh, Bhutan, India, Nepal, Maldives, Pakistan, and Sri Lanka.
4. David Devadas, *In Search of a Future: The Story of Kashmir* (New Delhi: Penguin Books, 2007).
5. Mufti Mohammad Sayeed was the chief minister of Kashmir from 2002 to 2005.
6. Author's interview with Javid Mukhdoomi, Jammu, 3 December 2016.
7. 'SSP, DySP arrested in fake encounter case', *DNA*, 4 February 2007, http://www.dnaindia.com/india/report-ssp-dysp-arrested-in-fake-encounter-case-1077754, accessed on 27 March 2017.
8. About this incident, Mukhdoomi holds: 'Parihar was a simple guy, who did not even go to the scene', author's interview with Javid Mukhdoomi, Jammu, 3 December 2016.
9. Author's interview with Javid Mukhdoomi, Jammu, 3 December 2016.
10. Another flyover began to be built in 2013.
11. Senior officials in the Government of India responsible for administering Kashmir had not heard of it when the author asked them about it.
12. This is a description of a check in which the author participated while being driven by a friend in 2002.

13. The author's private conversations with ranking diplomats of major Western countries in 2004.
14. Airtel in 2004. Aircel, Vodafone, and Reliance entered the Kashmir market between 2006 and 2008.
15. This was relatively uncommon among young women.
16. The British East India Company had recognized Gulab Singh, the raja of Jammu, as Maharaja of Jammu and Kashmir through a treaty following the Battle of Subraon, in which the British forces defeated the Sikh Maharaja, who had been Gulab Singh's suzerain. Gulab Singh paid Rs 75 lakh out of the indemnity of one crore rupees imposed by the British on the bankrupt Sikhs, in lieu of which the Company gave him control of all the Sikhs' mountain territories east of the Jhelum and north of the Ravi.

2

Mass Rage

One round of militancy had ended around 2007; a short decade later, another one had emerged with vigour. Three times during that decade—in 2008, 2010, and 2016—young Kashmiris rose in revolt against the state in angry mobs that pelted stones against police and paramilitary forces across the Valley. Even though militancy developed in tandem with these instances of mass rage, militancy did not initially lie beneath these acts of public fury. At least in public perception within Kashmir, militancy was as good as dead when public fury took over Kashmir in 2008. In 2010, even as new militancy had begun to emerge in a small way, there was very little support for it. Mass anger distinguished clearly between militants and non-combatants. The public was furious at that stage over the killing of those who many Kashmiris called 'innocent', that is, those who had nothing to do with militancy. At one level, the public fury was against the continuation of the counterinsurgency apparatus after the previous insurgency[1] had ended. The undercurrent of the 2010 agitations against the killing of innocents was a demand for the rule of law, the constitutionally guaranteed right to life of those who had not defied the state.

Although the apparatus of counterinsurgency was wound down to some extent in the aftermath of the mass eruption of rage in 2010, it was too little, too late. Continued harassment, torture, and injustice by the state police during the couple of years following that, and the unrespon-sive callousness of the state government, ensured that the new militancy continued to build quietly, and so did the public support for it. Indeed, since 2014, unarmed public mobs, including women, had taken to the streets during encounters between state forces and militants—to try and obstruct the forces.

When mass rage erupted in the latter half of 2016, public anger openly endorsed the new militancy. Overtly backing militants, the 2016 agitations represented a rejection of the state's legitimacy. That marked a sea-change from 2010, when the mass agitation was against the killing of 'innocents'; people had demanded the rule of law then.

The incredible fact is that the state seemed to not even have noticed the new militants until about 2015, even though the new militants had routinely snatched rifles from policemen or paramilitary CRPF men since around 2012. It was like a ritual of initiation, a test of courage and ability.

Several more boys than before went underground after the 2016 uprising subsided. Some of these boys were hiding from the police. Several joined the new militancy that had emerged gradually since 2008. The number of new militants in the field increased hugely in the two years following July 2016. The trend had begun as a little trickle around 2010; a boy occasionally slipped into a forest to join an established band of militants who still lurked there after the earlier militancy had petered out. What made the Kashmiri youth take this route was anger. And one major cause of their anger was the killing of innocents by armed forces looking for rewards. That had led to a furious uprising in 2010, when people demonstrated angrily on streets, highways, and byways right across Kashmir. Police and paramilitary forces deployed to control that uprising shot one or two boys almost daily. These forces apparently ignored repeated orders and appeals not to fire, or to aim at legs, not to cause fatal injuries.

GRADUAL EMERGENCE OF NEW MILITANCY

It was after 2009 that one first heard fresh talk in the Valley of boys having gone underground—boys from Shopian in south Kashmir, Tral in the east, and Baramulla in the north. One had not heard of these things for about a decade. This was surely a new round of militancy. By the middle of the next decade, militants from several outfits were said to be lurking again in Downtown Srinagar, though locals insisted that militancy was not active. Evidently, the militants were waiting for the right time, or for orders.

As for Sopore, that old centre of rebellion, a young Kashmiri journalist remarked in 2009 that it was 'back to 1992'. That had to be an exaggeration. For, between 1990 and 1992, Sopore had been as good as free of Indian control. Even army convoys would take a detour en route to the divisional headquarters at Kupwara, to avoid Sopore. A comparison with 1992 was a vivid comment on the extent to which the commercial hub of north Kashmir had once again become a stronghold of militants.

By 2015, it had become a well-known fact. There were several incidents of militant violence. In one of them, two young girls from a poor family were taken from their home and shot a short distance away. There were many other violent events in north Kashmir during the summer of 2015, mainly in two series. One targeted persons running telephone services or mobile telephone towers. The other targeted persons who were close to Kashmir's established freedom movement but who some militants suspected of playing both sides. That sent alarm bells ringing across Kashmir. But those who ran India only bothered with Kashmir when it exploded in rage. Generally, they seemed to have no idea about how to grapple with either the causes or the devious manipulations that contributed to causing those explosions.

Several of the new recruits to militancy were from south Kashmir, where many boys had been tortured and horribly humiliated in police stations in the months after the 2010 uprising. The worst month for detention and torture was February 2011. The Arab uprising in Cairo's Tahrir Square may have unnerved someone in the power hierarchy, for large numbers of boys were rounded up (though not formally arrested) immediately after. Most of them were released soon, but came out scarred. The anger and resentment that abusive captivity generated led a few more boys to become militants.

By 2013, militant attacks had clearly heralded a new militancy. Its emergence, in shadowy wisps, went largely unnoticed by the cumbersome and largely self-serving state apparatus. Policymakers and analysts in New Delhi chose to ignore it, for the various kinds of reports that shaped government responses (a flood of security-specific money and troops) and non-responses (neither worthwhile intelligence, nor sensitivity) reflected total control—on paper. Those reports used words like grid and domination—words that fit only in those reports and on the desks and shelves where those reports went. Those claims of control were an illusion. Grids and domination were not only useless, they were counterproductive if one wanted to nurture the desire for peace that had emerged among the new generation that began to come of age around 2007. The state's response was so unfocused that the new generation had become belligerently anti-state by 2016.

Assiduously ignored, the new militancy grew gradually until, by 2015, it could not be ignored. By then, militants had also come to Kashmir once again from across the Line of Control (LoC). These were Pakistanis, a few other foreigners intent on jihad, and some of the Kashmiris who had stayed behind when Pakistan had wound down support for militancy in January 2002. Most of the militants who crossed over now were highly trained and brought with them lethal arms; there was even some talk of relatively heavier weapons by the summer of 2017.

A very large number of training camps had dotted the regions around Muzaffarabad and Mirpur on the Pakistani side of the LoC since at least 2014, probably earlier. Some of them belonged to Lashkar-e-Taiba (LeT), an extremely narrow-vision Islamist outfit. Its members, generally from poor Pakistani families, were motivated to give their lives in jihad. The group had remained active even when Pakistan had wound down other militant outfits. By 2016, LeT fighters were joined by others from similar Islamist, jihad-inspired groups such as Jaish-e-Mohammed and Al Badr—which was affiliated to the Haqqani faction of the Afghan jihad.[2] These groups had not been seen in Kashmir for several years.

For the first time, militants from the Pakistani side had crossed the daunting, ice-bound LoC even through the winter of 2015–16.[3] During the summer of 2016, the inflow was at levels not witnessed since the 1990s. It was evident that these militants would join forces with the Kashmiri boys who had already stepped up the new militancy since at least 2012. Moreover, they would depend on common Kashmiris to rally to their support during battles. During encounters between the forces and militants since the beginning of 2015, residents of nearby hamlets had often opposed Indian forces with sticks and stones and slogans, in order to help cornered militants to escape.

DEMONSTRATIONS AND MILITANTS

This new militancy had a different pattern than the previous militancy. It developed quietly, as if wisps of mist were floating in. It was barely noticed for a long time. It drew to its ranks students who had often fared well in examinations and who were highly regarded by their teachers. This was a contrast to the militancy which lasted from 1988 to 2006. Only a few of those militants had completed high school, and most of them had not fared well at studies.

Generally, the new militants remained quiet, as if they were waiting for the big moment when they would show their hand. Militant attacks increased between 2015 and 2017, but were largely limited to south Kashmir. The moment when the new militancy would really show its hand in full force did not come until 2017, a decade after that year of beginnings and endings.

A significant factor had fallen into place by then: the angry street protests that erupted now and again finally converged with a new militancy. The three instances when Kashmiris rose in mass stone-pelting revolt showed that attitudes towards militancy had changed radically after 2010. Only by 2016 did those who were teenaged boys and girls by then valorize militancy. Most adults remained at best ambivalent about it. But they mattered little. The two trends—mass demonstrations and militancy—had begun to complement each other by 2015. The ranks of new militants swelled whenever state forces killed persons in those angry street mobs.

Those eruptions steadily became more focused, coordinated, and bold with time. There was also a major difference in geographical spread. The city of Srinagar and other urban centres such as Sopore and Baramulla were at the centre of the eruption of 2010. In 2016, these urban centres were much quieter than rural areas—even remote villages that had been relatively unaffected, not only in 2008 and 2010 but even through the 1990s. A third difference: mass anger built up gradually in 2008 and 2010, but the agitations of 2016 began with an explosive peak, as if a fuse had been lit.

BURHAN WANI

It was on the ninth day of July that public fury erupted in 2016. Large numbers protested angrily all across Kashmir over the death of a young militant in an encounter with forces the previous evening. That encounter led to the killing of three Kashmiri militants, but the widespread rage was over Burhan Wani, who had become an iconic hero in Kashmir over the previous year. In an intriguing change of strategy by those who were managing preparations for the new militancy, Burhan had been assiduously projected on social media platforms. Through the summer of 2015, pictures and videos of him remained on platforms like Facebook for several weeks at a time, and made Burhan a sensational youth icon.

Burhan was a soft-spoken, pleasant, smart young man. The darling of all, he was a natural leader. Those who knew him hero-worshipped him, even young men much older than him. Born in 1994, when Kashmir's militancy was at high pitch, and the place was being flooded with troops, Burhan entered his teens in 2007, that year of endings and beginnings. He was just finishing school when, close to his sixteenth birthday, Burhan slipped into the forests to join Kashmir's militancy during the autumn of 2010. A few weeks before, police and paramilitary men had wantonly beaten Burhan. All through that evening, his home was witness to his yelling about injustice, as he vented the anger and frustration he felt at the humiliation. He demanded to know what had he done to get a beating.

When Burhan and his brother had been returning home earlier that evening after buying provisions, some security men had questioned them. The movement of people was still restricted at the time, after the uprising that summer. The boys showed their identity cards and explained where they had been. The security men told them to bring some cigarettes. The boys did as asked and yet security men beat them before sending them on their way.[4] The security men included policemen of the Special Operations Group (SOG) and the CRPF.

The experience was humiliating. To Burhan, it felt like slavery. The injustice, violation, and helplessness of that power equation deeply upset him. Even as he tried to vent his anger and frustration that evening at home, it did not ease the pain in his mind. He slipped into the forests a few weeks later, to take up arms against the state. Burhan's experience represents the sort of experience that helped the new militancy that began after 2008 to take root.

Certain incidents shaped the response of the community at large, as well as of particular individuals. Sabzar Bhat, one of those who succeeded Burhan as the commander of Hizb-ul-Mujahideen in south Kashmir, snatched a rifle and became a militant an hour after the army sent home the body of Khalid, Burhan's elder brother, with brutal torture marks. Among the first of the new militants were four boys who were said to have slipped underground from Shopian in 2009, a few weeks after all of Shopian had shut down for weeks on end to protest the rape and murder of two young women. Investigators declared that the two women had drowned, not been raped or murdered, but people by and large were not convinced by those investigations.

The fact that they perceived Burhan rather than his brother Khalid as their icon indicated that what mattered most to this generation was what they experienced and saw around them. Horrific torture by the Border Security Force (BSF) or a police Special Task Force had largely become a thing of the past during the decade after 2005. But those who had been born around the turn of the millennium could relate to the arbitrary humiliation and assault that had made Burhan shout angry questions through an evening, and then take up weapons. He was the perfect example of a soft-spoken, innocent victim of outrageous impunity—which is how most Kashmiri youth saw themselves, based on the perceptions that followed the uprisings of 2008 and 2010.

No lessons were learnt until the new militancy became too obvious to ignore, around 2015. Police insensitivity and brutality still occurred, even though the police's functioning became far more professional thereafter. Even in June 2017, young Zubair Bashir Turey[5] got away from police custody and became a militant. On YouTube, he stated that the police had relentlessly harassed and humiliated him, even keeping him in lock-up for three more months after the High Court had quashed his arrest under the Public Safety Act (PSA), which allowed for extended detention without evidence. That was after he had already endured jail for four years before that case was quashed. Determined to keep him locked, the police slapped another case under PSA, after which he escaped through what he called a 'painful' story.[6] The police had first charged the Shopian millennial with the Arms Act in 2009, when he was eleven-years-old; the state appeared to have no other tactics or methods to engage with angry boys, even pre-teens.[7]

Dressed in a green uniform as a soldier of Islam with grenades and guns around him, Turey announced on YouTube that his traumas had been as painful as the horrors 'our sisters have suffered'. Like so many others of that age, this teenager contrasted the pellet guns, which frequently harmed Kashmiris' life and sight, with crowd control methods (such as water cannons) used elsewhere in India; he, and other young Kashmiris like him, considered it discriminatory.

This generation sought a just world—and ideals in terms of nature and personality. Another factor that turned Burhan into such an iconic hero was public projection. Videos of him went viral on the internet, particularly Facebook, during the summer of 2015. Several of these showed the boy playing cricket, or chatting with other youth, often near a stream or in a green clearing of a verdant forest. The happy spaces in his videos illustrated an ideal retreat from the confusing, humiliating world in which nobody seemed to understand young people, too many teachers did not satisfy quests for insights, and parents unfamiliar with unitary families struggled to cope.

Another factor was implicit empowerment. Those verdant video retreats were a world in which the boy was master, surrounded by loyal comrades, nature, or a traditional house, and the elevating symbols of religiosity. Expertly put together, the visuals in the videos must have subconsciously seemed like a millennial teenager's paradise. The desire for empowerment animated many of the boys who barricaded the streets in 2010 and 2016 too. They sometimes had a boss. Those wanting to pass a posse of menacing 'stone-pelters' would be referred to a 'sahib' who might turn out to be a puny boy in his pre-teens. With an air of machismo, he would decide on the pleas of each vehicle wanting to pass. The boys' targets were ordinary, generally older, Kashmiris as much as police or other forces. Such behaviour patterns were, at least at a subconscious level, their response to the arbitrary, humiliating, violative impression of the state and society in their minds—which had potently contributed to the emergence of the new militancy.

INSENSITIVITY AND WORSE

Burhan was a charismatic boy-leader during the almost six years he remained underground, just as he had been before he went underground. He had amazing charm, combined with steely resolve and resilience.[8] People with whom he interacted respected and loved him. By the time he was out of his teens, he was the prime motivator to take more young men in south Kashmir into militant resistance. Lt General D.S. Hooda, who had been Commander-in-Chief of the Northern Command of the Indian Army when Burhan was killed in 2016, stated at a seminar in December 2017 that Burhan had never himself killed anyone. That was a crucial part of what made him seem like a hero among Kashmiri youth. In fact, some youth in south Kashmir believed that the only person Burhan had killed with his own gun was another militant, who had crowed to Burhan that he had molested a woman.

Burhan found it easy to motivate young Kashmiris. Since 2008, and more so since 2009, many of them had felt increasingly distressed at their situation. For, although those who had grown up amid violence and turmoil had become convinced of the futility of militancy by 2007, their sentiments were brittle. Although at that point the 'azadi' objective did not excite them much, the perception of a cruel, unresponsive state that killed as a first response, which developed during the uprisings of 2008 and 2010, made them receptive to the new narratives that had come into play since 2008. There was, after all, a well of pain beneath their placidity. They were all in trauma—adolescent trauma layered over childhood trauma, layered over infant trauma, layered over postnatal and even prenatal trauma. For, most of those who exploded in anger in 2010 and 2016 were born in the time of violence that began in 1988. In Kashmir, the 1990s had been nerve-wracking. The lives of this generation had been unstable and troubled at several levels—political, social, cultural, personal—and they needed extraordinarily sensitive handling.

The youth of Kashmir had aspirations. They had hopes. They wanted to get on with their lives in peace—but with dignity. What some of them saw after the uprising of 2010, and many heard about through social media, was humiliation, cruelty, and extortion. The infrastructure of counterinsurgency, and the elastic powers that went with it, remained largely in place. It particularly irked because, between 2000 and 2005, Kashmir had got used to the easing of restrictions and a tightening of reins over those engaged in counterinsurgency. An apparently earnest India–Pakistan peace process had also picked up during that time, and it gave people a sense of hope that the violence and turmoil that had dominated their lives would soon be consigned to the past.

A deep sense of betrayal gradually took root in the years after 2007, and the hope that had encouraged Kashmiris started fading. Before long, hope was replaced by fury. As we have noted, that sense of betrayal led the young in two directions during that decade: while a few took to militancy, a very large number periodically erupted in street protests. The new militancy emerged very slowly soon after the first round of street protests in 2008. The two trends were still separate when street protests occurred again in 2010. But by 2015, the two trends had begun to complement each other: stone-pelting protests sometimes occurred around the site of an encounter between forces and militants.

Both trends were pushed by the cynical unresponsiveness of the state government. Officers charged with controlling the demonstrations were unable to prevent their men from killing one or two protestors with either gunfire or with teargas shells shot at close range—almost every day during the protests of 2010. What made it worse was that those in charge of deploying 'non-lethal' weaponry, so that demonstrators may not get killed, bought vast numbers of pellet guns. In 2016, these pellets blinded many protesting youth—some in both eyes. Pellets fired from close range even killed. This enraged young Kashmiris even more, especially when they compared pellet guns with the deployment of water cannons to control violent mobs in areas like Haryana and Rajasthan nearer New Delhi.

A large number of young men became enemies of the state after being locked up in police stations across the Valley in 2010, and during the following winter and spring. They were assaulted, abused, and threatened with the PSA while there. They felt brutalized by the time they emerged. Thrust onto the statute by Chief Minister Omar Abdullah's grandfather, Sheikh Abdullah, the Act allowed the police to lock up anyone for two years without evidentiary judicial process. That happened again in 2016, as if the state were intent on generating more violence and conflict. Money was extorted from many of the parents and most young men were released. But they came out scarred by the experience, and often became determined to oppose the state even more strongly.

In early 2011, as in most years, the objective of the government was short term: to 'get through this summer' somehow.[9] Since generalist bureaucrats and elected politicians formulated government policies, these tended to be very short term. The bureaucrats knew they would be transferred (to, say, wind power or drainage management) in one or two years. The politicians expected to lose power in a couple of years, or at most five. A degree of cynicism marked Omar Abdullah's approach: according to him, young people used to throw stones in the 1980s, had taken up arms around 1990, and had gone back to throwing stones.[10] He was dismissive of the idea that they might take up arms again. To him, the pelting of stones was normal.

Normal. Those who ran governments loved that word. They had spent the past few years strenuously telling all who would listen that Kashmir was normal. They projected normalcy by pointing out that large numbers of tourists roamed the place, and large numbers of Kashmiris turned out to vote in elections. That was all true, but none of that reflected the changing attitudes or aspirations of young people. The only people who really believed those versions of 'normal'—electoral turnout and tourists—were Indians who wanted to feel good about the situation in Kashmir. On the other hand, many young Kashmiris' experiences with the police and exasperation with the cynical attitudes of politicians affected their attitudes and aspirations. To be sure, the police and politicians were not much better, and often much worse, in many other states of India, but their impact on a traumatized and volatile population was far more incendiary in Kashmir.

FORMATIVE FACTORS

Several factors contributed to the mass rage, like the rage of a jilted lover, that surfaced off and on through that decade. The first factor was the sort of police brutality that pushed Burhan and others like him to become militants. The second was the incompetence and cynicism of the state government that New Delhi installed at the end of 2008, and insisted on retaining in power through that terrible time when a new generation of Kashmiris was lost. The incompetence of Omar Abdullah came to the fore in less than six months of his taking over as the chief minister, when he hemmed and hawed and repeatedly changed his stance over allegations that armed forces had raped and murdered two young women in Shopian in southwest Kashmir. That was when the Kashmiri people largely lost trust in his regime—and in the system that sustained it.[11]

These two primary factors created a fertile ground for the third, which was the masterfully orchestrated set of narratives that went into high gear in 2008. These came into play just when the submerged rage of the new generation was brought to the surface by a controversy over the transfer of land to a Hindu shrine board—a controversy that was manufactured by politicians. New narratives of colonization, occupation, exploitation, mass rapes, and mass graves were the order of the day. Narratives about what had happened during the previous insurgency, which many millennials did not remember, made a huge impact on them. Their experiences of police high-handedness, such as Burhan's in 2010, seemed to confirm the impressions generated by those influences. Unlike their parents, they had not experienced, and so did not know, the nuanced realities of the 1990s—patterns of those militants' as well as those security forces' behaviour. Post-truth shaped their responses.

The Kashmiri youth's experience of humiliation and cruelty—of the sort Burhan experienced at the hands of Special Operations Police—dovetailed neatly with the image of a Muslim *ummah* under occupation, siege, violation, and exploitation globally. This was the fourth factor that shaped this generation: ideas of Islamic exclusivism that revolved around Muslim superiority, and the compulsion to strictly follow a narrow interpretation of correct Islam. For two centuries, religion had been co-opted as symbol of an identity that revolved essentially around victimhood; the oppressor, even if nominally of the same religious and linguistic identity, was othered as collaborator–oppressor. So, for example, many young Kashmiris contemned the local police as 'Ponda police', a moniker that some said was invented during the British Raj as a corruption of 'Pound'. So intense was that process of othering that many Kashmiris defended the horrific lynching of a police officer in the heart of Sringar during Ramzan in 2017.

GENERATIONAL CHANGE

Generational change had been intense within Kashmir during that decade. After the first few days following Burhan's death, most of the youth on the streets, imposing blockades and shutdowns, were younger than Burhan had been. Most of them were teenagers, or in their pre-teens. They had been little children in 2008. Most of those who had participated in the 2008 demonstrations were already adults; many of those who were relatively young then were in their thirties by 2016. More teenagers had participated in the 2010 agitations than in 2008, but even those who were in their early teens in 2010 were past their teens by 2016, six years later. After the first day or two after Burhan's death, relatively few of those who were older than Burhan had been (almost twenty-two) participated in demonstrations. The generation that had been children during the 1990s had become enraged between 2007 and 2011. By 2016, they had already become the second tier—behind the generation that was born around the turn of the millennium.

In different parts of the Valley, several of those who had been born around 1990 spoke during 2016 of having introspected since the previous winter, when violence and agitations had picked up. While their adolescent younger brothers pelted stones, many of those now aged around thirty weighed the meaning and impact of global trends—of Islamic State, of other narrow-vision versions of religion, of the kinds of values by which they wanted to live, the divisions and fault-lines in their society, and the consequences of war.

On the other hand, most of those—mainly teenagers—who were at the core of the 2016 protests were enamoured of those sorts of narrow-vision, exclusivist ideas. Most of them may not even have participated in 2008 and 2010. Those among them who had been on the streets in 2010 too had been little boys then. But pelting stones was literally child's play to them. It had become a commonplace form of play in Kashmir since 2008. Even two-year-olds chucked little pebbles at each other in their driveways and front gardens, yelling slogans in their high-pitched voices. Many had honed the craft since infancy; their aim was sharp, and they knew the art of lobbing.

Why did they hit out at police and paramilitary troops? Conversations with young men who led the 'stone-pelting' in such epicentres of the 2016 uprising as Pulwama confirmed that, while those in their twenties had some sense of the counterinsurgency excesses of the 1990s, those in their late teens did not remember what had happened. They went by the narratives that had helped to form them as they grew up. Some of the leading 'stone-pelters' in Newa near Pulwama in south Kashmir said in December 2016 that they had routinely played with and shared food with army soldiers deployed near their homes when they were children, but had learnt to hate them from 2008 onwards.[12] Narratives shaped their minds, and their hatred. Broadly speaking then, the experience of the 2008 uprising, and the narratives that vigorously circulated since then, shaped and animated the majority of those who took to the streets in 2016.

The teenagers who were at the forefront of the 2016 protests had no direct memory of the peace process which Prime Minister Vajpayee had initiated in 2003, when they had been little children. They had grown up amid the concerted construction of a narrative of military occupation, horrific repression, and exploitation—a narrative construction which had got going around that year of endings and beginnings, 2007. They had only heard the narrative, not experienced the more nuanced reality of the 1990s. Burhan was such an iconic object of hero-worship for them since his story, and that of his elder brother Khalid's horrific death, was like a metaphor for that entire narrative. That narrative dovetailed with the discourse about Islam, jihad, and martyrdom that Burhan's videos reflected.

Those charged with upholding public order, including those under oath like Omar Abdullah from 2009 to 2014 and Mehbooba Mufti in 2016, should have been very seriously concerned about the changes in focus each time young people erupted in anger and protest. For, the 2010 protests were specifically against the killing of innocents—those not involved in militancy. At that stage, one might argue that the protestors obliquely accepted the legitimacy of forces' action against militants, that they wanted their constitutionally guaranteed right to life, the mandated rule of law. At any rate, they did not interfere in forces' operations at that stage. The 2016 protests were specifically against the killing of Burhan, an acknowledged militant. And, by then, people from neighbouring homes and even nearby villages, had begun to turn out to try and prevent the forces from acting against militants during searches and firefights. While 2010 represented a cry of distress at innocents being clubbed with militants, 2016 witnessed an endorsement of militancy. Erasing the line dividing militants from others, it turned the population at large, at least in some pockets, into combatants.

MULTI-ROOTED ANGST

The eruption of rage in 2016 must be understood at several levels. At one level, it was a protest at the killing of Burhan. To many across India, that was unacceptable simply because Burhan was, to them, a 'terrorist'. If one wishes to get beyond a cycle of violence and hate, one must understand that most people in Kashmir saw Burhan as a hero. Focusing on the arbitrary humiliation he suffered before taking the militant path, they saw him as personifying victimhood and an insistence on dignity.

In any case, the uprising of 2016 was only partly about Burhan. At a geopolitical level, it was a cry for freedom, a ringing protest against India. Two factors are important at this level. One, activists of the Islamist Jamaat-e-Islami largely managed the eruption. Two, those who ran protests on the ground were coordinated from Pakistan far more than in 2010. At this level then, the eruption of anger potentially laid the ground for war.

At a third level, the eruption of 2016 was a cry of resistance against the coalition alliance of the Kashmiri People's Democratic Party (PDP) and the Bharatiya Janata Party (BJP). Resentment against it had built gradually over 2015, stemming both from disappointment over funding for Kashmir, as well as the Hindutva agenda of BJP activists. That the 2016 eruption was concentrated in south Kashmir, the PDP's putative stronghold, was a measure of how deep was the sense of betrayal over this alliance and its agenda.

These first three levels were readily recognized, and widely analysed. I have pointed out two more levels—of generational differences, and the role of narratives in shaping collective memory. Although the millennial generation had not experienced the worst of counterinsurgency excesses when insurgency actually raged, the cynicism and extortion they had experienced gave those narratives salience. In this light, the agitations of 2016 represented a response to counterinsurgency excesses. The cruel ways in which the insurgency of the 1990s was repressed were bad enough on their own. But resentment against it had been exhausted, and so had died down in the period leading up to 2007. However, resentment rose again when the violations of dignity and peace of mind continued, as the counterinsurgency regime continued to hold sway even after the insurgency had petered out.

The Indian state was reaping the whirlwind, since it had not nurtured and responded to the widespread disillusionment, and desire to move on towards peace, that had dominated for a while around 2007.

NOTES

1. The author lived in Kashmir and witnessed the uprising.
2. Based on the author's interviews with citizens and army officers in Kupwara in August 2016.
3. Author's interactions in August 2016 with officers directly engaged in foiling infiltrations in Kupwara district.
4. Based on author's interview with Burhan Wani's father at Tral on 10 August 2016.
5. This was his name in official records, though it was often spelt differently.
6. https://www.youtube.com/watch?v=wRx1jrvHHNE&feature=youtu.be, accessed on 5 June 2017.
7. https://www.thequint.com/india/2017/05/18/zubair-ahmed-turay-kashmir-shopian-militancy, accessed on 4 June 2017.
8. Author's interviews with people in Tral, including Burhan Wani's father, brother, and grandfather.
9. Author's interactions with senior officers and other state functionaries that year.
10. Author's meeting with Omar Abdullah in the chief minister's office at the Secretariat in Srinagar in September 2011.
11. http://www.hindustantimes.com/india/frittered-mandate/story-Mrmnf2IUT-PZw5eNGhQyWDO.html, accessed on 13 February 2017.
12. Reported in http://www.firstpost.com/india/farooq-abdullahs-pro-hurriyat-line-shows-once-again-that-dividing-lines-in-kashmir-are-only-on-paper-3144650.html, accessed on 16 December 2016.

3

Caged Childhood

In order to understand the responses of young Kashmiris, it is important to visualize the world in which they grew up—the world that shaped their psyches and responses. It is hard to imagine how insecure a family feels when there is virtually no state, and anybody with muscle power and a gun rules. Through the first half of the 1990s, most rural areas felt totally exposed, vulnerable. The city got by a little better than most rural belts, since the arms of government did not abandon it for as long or as completely. The city did not endure the excesses of its freedom fighters the way rural areas did. It felt the terror of those bunkers spewing bullets, though—and curfews, and fearful lifelessness from dusk to dawn.

For individuals, life in the early 1990s was a constant battle with fear and uncertainty. Rural or urban, hardly anyone ventured out after sunset. Most people sat indoors without lights, with a blanket stretched across every shuttered window—so that not even the flicker of a candle might be seen outside. In those dreary homes, they would creep about, desperately shushing babies and noisy children. In an article that appeared in *Business Line* on 22 October 2010,[1] Marryam H. Reshii, a Kerala-born journalist and cuisine expert married to a Kashmiri from Downtown Srinagar, gave a glimpse into the Downtown Srinagar she came to know as a bride. She evocatively described the tense challenge of preventing a baby in the family from crying, the entire family hardly daring to breathe in the enveloping darkness, in their desperation to not attract the attention of troops crunching the lane outside with their boots.

Focusing on the generation that she watched growing up in the time of militancy, Reshii described the ways in which violence had shaped her nephew. Born in 1988, he was typical of the city-born Kashmiri generation that came of age around 2007:

… Elder sister's son, Omar Jan, had a shockingly violent childhood, quite beyond the comprehension of most of us in the rest of the country. …

… When Omar Jan came to our part of the city to visit, come night-fall and the street outside our home would be deserted. You could hear a pin drop in that blank silence, because when the military men from the nearby bunkers went off duty, they'd be as inwardly terrified of leaving the relative safety of their sand-bagged bunkers as we would be of the consequences of their skittish nerves. A man with a gun walking down the street at dead of night, conscious of being a target of hatred by the public, is apt to react violently at any unexpected sound, so our one-point agenda was to keep Omar Jan quiet.

We would all be huddled in an inside room—Mum, Dad, the three brothers, of whom my husband was the eldest, and the two sisters, including Omar Jan's mother who had come to visit her parents. As usual, there would be no electricity and little Omar would be on my lap. I would whisper nursery rhymes to him, my heart pounding so loudly in my rib cage that I would always wonder why the frog-marching army outside didn't hear it. The family would be wound tight with tension. What if Omar Jan began crying or talking just that very minute that the jackboots were marching outside our front door? What if they reacted instantly, by pulling the trigger? What if … ?

Nineteen years later, I now realise that the childhood that Omar Jan was subjected to made him the hardened young man that he is today. He is as adorable as he ever was, as caring, as affectionate and ready to learn. But fear, as an emotion, is an alien beast to him. So it would be to you, if you had seen humans blown to bits before your eyes when you were three.

The first inkling we had of it was during the Amarnath land transfer agitation of 2008. Mum and I were peeling vegetables in the kitchen, with the front door firmly bolted. By then, both brothers as well as little sister were married. Mum and I were as nervous as we had always been, but all throughout the agitation, Omar would breeze in and out of the old house with supreme confidence. When the police, in an effort to control the crowds at the seventh bridge, fired rubber bullets, Omar was injured. Everyone was aghast, except Omar himself.

The confusing efforts of mothers, grandmothers, and aunts to shush them with a terrified edge of desperation, while men with guns prowled, were among the earliest memories of many among the Kashmiri generation that came of age around 2007. Many whispered memories of peril lurked in the subconscious layers of their minds. As Reshii pointed out, danger had been such an immediate and constant fact of their lives since their infancies that they were inured to it.

The very tactics that the armed forces used to terrorize adults into submission hardened children to the terrors of a war zone. They were at home with silences, the dark nights when lighting a candle might attract a bullet, braving bullets to go out for a vegetable or milk for a home with nothing to eat. Most boys of that generation could take apart any gun smaller than a machine gun, and put it back again. They could recognize a gun from its sound. Their toys were guns, their games were of terror.

MACABRE MEMORIES

If one got used to seeing shattered bits of bodies when one was just an infant, one had to deal with such bodies when one was older. Imtiaz Khanday describes how he helped to carry the body of a neighbour who had just been shot in the head a couple of hundred metres from his house. In a matter-of-fact voice, as if he were talking of a car breakdown, he says that the wife and sister-in-law of his neighbour gathered the dead man's spilled brains and wrapped his shattered head in their scarf before he helped them to carry the man's body to their home.

A few minutes earlier, 'two gunmen' (as Khanday describes the militants) had come to that house, next to his, and called the man out. They took him about 200 metres away from his home, says Khanday, and shot him in the head. He was 'thought to be an informer', Khanday adds by way of explanation. This happened in November 2011, when Khanday was still nineteen years old. From his village near Kreeri in the Baramulla district of north Kashmir, one could see the ridges that marked the LoC; violence and horror had been a much greater part of his life than that of a city child, ever since he was born.

Although this sort of experience did not last beyond the mid-1990s for boys like Omar Jan in the downtown city of Srinagar, Kashmir's leading psychiatrists confirmed that levels of harassment and uncertainty remained high enough to cause just about everyone in the population to suffer some degree of post-traumatic stress disorder. For rural youth who were born in the late 1990s in some pockets of Kashmir, the experience of macabre things such as blown up body parts continued until about 2005. Carrying the freshly killed body of a neighbour is only one of the several stories that Khanday related from his deep store of memories.

Another is that soldiers took Manzoor Ahmed Mir from his home in Delina village near Baramulla on 7 September 2003, and that Manzoor never returned. Khanday names a Captain Sharma as the one who promised Manzoor's wife and three little children when they took him away that he would be back the next day. Manzoor was twenty-five, says Khanday, and worked as a mason.

Khanday became a student of biotechnology at Sharda University in Greater Noida from 2012. Quite comfortable among his friends in the ambience of Greater Noida and Delhi, he got involved with organizing student activities at his university. But the narratives of his traumatizing childhood came back quite easily, in a matter-of-fact way, during one weekend of remembering early in 2015. He talked, among others, of a boy who had been just a little older than him. Khushi Mohammed was fourteen when he stepped on a mine while grazing his cattle in a field next to his home on 11 March 2003.

FEARSOME 'CRACKDOWNS'

The 'crackdown' was the most commonly resented symbol of trauma and violation during the second phase of counterinsurgency. 'Crackdown' was the word among Kashmiris for the cordon-and-search operations through which the army tried to discover militants and arms dumps. They were nightmares for adults. It is difficult to imagine what kind of impact they had on children. Nazar-ul Islam Wani was a PhD scholar at Kashmir University in 2015,[2] when he described his personal experience of crackdowns. It indicates that this generation experienced a great deal of fear and confusion when they were children, before those experiences immunized them to fear.

My life started in village Naibugh, Tral, some 45 kms away from Srinagar. I was pretty well-off. Like other children anywhere in the world, my desire to play with toys and other boys would take me to the outskirts of my village, my first long journeys. While playing one day, we saw army patrolling in the evening.

Fearful, we returned home and squatted. Fear of the army had got transferred irrationally into me; it was more in my culture than in my mind. Army patrolling in the distant fields was the first indication of a 'crackdown'.

Crackdowns in my village usually began at midnight. The patrolling of army in the fields, circumambulating the whole village, marching, trampling, gushing, yelling, and dogs barking, would implicitly announce that your whole village is cordoned/circled and ambushed by the army with no chance left to leave.

The azaan (call for prayers) in the morning would create an image of crackdown because the muezzin would sound very low on that day. Technically, this was followed by announcing the 'crackdown' on the only loudspeaker of the village mosque by an Imam. The words were announced in Urdu and then translated in Kashmiri: *'Tamam logun say guzarish ki jati hai ki wo ground main jama hojaye. Tamam mard our auratein apnay garun say bahar niklay our ground main jama hojaye. Boday our bemaar garun main rah sakhtay hain.'* 'All the men and the women of the village are requested (in high tone) to assemble in the school ground. The old and ill may stay in their homes.'

Immediately, though reluctantly, people would get out of their beds, put on their pheran, carry the identity card and run off to the school ground. On the way, we were all regimented to parade in a straight line, like school boys in the morning assembly. I was in the queue, with my pheran on my shoulders. My first interaction with the Indian army and with the Indian state was when army yelled at me to put off the pheran. Indian Army developed huge hatred for Kashmiri pherans. My dress was hated! I pondered about it throughout my life.

I was growing up in these queues and parades, and so did my impression about the Indian Army grow. So many people were beaten terribly because they did not have an identity card in these long queues, which would also formally announce the threat people would have to face the whole day.

In the assembled ground, people would sit, frightened, in a terrible disposition, dull. The atmosphere would turn into grieving. Suddenly, an officer wearing a greyish-green uniform would come and decide on the youth with long beard. They were dragged behind a hay rick and beaten. I couldn't understand the connection these men had with militants. I only knew they were my own people who were beaten ruthlessly and hence developed my hatred towards the army. Hundreds of men of each profession and age would squat before the army.

Technically, the next stage of crackdown was making search parties, commonly known as *talashi* party, to search all the houses, cowsheds, and storehouses of the village. Parties were chosen by the army. Each search party was shaped by one dozen army men and four civilians. Civilians were chosen on the basis of physical strength so that they could move the heavy stuff, climb and run fast. I was always made a *talashi wala* (one who accompanies the search party). I was made to move the heavy stuff; search the bathrooms, chimneys, granaries with iron rods passed through grains and many times gun was put on my shoulder to shield army in anticipation of any danger.

Back in the ground, even while talashi was underway, people were selected one by one. They would be presented before the collaborator or informer, who would single out the relatives or friends of militants. This was the most gruesome part of the 'crackdown' as the people pointed out by collaborator were tortured in schools, whipped with willow sticks, suffocated in unpleasantly cold water, and most of the times chilly water was poured through their nostrils. The interrogated men would yell so loud that their echo was heard in the mountains.

The atmosphere of fear could be smelt in the odours of vomit and other involuntary bodily emissions in my grandmother's house, where children and women were assembled.

Our search party soon returned to the school assembly. Army would make us sign the documents which explained that army had not stolen any property. I have never seen the army stealing but most of the people would complain about it. We were given back our identity cards and pherans and were made to sit in the ground. My evaluation about this kind of slavery had a negative impact on the rest of my life.

The final stage of crackdown was the arrests. The close relatives of militants—'mujahids' as locals call them—were arrested and tortured in military camps for several days. One day my father was pulled out from the assembly of torture and released after 15 days, leaving the family in shambles. The release was made possible only by begging before a military officer.

The aftermath of a crackdown would create hysteria in families. Most of them found their houses in a mess, with the stains of army boots on beautiful carpets. Everything was misplaced in my house. It took my mother a day to re-arrange the stuff.

Some families were heard wailing and moaning over the arrests of their husbands and sons. Depressed, the whole village discussed the brutalities of the crackdown at shop fronts in the evening. When the muezzin called for evening prayers, the knock on the loud-speaker would bring up the horrible memory. But this time, it was an evening prayer.

Nazar-ul Islam mentions soldiers' aversion to beards. That was common during the mid and late 1990s. Most Kashmiris shaved off or at least trimmed their beards at that stage. For, an open beard was likely to get the man beaten and tortured for no other reason than that he fit a soldier's stereotype of an 'extremist'. The tables were turned early in the new century. Then, a long, open beard was treated with respect rather than suspicion. Apparently, someone high up in the army brass had become convinced that Tablighi Jamaat activists, who most commonly kept long open beards, only preached about piety and heaven, and discouraged not just sedition but politics in general. Both sorts of presumption were simplistic and completely inadequate. One size does not fit all!

Crackdowns, barricade checks, and bunkers became the invasive shorthand of counterinsurgency. To Kashmiris who grew up during those years, India was the army (the generic term for all counterinsurgency forces). And, in their minds, the army meant the frightening power to enter anywhere, to humiliate, and to mete out horrifying punishments and torture. It was also decidedly alien—from a culture that disliked and punished one for wearing a pheran, the traditional Kashmiri dress that most Kashmiris found as comforting as Linus's blanket, almost like a protective womb. A child might not easily understand that a soldier viewed its enveloping wrap as a perfect cover for guns, bombs, or grenades.

Although such operations had ceased by 2007, the narrative, if not the direct memory, of the 'crackdown' was deeply embedded in the minds of Kashmiris who grew up in those years of terrible violence.

LONELINESS

On the one hand, young people of this generation had had to get used to violent death and destruction. On the other, they had never experienced life the way children elsewhere did—the joy of going out for an ice cream in the evening, a weekend picnic, a drive in the countryside, or even the fun and frolic of a family wedding. Life was a cage. Parents were often too paranoid to let them go out to play, at least after sunset. During the early and mid-1990s, no child in Kashmir had been out for an after-dinner stroll—or even a pre-dinner walk. They had to be indoors well before it got dark, which meant 4 p.m. in winter. Even then, their mothers and other family members worried ceaselessly as long as they were out of the house. They were almost never allowed to go far. Picnics, weekend excursions, and evening outings were unheard of. For the most part, the only leisure activities for boys were street cricket, or possibly football or volleyball on a rocky patch. Most girls were not allowed outdoors except for school or perhaps religious instruction at a neighbourhood *darasgah*.

Listless, they spent the long hours at home watching television if there was electricity—until their elders made them turn off the lights, generally quite early. During most of that awful decade, the 1990s, they could not even pass the time during those lonely evenings by chatting with friends over the telephone. Telephone services were so bad during that decade that it generally took several minutes to get through to a number. To be sure, when telephone connectivity became easier towards the end of that decade, young people took to the telephone, whispering to friends for hours in the darkness of the night. Many teenagers kept extension wires at hand, so that they could take the telephone instrument into their bedroom at night, unnoticed by their parents.

Their loneliness was heightened by the ways in which the architecture of Kashmiri houses changed during that time of violence. Families began to move from rural areas to the outskirts of cities. Sprawling suburbs came up on what had been agricultural land, or wetlands, even marshes. Families began to move to these from the inner city too. To own a house in one of these suburbs was the new fashion, a sign of upward social mobility. These houses were generally large and opulent, often a dozen rooms occupied by just three or four members of a household.

Until the 1990s, the typical Kashmiri house was never locked but, during the time of violence, people began to lock themselves indoors for fear of both kinds of men with guns. High walls were built around new houses, until it became the norm by the beginning of the new century to build eight-foot-high walls around new houses—even in villages, by the second decade of the century. Gates too were high and covered with thick iron sheets, so that no one could see across. In upmarket suburbs, those gates were generally bolted shut.

SOCIAL TRANSFORMATION

Social cohesion was under huge stress. Largely unnoticed, Kashmiri society had changed unrecognizably during the couple of decades before 2007, and this too caused alienation—disharmony with the social environment. First-generation unitary families had often come to live in huge mansions behind high walls, not coping very well with bringing up children. Bonds in what were once closely knit extended families had strained. Education was in shambles. All this had occurred in tandem with political and geopolitical ferment and tremendous, often competitive, pressure to conform to revised religious practices that were projected as pristine, original, and exclusively correct.

Adolescents felt the turbulence of all these changes most intensely. Most of this generation had rejected various sorts of role models. They needed to overcome disappointments and deeply felt betrayals—in the political, familial, and other dimensions of their lived realities. Bringing life to a halt, as they collectively did in 2016, was at one level also a way to stop the betrayals and disappointments. Those strutting boys were grappling for empowerment in many senses, and at various levels. They needed to physically dominate their environment, their society. Lurking throughout their charged eruptions was hope for a better reality, a more responsive social, economic, and political milieu.

Social changes that occurred during the time of violence plugged into this unprecedented intergenerational change. Social hierarchies were reordered chaotically, sometimes violently, in the early years of militancy. Two factors were at play. One, land reforms had already destroyed the Valley's existing social hierarchies during the 1950s. Two, the social turbulence wrought by militancy and the eviction of Pandits took that process much further during the 1990s. There was a great deal of churning beneath the social surface, as members of the Valley's highly status-conscious society struggled to establish precedence in a putative new social hierarchy. This too led to a great deal of societal stress and resentment.

As militancy and unaccountability generated a huge black economy, the new houses that came up behind those high walls and gates were often large opulent mansions. These reflected the urgent need to establish social status in the fast-changing milieu. So, within two generations from the time before Kashmir's land reforms,[3] when it was common for large extended families to sleep together in one or two rooms under a thatched roof, it became common for each child, particularly a boy, to have his own room. Too often, those rooms, and those mansions, were another sort of cage of isolation.

The wealth that accompanied social transformation since the 1950s was also beginning to reshape family life, cultural norms, and social milieus. Almost unnoticed, families had turned unitary. Grandparents might come to stay for a few weeks or months but, more often than not, returned to their ancestral home or to another child's house for the next few months. In the past, Kashmiri children had traditionally grown up in the nurturing environs of extended families and neighbourhoods, with several parent figures and role models. It had been normal for children to eat at whichever house they happened to be playing, even sleep over. During the time of violence, many parents had to adjust not only to their traumatizing circumstances but also to parenting in a unitary family without additional societal assistance. A very large number of mothers were hardly able to cope without support or role models amid the traumas of the violence around them. As in the past, a number of children grew up in their *matamal*, maternal grandparents' home—but lifestyles were under strain there too.

Fathers found the transition particularly difficult. Growing up in large, joint families, their interactions with their own fathers had been limited. The lack of intimate interactions had made them fear, and avoid, their fathers. But with the social transformation to unitary families, and the loss of bonds with extended families, their children expected more intimate interactions from them. What these fathers had not experienced from their own fathers while growing up, they found it difficult to provide to their children. Intergenerational conflict increased within homes, particularly between fathers and sons. If these young men were not willing to bow before repression by state forces, they were even less willing to be obsequious at home. Their fathers often found it tough to cope with them.

So, young people adjusted to violence, fear, and uncertainty in the isolation of their private rooms in large houses. In the seclusion of those rooms, boys could indulge themselves in all the things boys try out in order to overcome depression. Drug abuse became commonplace, smoking much more so. In fact, many nine- and ten-year-old boys smoked. Alcohol abuse too was common in the new century—in secret of course, since it was a major religious taboo.

When boys did go out, at least during the 1990s, the cage only changed its dimensions. There were barriers and checkpoints everywhere.[4] Passengers would be forced to get off a bus or other vehicle, to walk in line to a point where they were searched and questioned. To be without an identity card was suicidal. Everyone learnt to address a soldier as 'sir', and to remain silent and look respectful even while being abused or roughed up during a check. Paramilitary soldiers routinely slapped and humiliated people at these checkpoints. It was common for Kashmiris to be made to stand on their hands, with their feet propped against a wall, sometimes simply because a soldier did not like the look on their face, or he was having a bad day himself, or was Islamophobic. General M.A. Zaki, who was Corps Commander in 1989–91 and then Advisor (Security) to the Governor until 1995, observes that Kashmiris have a refined culture and were not used to the language and abrasive culture of many of the troops from some other states.[5]

CRIPPLED EDUCATION SYSTEM

Militancy crippled the education of this generation. Through the first half of the 1990s, most schools were more often closed than open. Even when they were open, teachers and students frequently could not get there. For, roads would be closed after a militant attack or for a cordon-and-search operation, or students and teachers were delayed so long at a checkpoint or by a search that they turned back home. School was missed more often than attended. If a child did reach school, teachers might not—or arson might have reduced the school building to a smouldering wreck.

Even when they functioned, schools were no safe havens. Paramilitary forces searched educational institutions too. In the early years of the insurgency, even the vice-chancellor was forced to line up on the university grounds for identification during a cordon-and-search 'crackdown'. And soldiers sometimes set up camp in a part of a school or a college. What this meant was that barbed wire fences, bunkers, rude searches, and mines surrounded the children near the outside perimeter. Forces only stopped using schools as camps in 2007, after a brave young student-journalist from Delhi[6] wrote about it and then personally pressed the Defence Minister to ban the use of schools and colleges to billet soldiers.

In the mid-1990s, Kashmiris spoke of middle-aged, sometimes grey-bearded, men walking into examination halls, placing a pistol on the desk and writing the examination on behalf of a student. Nobody dared question the man's identity. After things returned to a semblance of normalcy in 1997, the examination system began to be subverted in other ways. In the new century, parents and teachers sometimes collaborated to assist cheating so that their wards would pass examinations.

By the time the government pushed hard to revive and expand the education system,[7] a large number of young teachers had been educated during the time the system had been crippled. The government needed an army of teachers for the new colleges and schools it opened in the early years of the new century, but even the Education Minister of the time acknowledged that the quality of teachers was a problem.[8] Some colleges and universities were devalued into mass production degree factories. The liberal arts, which could have shaped thinkers who could rebuild society and lead its cultural and political life, were devalued the most.

The pressure of parents and society resulted in students generally pushing hard to get admission to medicine, engineering, management, media, or computer science courses—in more or less that order of preference—before finally opting for the arts, if they could not get admission to any of those other courses. Insightful analysis, rigorous research, and critical questioning were casualties of the times. For, to cover up their insecurities, many teachers shouted down students' questions, punished curious students with bad marks, or resorted to corporal punishment.

A generation left those educational institutions with degrees and with training against independent thinking. In his keynote address at an event organized by a university's Islamic Studies department, a vice-chancellor stated that Islam does not allow for theology or questioning. 'Just do it', he said, specifically citing the Nike advertisement.[9] As was standard practice, the vice-chancellor got a standing ovation. Nobody pointed out that the Prophet of Islam had prioritized learning, and that reasoned scientific innovations and discoveries were highlights of Islamic history—even as taught by that Islamic Studies department.

The hollowing of the education system meant that armies of men and women roamed the state with degrees. Many of them were barely employable but expected that the government owed them a job. A few months after that summer of stone-pelting in the Valley in 2010, an older man in a village observed that his school teacher had been 'fifth pass', but taught far better than contemporary PhDs. As if to prove his point, a graduate in English literature who planned to get a PhD and become a lecturer said that his favourite literary works were Shakespeare's novels. (Novels, in fact, emerged a couple of centuries after Shakespeare, who wrote plays and poems.) Indeed, one could find young people with PhD degrees who were hard put to express a cogent sentence—in any language. Some people said the safest way to get a PhD was to carry groceries for one's PhD supervisor.

NO SPACE TO SOCIALIZE

Despite all these infirmities, the ironic fact is that educational institutions were about the only places where students could socialize and learn to be members of society. Opportunities for entertainment were largely limited to television and, later, to phones and computers. For, militants had destroyed all of Kashmir's cinemas, clubs, and bars in 1990. There were few restaurants in the entire Valley except on a tiny strip in Srinagar. After 1995, that strip expanded a few kilometres up to Dalgate[10] but, until the beginning of the new century, that was more or less all.

Kashmiri weddings had traditionally involved multi-course *wazwan* feasts in the late evening, after which the groom's family would take the bride home at night. During the 1990s, weddings became hurried daytime events attended by not only guests but also fear. The wazwan was served as a late lunch instead of an evening feast, and every effort was made that the bride should reach the groom's house before dusk.

Hardly anyone was on the streets after dusk. Getting to a doctor or hospital after dark could be like running a gauntlet of cajoling, pleading, convincing, and racing. For many years, Kashmiris got used to driving their vehicles right off a road or highway if they saw an army vehicle approaching from the other side. If the driver and others on the army vehicle thought the civilian vehicle had not given their vehicle enough space to pass smoothly, they would most likely stop to assault the vehicle and its passengers. For a few years, they just wielded long staffs to assault the vehicle as the army vehicle passed. One had to be very wary of tossing anything out of a car window, for a soldier might mistake it for a grenade and respond with a bullet.

For some years, Kashmiris were forced to keep the windows of their vehicles rolled up. It seemed like a thing of yesterday to Mohsin Haider Ali of Srinagar, who could recall even many years later the horror of warm blood gushing from his head after the long baton of an army man crashed on his head through the open window of the bus in which he was sitting.[11] He was a little boy then, on a school excursion. It was the period during the second half of the 1990s when some schools were tentatively trying to revive such excursions. The child had just been for his first picnic and was delightedly feeling the breeze in his hair on the return journey when the baton blow landed. It was not meant specifically for Mohsin; it had been aimed at whoever was behind that open window. However hot it might be, open windows were not acceptable to the armed forces in that phase. They feared that a militant might shoot, or hurl a grenade, at them from a passing vehicle.

TRAUMA AT BIRTH

Some of the most traumatizing memories of that generation were not even memories but terrifying tales they had heard of how they were born, or borne. During those horrific early 1990s, at least one Kashmiri child was born on freezing snow, out in the open. An army company had surrounded the village near Khrew in Pulwama district. Some militants who had been hiding there fired and killed some soldiers, and then escaped. Irate at having thus been outmanoeuvred, the army men punished the entire village by forcing everyone, old and young, male and female, to squat in the snow outside the village all night. One of the village women was pregnant. She gave birth out on that snow.[12]

Shakeeb of Anantnag recounted his continuing trauma at the knowledge that his mother had been about to be battered by army men while he was in her womb. Only the chance intervention of an officer saved her from what could have resulted in a miscarriage. Shakeeb went on to study at one of India's most prestigious institutions of higher learning, but his life could have been over before it began. In July 2010, when Indians by and large were agog over daily 'stone-pelting' by Kashmiri youth, *Governance Now* magazine published Shakeeb's unedited account of growing up:

> Psychologically, the scenario leaves an indelible mark on a teenager and he becomes acquainted with things he need not be; things far beyond his age. On a normal day, before leaving for school, it is habitual for him to ask his dad (quite inadvertently), 'Is there a strike today?' A regular feature of his daily routine is the list of grueling incidents he hears about on local news channels, the radio or elsewhere. Curfew, protests, custodial killings. Ask any tender-aged kid in the valley and he will fully explain to you the meaning of each term. His days are marred by gory tales. Corny as it may sound, but at an age when he is supposed to be playing with friends without caring for the 'conditions' around, he has to deal with terms like those mentioned above. Curfews in the daytime and sheer horror at night is his quota.
>
> To an outsider, he might come across as a detached, unaffected observer of the state of affairs who is more interested in going out with friends and having fun. But, his psyche is deeply affected, though he doesn't show it. And when it comes to incidents such as the ones that have happened over the past couple of years, he shows his dissent. And his way of showing it is: pick up a stone and hurl it with all your might. What else can he do?
>
> A recent incident: a group of boys was playing cricket in a playfield. The 'law' enforcers arrived and started beating them ruthlessly. The videos of the incident were circulated throughout the place. Anger piled up inside the meek and tender hearts. You can't blame them for that. An outsider cannot imagine the humiliation felt when a burly, ridiculous looking man whacks you. I have felt that humiliation. One morning, I leave my house to buy some commodities. As always, I take a short route to the market. On arriving there, a deserted scene greets me. A grocer's belongings spilled on the road. I am about to turn back, when a jawaan grabs my collar and lashes at me with his gun butt. What I want to ask is, what reactions do

the authorities expect from the fuming teenager. The best (and it would be safe to say the only) way he knows: pick up a stone and hurl it at the tormentor with all his might. Though that's not what I did.

I haven't had a first-hand experience of the times when the fervor for azaadi was at its peak—the late 1980s, early 1990s. But, tales of those times form our bedtime stories wherein the young martyrs are the heroes and the villains quite obviously are you-know-who.

Growing up in the valley, I have had a few experiences and heard of several such heinous crimes against humanity. A teenager grows up nurturing a sense of being cheated of his right and destiny. Call it political catharsis, emotional purgation or economic disempowerment; the youth of our strife-torn valley is filled with dissent. How does the so-called representative of the masses expect a man to react when he learns that the guy who used to accompany him to the mosque everyday was mercilessly killed? And what's worse, the poor martyr is labeled as a 'miscreant', an 'anti-social element'. Ridiculous. The subjugation that follows only adds to the fumes which look for vents via a preferred route: protest. The law enforcers always try to choke up the voices of the youth and hence the only ways they can find to give vent to their sufferings remain sloganeering, stone-pelting and the not-so-famous and yet popular Ragda Ragda.

My mother often tells me a story. A pregnant woman went to submit her maternity leave application to the school authorities. On her way back, she learnt that her town was gripped by the devil–curfew. So, she and a group of people including some women decided to take a short route. On their way, a group of jawaans intercepted them. They were asked to line up and the jawaans started beating them. They hit one of the women but just then a high-ranking officer arrived and told them to go before something bad happened. The pregnant woman in this incident is, by sheer coincidence, my mother and the baby sprouting tiny legs and hands in her womb is writing this. When I hear my mom narrating this, what do you expect me to feel? The very thought of the episode sends shivers down my spine and, honestly, angers me to an unimaginable extent. There are hundreds of untold tales of sorrow that can melt even the hardest heart.

Now that I'm a teen, it's a daily routine to wake up every day to get ready in time for the college and very often going back to sleep again because curfew was declared in the dead of the night. Now that I'm a teen, the voices of my mother imploring me to stay indoors whenever khaki-clad brigades are on the prowl on streets are a regular feature. The aunt who lives next door has to keep shouting her lungs out to keep her 16-year old from joining the furious mobs. Particularly the time for prayers is jitters time for my mother. She sees me off at the door and waits till I come back from the mosque, praying under each breath that I return unscathed. How many mothers in the largest democracy (ahem) in the world have to undergo that sort of frustration? The guys who live along the lane on the other side of the streets wreak havoc every day. Very often in the day, they try to target the important-looking fellas (jawaans) roaming about (God! Everybody is an IGP here) from over rooftops. And very frequently, their stones find the window panes of our house in particular (don't know why) and other houses in general. You are having dinner with your family when suddenly the mosque loudspeakers are turned on with announcements like '10 boys have been detained by security forces in the adjoining locality. Please come out of your homes.' To hell with the dinner. These are our friends. Let's go out. And the night passes in suspense and anxiety. The very thought of spending a night in jail is harassing enough. Plus, the hound-like nature of those who detain our brothers is the topping on the cake. The punishment inflicted there rattles the very being of the victim. I can never forget the condition my friend was in when he was let off three days after detention.

The lanes remind me of Auschwitz. The camps of the exposed barracks that held back men, women and children alike and the centres wherein millions were incarcerated and gassed.

Switch on the TV, set your eyes on any news channel; you will hear 'Four people killed in clashes between security forces and stone-pelters in Srinagar.' That dampens the heart. That sure does. And what irks us more are the statements issued by the government. 'Controlling mob-fury', 'self defence', 'maximum restraint'. Heartrending tales ignite the urge to carry this to the end. The recent killings in Anantnag are classic examples of the dastardly crimes committed against us. What harm could a 15-year old cause? This is nothing but cold-blooded murder. The youth of Kashmir is fed up of the probes, the investigations that are ordered but never carried out. The fake encounters to win accolades. The high handedness of the troopers. Why aren't they held responsible for the crimes they commit? And what we want to know is: where to go for the answers? For those sections of society who believe that there is no issue, no dispute worth the name, all we ask is whether they have ever felt the pain we live with every day.

The life of the average Kashmiri youth is marred with horrors. Labeled as an anti-social element for protesting what's inhumane, for speaking out against suppression. What do we call the freedom fighters of India then? But what they don't realise is that this kind of crackdown will never silence the youth of Kashmir. This has gone too far. There is no alternative route to peace. What the youth of the state want to say is; We are the future of the society and we will decide its destiny. The hope of the Kashmir of my dreams stands and stands tall.[13]

This was the generation that came of age after 2007. Shakeeb was a teen-aged schoolboy when he wrote this in 2010. The intelligent and thoughtful boy did not pelt stones. But his article shows the depths to which the generation that was born in the mid-1990s had been scarred by the violence of their childhoods. It demonstrated how the narratives they heard dovetailed with the militarization they saw. Shakeeb gives a perspective on how alienating and frightening troops can seem to a child, even if those troops see themselves as guardians. The starting point of a narrative determines how the rest of the narrative is received. The boy's narrative reflects a common ground-level perspective on who started it, and so who is responsible for conflict. Soldiers and policymakers generally have a very different narrative about who started it, which is why both sides so often fail to understand the other side's angry responses.

Image, memory, and perspective often determine how people see things. When they faced bullets for stones in the summer of 2010, the image of being caged easily came to dominate the discourse of many young Kashmiris. The explosions of rage, and the new militancy, stemmed in part from that psychological feeling of being caged. Tragically, those who ran the state too often saw them only as errant boys disturbing law and order. Policymakers, and the instruments of crowd control that those policymakers used, generally lacked insights into the traumas, insecurities, and lived experience of the youth.

NOTES

1. http://www.thehindubusinessline.com/todays-paper/tp-life/article1015372. ece, accessed on 24 May 2017. Reprinted here with permission.
2. This was written when Wani was a PhD candidate. He subsequently became a lecturer at a government-run college.
3. From 1949 to 1975, Kashmir had radical land reforms in the world outside the Communist bloc. A succession of laws lowered the ceiling on land ownership. Remaining land was given to tillers, without compensation to the landlord. Those land reforms transformed rural society in the Valley.
4. Much of the city experienced bunkers and checkpoints from the early 1990s, including many rural areas. Many other rural areas experienced them from 1994. In the second half of the 1990s, it was the reality of the entire Valley.
5. Author's interview with General M.A. Zaki.
6. Appu Esthose Suresh wrote and campaigned about it after a visit to Kashmir during summer vacations while he was an undergraduate student.
7. When he was chief minister from 2002 to 2005, Mufti Mohammad Sayeed's government opened large numbers of new high schools, colleges, and universities across the state.
8. Author's interview with Harsh Dev Singh at his residence in Gandhi Nagar, Jammu, in March 2010.
9. The author witnessed (the then) vice-chancellor's address in the hall of the Islamic University of Science and Technology in 2007.
10. In May 1995, a friend (who later became a newspaper editor) persuaded the author to stay at a freshly reopened hotel on the Boulevard leading to the Dal Lake. Only one other guest was at that hotel, which was the only hotel functioning in that area.
11. Author's interview with Mohsin Ali in Srinagar in 2010.
12. General M.A. Zaki, former Corps Commander in Srinagar, told the author during an interview that he drove to the village as soon as he heard of this, and found that it was true.
13. This first appeared in *Governance Now*, Volume 01, Issue 12 (16–31 July 2010), http://www.governancenow.com/news/regular-story/angst-kashmiri-teen, accessed on 25 June 2017. Reprinted here with permission.

4

Varied Opinions

Living in Kashmir, I had realized by 2008 that the Hurriyat Conference and other political leaders of the 1990s, and the militant commanders of that decade, had become largely irrelevant. Leadership had passed to the generation born around 1990. I also realized that, in the age of the internet, initiative and leadership were far more diffuse than before. From 2007 to 2017, I interacted with Kashmiri youth, particularly students, whenever I could. I did so mainly in schools, colleges, and universities, but also in more informal settings—particularly in the localities in which I lived for several months or years. To get an overall sense of the experience, aspirations, and frustrations of youth, several Kashmiri youth joined me to formally survey school and college students across the Kashmir Valley in July 2011, halfway through that decade. We went to a couple of madrasas too. By the end of that month, we had had intensive interactions with more than 7,000 youth.

Wherever principals and other authorities allowed us, we invited students to fill questionnaires. All the questions were qualitative. Each time we distributed questionnaires, we announced that sharing personal identity details while filling the questionnaire was not mandatory. It was also okay if someone did not answer all questions; students could answer as many as they pleased. I was surprised at the large number of students willing to answer the entire questionnaire, even though it would take them about an hour to do so. Many others answered some of the questions.

What this meant was that the total number of respondents varied for each question. However, since we reached out to a large number (more than 3,000 filled at least some part of the questionnaire), the survey gave us a fair insight into the thinking of students that summer—halfway through that decade of change.[1]

While many respondents did not fill the columns asking for information about parents' occupations and the monthly family income, there were some who did—and it revealed a correlation between aspirations and family income. A pattern emerged from the questionnaire responses: three categories of respondents were almost certain to focus primarily on peace, stability, and economic opportunity as against regime change: one, respondents whose family earning was from tilling land; two, respondents with a family income less than Rs 10,000; and three, respondents based in a remote location. Judging by the geographical pattern of agitations following the killing of Burhan, this trend may have changed between 2011 and 2016. Agitations between July and October 2016 were most intense in rural and remote areas. There were angry demonstrations in hamlets tucked into the mountains that most people had forgotten.

Differences in attitudes and aspirations between young men and young women too were clear in 2011—not only in their written answers, but in classroom discussions too. As against their male counterparts, young women generally seemed far more eager to settle down to peace.

There were indications that these differences narrowed close to an explosion of rage. This became evident in my interactions with students at some schools and colleges in April and, later, in December 2016. In April, eleven weeks before rage exploded on the streets, the difference between young men and young women had narrowed, if not disappeared. As before, a larger proportion of young women than young men remained silent. But among those who did speak during classroom or campus discussions, anger, a push to resist, and a willingness to take up arms was common across genders. By December, after youth had vented anger through stones and barricades, difference was evident again, even though passion seemed to have dissipated even among the more feisty boys.

The rural–urban gap too seemed to have narrowed—even reversed—during the 2016 protests: youth from poorer families and more remote areas were at the forefront of the 2016 protests. This owed largely to the changed issues. Rather than resisting the possible ethnic dilution of the Valley, as in 2008, or the murder of innocents, as in 2010, the 2016 agitations brought to the fore an increased rejection of the entire system.

DIFFERENCES AND CONTRADICTIONS

Such changes in mood were at best trends. There were counter-trends and several currents to leaven those trends. Although a single, insistent, shrill voice was heard from Kashmir in times of collective rage, there were variations and even contradictory trends at most times. There were dissimilarities with regard to self-perception, religious dedication, ethnic aspiration, even with regard to approval for the tactics of resistance.

One may not expect teenagers' perceptions of self and identity to be deeply thought through, but the way identity self-perception played out in many minds was ironic. Although the youth mostly identified with the Kashmiri linguistic-ethnic identity, the idea of what it meant to be Kashmiri was itself reduced in many young minds to being Muslim. It seemed that consciousness of religious identity increased in times of rage, as during the summer and autumn of 2016. It became a rallying motif for resistance—amid widespread talk of ummah, global war, persecution, and Islamic solidarity.

This plugged into the widespread ideal of 'azadi' for those who belonged to the Kashmiri identity. The range of meanings that students assigned to the term 'azadi', as reflected in the survey responses, was baffling. Generally, their responses were framed in terms of rights, benefits, and environment (of security, not fear) created by those in power, rather than concerned about the structures of governance or statehood. To a large number of young women and many young men, the word 'azadi' signified the liberty to live with dignity, with rights, and without humiliation—at least it did in 2011. The majority of the youth felt deprived of rights that Indians in other states could take for granted. It was ironic that many citizens in other parts of India, more so in the Jammu region of the state, felt that Kashmiris benefitted from special privileges. In fact, most Kashmiri students thought they lacked the rights other states had.[2]

Young men and women deeply resented the deployment of soldiers all over. They particularly disliked having to prove their identities to an 'outsider'. Women were also uneasy about being watched by strange men with power. They had grown up this way, and it had taken a toll. Now that such deployment seemed unnecessary in the years from around 2007, they viewed it as a nasty imposition.

Particularly in the earlier parts of that decade of change, hardly any Kashmiri youth wanted to associate their destiny with Pakistan. Even by the end of that decade, in 2016, the large majority did not. For, at most times, being Kashmiri was the essence of identity. The questionnaire responses reflected a deeply embedded Kashmiri identity based on language and geography. About half of those who responded to the question 'What is a Kashmiri' spoke of region—the Kashmir Valley—while more than a quarter wrote of language. Almost 10 per cent wrote of culture. Seven per cent described Kashmiris as Muslim. The concept of a Kashmiri was romanticized, at least privileged, in many answers to this and a related question about whether, and how, Kashmiris are different from others. More than one-third of respondents wrote that Kashmiris were good, trustworthy, helpful. Another 6.5 per cent wrote that Kashmiris were superior.

A few of the answers to that question were overtly political. One student wrote that 'Kashmiri means slaves of India', and another wrote 'Geelani sahib' (is a Kashmiri). One wrote that a Kashmiri is 'a person who is patriotic to Kashmir and remembers its martyrs'. Two per cent wrote of victimhood. One wrote that 'Kashmiri is a normal person with a stone in his hand for freedom'. There was one respondent who was more universalist than Tagore; he wrote: 'There is no Kashmiri, no Indian, no Pakistani. It is just our thinking.' Others focused on deprivation as part of India. One, for example, wrote: 'Kashmiris are loving. Kashmiris are poor because of unavailability of resources and other facilities while people of other states are rich.' Another wrote that a Kashmiri is 'a helpless person with nothing to gain and every thing to loose [sic]'. Yet another wrote that a 'Kashmiri is a toy in the hands of Indian govt and Indian military.'

We also tried to get a sense of what Kashmiri youth thought of other parts of the state of Jammu and Kashmir. In response to the question 'Are Jammu, Kashmir and Ladakh different from each other? If yes, how?' most respondents noted differences between Kashmir and the other two. Many wrote of Kashmir as being more beautiful and better in other ways. Some responded with the clichéd comparison of Kashmir being like paradise. Most respondents said Kashmiris were distinct, different from others. Some respondents made a mention of physical beauty; some focused on culture, including modes of dress, to define what was distinctive about a Kashmiri.

Many wrote of a combination of two or all three factors: Kashmiris are those who live in Kashmir, speak the language, and have absorbed the culture. The category 'Kashmiri' tends to be used without nuance, as pristine and unidimensional, but it is actually a complex category with several nuances. Indeed, if one uses the term Kashmir to talk of the entire state of Jammu and Kashmir—even if only the state on the Indian side of the LoC—one would be referring to a sociological reality more diverse than the Balkans. For, different people in the state identify themselves as Gujjar, Dogra, Kishtwari, Poonchhi, Bhaderwahi, and so on. Others identify as Sheerazi, Gaddi, Sippi, Balti, Purig-pa, or Brok-pa. Brok is a form of Shina, as are Gurezi, Tulaili, and Drassi. Some identify as Karnahi or other kinds of Pahari.

Most respondents in our survey identified Pahadis and Gujjars in a stereotyped way. Most students described these categories as people who live in forests and high mountains, herd sheep and goats, and live in primitive ways. These responses indicated that most students were not aware of the extraordinary changes in lifestyles, dress codes, locations, and self-perceptions of the majority of those who might have identified as belonging to those categories. At the time the survey was conducted, the Divisional Commissioner, the officer in charge of Kashmir's administration, was identified as a Pahari.

There are differences even among those who call themselves Kashmiri. Differences between south Kashmir and north Kashmir within the Kashmir Valley had been evident over the year or two before Burhan's death. Tral, Shopian, Baramulla, and Sopore were among Kashmiri towns that have had distinctive self-perceptions of identity through history. A privileged self-perception among residents of the city of Srinagar had long been evident. Despite huge migration to the city since around the turn of the millennium, long-time city residents often treated those from beyond the city with contempt.

Voting trends in the 1996, 2002, 2008, and 2014 elections reflected urban–rural differences. Overall levels differed each time, generally showing an uptrend, but the turnout of rural voters was always substantially higher than that of urban voters. One reason for this was the wide-ranging land reforms that rural belts had experienced since 1949. Another factor was their experience of counterinsurgency. Largely, city residents had experienced the excesses, including horrifying torture, of the BSF, from the early 1990s to 2005. Rural areas more often experienced the army; these areas had also experienced excesses by Kashmiri militants before Pakistani and other foreign elements came to dominate militancy during the second half of the 1990s.

There were also differences—in perceptions, attitudes, and aspirations—across time. For example, most of the Kashmiri Muslims who had matured politically between 1965 and 1990 had been dedicated to becoming Pakistanis. The social transformation caused by land reforms during the 1950s had shaped the minds of many Kashmiri Muslims who had matured before 1965. 'Azadi', generally very fuzzily imagined, became the common aspiration from 1990. And in the new century, ideas about identity and aspiration were often based on Islam.

FASHIONABLE ISLAMIST IDEAS

Many young people had begun to reject a political system not based on Islam. As an organization, Islamic State did not have a base in Kashmir, but some of its foundational ideas had seeped into several young minds.

However, most young people had romanticized the idea that Muslims were better, and that they were victims of unfair biases and of global, national, and local conspiracies. Responses to the survey showed that this often shaped students' responses to the world. Their responses about Muslims were as romanticized as answers about Kashmiris. A very large proportion wrote of Muslims as good, merciful, helpful, generous, and so on—'sympathetic and merciful', for example. When asked 'What do you think about Muslims?' 697 of 1,947 (35.8 per cent) respondents wrote that Muslims were good or had positive qualities, 26.42 per cent that they follow Allah, and 23.21 per cent that they are followers of the Prophet Mohammed.

However, although they tended to privilege their co-religionists and their religion as the best, most respondents had only limited knowledge about even their own faith, leave alone other common faiths. For example, a large proportion of respondents did not attempt the question 'How many types of jihad are there? What is the great jihad—jihad-e-awwal?' Of those who did, only a quarter (235 out of 961 who responded, 24.5 per cent to be precise) answered that it is the struggle to improve oneself or to purify one's soul. On the other hand, many of those who gave other answers did not associate jihad with violence. One, in fact, wrote that 'peace is the best jihad all over the world'.

Another common belief was that sectarian unease was increasing. The survey discovered that sectarian animosity was in fact expressed much less than it might have been some years before. To the question 'Who are Sunnis? What are they like?' 524 of the 1,213 respondents (43.2 per cent) wrote that they are Muslims. A hundred and twenty-one respondents (10 per cent) wrote that believe in one God, and 298 (24.56 per cent) that they follow the Prophet. Another 73 (6 per cent) wrote of positive qualities such as goodness or honesty. As many as 469 of the 1,261 (37.19 per cent) who answered the question 'Who are Shias?' described them as 'Muslim', 78 (6.18 per cent) as non-Muslim, and 48 (3.8 per cent) as 'our brothers'. Another 315 (24.98 per cent) described Shias as followers of Ali, Hasan or/and Hussain. Twenty-eight (2.22 per cent) attributed negative qualities to Shias, but 11 (0.87 per cent) spoke of Shias as 'loving'.

There is a long history of distrust between the majority Sunnis and minority Shias of Kashmir, although the issue is often brushed away. Over the past decade or so, Salafist thinking has given it a new edge. The chief propagator of Salafism in Kashmir is the Ahle-Hadith movement. The proselytizing Tablighi Jamaat movement was popular, particularly from around 2007 to 2011, and had a wide impact. It claims to have nothing to do with politics, but promotes orthodox piety similar to that of the early Taliban (when it developed in Pakistani madrasas in the mid-1990s).

Asked which was best among Jamaat-e-Islami, Ahle-Hadith, Tablighi Jamaat, Hanafi, etc., most respondents did not answer. Of the respondents who did answer the question, 57.14 per cent wrote approvingly of the Tablighi Jamaat, 9.38 per cent of Jamaat-e-Islami, and 4 per cent of Ahle-Hadith. The proportion of support for the Jamaat-e-Islami reflects the organization's established base of membership and active supporters in the Valley—around 10 per cent of the population. Since members are generally strongly dedicated and are often professional lawyers, teachers, or government officials, that one-tenth of the population has had great influence. During the latter half of the decade of growing rage, the proportion of young supporters of the Jamaat-e-Islami has increased; the Jamaat's youth wing, the Islami Jamiat-e-Tulaba, has done tremendous work in colleges and high schools.

Notably, only 2.8 per cent listed the inclusive Hanafi school as best in 2011, though it has for centuries been predominant across the Indian subcontinent, including Kashmir. It is quite possible that a much larger proportion would have identified with the Hanafi school a quarter-century ago.

OTHER FAITHS

Romanticization of Muslims did not necessarily extend to disparagement of other religions. Answering questions about Hindus, Sikhs, Christians, and Jews (for example, 'What do you think about Hindus?'), most respondents wrote of the belief systems of those faiths—some positively. For instance, the one who wrote that Muslims are 'sympathetic and merciful', wrote about Hindus: 'They are also sympathetic and merciful. But they are different from Muslims. They are going to temples. [sic]'

Some of the respondents were misinformed about those belief systems. A few were judgmental. For example, 167 of the 1,009 who attempted the question 'What do you think about Sikhs?' wrote that Sikhs worship Guru Nanak and another 31 wrote that Sikhs have many gods. In fact, the Sikh belief in a formless, timeless, singular God parallels the Islamic concept of *wahadat* (the singular unity of God).

Only 605 respondents attempted the question about what Jews were and what they were like. A third of them (201 of 605) explicitly wrote that they did not know. Others too did not know: 43 (7 per cent) wrote that they are followers of Jesus and six (1 per cent) that Jews worship Jesus. One wrote that the word is 'derived from jeans which we wear'. Of the 605 who attempted this question, 37 (6 per cent) wrote of Jews' positive qualities, and 48 (8 per cent) of negative qualities.

This was one of the questions that led the research team to the realization that trying to extrapolate ground-level trends in thinking and aspirations from social media platforms can be misleading. Posts of Kashmiri youth active on Facebook might lead an analyst to presume that many young Kashmiris hate Jews. That presumption would be off the mark. The survey indicated that a very large majority have no idea about Jews. Most respondents knew something about Pandits—Kashmiri Hindus, the large majority of whom migrated from the Valley in terror, mainly between February and August 1990—but their answers were scattered. The question 'Who are Pandits? What are they like?' elicited such a wide variety of answers that my co-investigators categorized 751 of 1,343 answers (56 per cent) under the category 'other answers'. In response to the question, 283 (21 per cent) answered that Pandits are 'Kashmiri' and 57 or 4.24 per cent described them as 'migrants'. Another 58 (4.3 per cent) wrote specifically of Pandits' good qualities while 20 (a mere 1.49 per cent) described negative qualities (such as oppressors). Pandits were described as polytheists by 142 (10.57 per cent), 21 (1.56 per cent) described them as worshippers of Shiva, and 6 (0.44 per cent) as worshippers of Vishnu. Three respondents called Pandits 'brothers'.

WOMEN'S RIGHTS

The increased influence of religion on everyday discourse, behaviour, and dress codes during that decade of change was obvious. Beards and hijabs became the norm, although a few students (and others) did not conform. Interactions between young men and women became more covert, although the difference was more in their visibility than their frequency or intensity. Boys and girls met each other more secretly than they might have done earlier. Responses to the survey question 'Is it right for a boy to make friends with a girl, and a girl with a boy?' evoked an almost evenly divided response. Almost 50 per cent said it was wrong, around 1 per cent wrote that it should be according to Islamic codes, slightly more than 1 per cent wrote that they could not say, and 47 per cent said it was right.

It is possible that many of those who wrote about preferring conservatism, in gender relations, laws, or rights, had not imbibed those values deeply—or wrote what they thought was expected, or acceptable. For, answering another set of questions, a majority of the same respondents wrote of romantic films and film heroes (Salman Khan most often) as their favourites, of using phones and the internet, and of their favourite sports heroes.

Although most women wore headscarves by this time, some did not cover their hair at all. Whatever their dress code, many of those who grew into womanhood during that decade were energetic, poised, and articulate. Their aspirations were unsubdued. The survey showed that young women generally aspired for equal opportunities, although their discourse was often couched in the idiom of correct Islamic practice—for that had become the cultural norm.

Asked 'What rights do you think a woman should have?' a very large majority of women respondents wrote that women should have the same rights as men. In fact, 1,165 of all the 2,007 students who responded to this question wrote that they should have equal rights. That is 58 per cent of all male and female respondents. On the other hand, 538 or 26.8 per cent wrote that women should have the rights that Islam mandated for them. Thirty wrote that women should have the freedom to study what they choose. Most of those were perhaps women respondents under family pressure to take courses that would ready them for an easy marriage rather than an ambitious career.

BIGGEST PROBLEM

During times when rage has peaked over the decade of change since 2007, high-decibel speeches and slogans had made it seem as if all of

Kashmir spoke with a single voice, and had a single, focused agenda. At other times, however, there were several variations. For example, during a 'peaceful' phase of the decade, students in their early teens in a school classroom in Pulwama told me of their aspirations to be a judge or an astronaut, ignoring their teacher's urgent whispers that they should say they want freedom.

'Azadi' is the almost reflexive battle cry of most Kashmiris, but since 2007 my extensive conversations with many Kashmiri youth indicated that 'azadi' was often a nebulous concept. This was confirmed by interactions with students before, during, and after the uprising of 2016. Hardly anyone had a cogent idea of the borders, programmes, or agenda of this freedom. The Hurriyat Conference was its flag-bearer, but each member of that organization's executive had different responses even with regard to its putative borders, and the extent to which it was to be Islamic, secular, or democratic. To very many young people, especially young women, 'azadi' denoted freedom from fear and humiliation. To many, it meant a regime of rights. Many young Kashmiris imagined that rights were easily available in other states of India but stopped short (as the narrative held) at Banihal, the entrance to the Kashmir Valley.

The survey also revealed a range of aspirations and problems. The single most common answer to the question 'What is Kashmir's biggest overall problem?' was 'independence' (or some form of that answer, for example, 'freedom'). That was predictable enough, but it was nowhere near the majority opinion: at 349 of 1,612 respondents, it was the answer of only 21.65 per cent. Another 118 (7.32 per cent) wrote 'rule of India' and 60 (3.72 per cent) wrote 'military rule'. The sum of these three categories is just over a third of the total. As many as 333 or 20.66 per cent of respondents gave the second most common answer: 'unemployment'. Another 87 (5.4 per cent) wrote 'poverty' and 91 (5.65 per cent) 'corruption'. One respondent wrote 'industries and food production'.

Other answers showed that some students had complex, even laconic, observations on politics. For example, 113 respondents (7 per cent) considered 'bad leadership' as Kashmir's biggest problem, while 66 (4.09 per cent) felt it to be 'negative thinking'. One student wrote that 'neighbouring countries including India want to get their own interests fulfilled but don't think about Kashmiris'. At the other end of the spectrum, one wrote: 'Bad leadership bcoz leaders only look after their own houses.' One respondent wrote 'anger', another 'Geelani', and a third considered 'Kashmiri itself' was the biggest problem. As if to complement that, a student wrote in response to another question that 'Kashmiris lack exposure'.

The survey made it clear that, at least in the periods when rage is not surging, Kashmiri youth respond to, and criticize, the entire spectrum of leaders, including those who are generally categorized as 'mainstream' and 'separatist'. However, this changes during Kashmir's explosively angry phases: during such times, the general narrative is that everyone rejects 'mainstream' politics and leaders, and that 'separatist' leaders and politics have the backing of the people. The fact that vast numbers turn up to vote in 'mainstream' elections (the voter turnout being as high as 70 per cent at times) is explained as 'only meant for governance'—not a vote to stay in India. Such narratives tend to overplay the popularity of 'separatist' leaders, and underplay the popularity of 'mainstream' ones. The survey in 2011 clearly reflected a mixed picture with regard to 'mainstream' and 'separatists'. When asked who is 'the best leader for Kashmir', the largest number by far named Syed Ali Shah Geelani, but the second largest number listed the then Chief Minister Omar Abdullah, and the third largest listed the then opposition leader Mufti Mohammad Sayeed.

RESPONSES TO STONE PELTING

The survey revealed a striking change between periods of great rage and more sober times. During the uprising of 2010 and, to some extent, during 2008 too, there had seemed to be widespread support for the pelting of stones as a method of protest. In 2016 too, there was a large measure of support, although many adults were unhappy. Some thought it was a bad idea, but did not advertise those thoughts; especially in times of great public anger, discretion can be the better part of valour.

It, however, seems that general approval for stone-pelting greatly reduced in the absence of mass rage, even among young people. The majority of students in precisely the age bracket most likely to pelt stones disapproved of it just a year after the ferocious stone-pelting of 2010. Classroom discussions showed that this was particularly true of young women. On the other hand, classroom discussions a few weeks before the uprising of 2016—when rage was evidently building again—indicated that young teenaged women were as supportive of active resistance, including with stones, as teenaged men. In response to the question 'What do you think about stone-pelting?' 848 out of 1,610 (52.67 per cent) respondents considered it to be wrong in 2011, while 596 (37 per cent) thought it was right. Only 5 (0.3 per cent) described it as 'Islamic jihad', three ascribed it to 'unemployment', and 14 (0.9 per cent) wrote that it was done by the 'uneducated'.

The disapproval rate was striking. For, I discovered during classroom interactions how dangerous it could be for young people to defy the popular mood and narrative. Two young women, sitting beside each other in one school classroom on the outskirts of Srinagar, stood up together and spoke with poise about the great harm that the pelting of stones had done to education and society at large. A boy on the last bench suddenly leapt to his feet in rage and yelled, *'Mai tujhe zinda nahi chhorhunga'* (I won't leave you alive). The girls were unruffled. 'Don't bother about him,' they said. 'He's a pelter.' At an Ahle-Hadith-affiliated school in an upmarket part of the city, I found that the discourse (particularly among young women) became less 'separatist' when their teachers were not present.

In response to one of the survey questions, a student from a different school wrote that 'stone pelting is right for Kashmiris but poor and students suffer. So there is a need of some other form to avoid the problem'. Another described it as the 'national game of Kashmir'. A third wrote: 'Stone pelters have close contact with political leaders who gave them money to pelt stones.' Another held the government responsible for stone-pelting, explaining that there were no playgrounds or ways to pass time. One wrote that people do 'not know why are we doing and what are we doing'.

Of course, this was in 2011, when the intense anger of 2010 had subsided. When stones emerged again in 2016, it seemed that acceptance had increased among teenagers and those in their pre-teens—who would have been little children in 2011. However, approval for stone-pelting seemed to be at best ambivalent (if it had not actually decreased) among the generation we had surveyed in 2011 in colleges and high schools—many of whom were in their mid- to late twenties by 2016. Relatively few in that age bracket seemed to be pelting stones in 2016.

In response to the question 'Is militancy a jihad?' opinion was almost evenly divided in 2011. A slightly higher number of respondents answered in the affirmative (818 of 1,681, or 48.66 per cent) than in the negative (774 or 46 per cent). On the other hand, most students rejected suicide attacks. Asked 'Do you think suicide attacks are acceptable in Islam?' 84.5 per cent (1,517 of 1,794 who answered the question) wrote that they were not, while 10.25 per cent (184) considered them acceptable. About 5 per cent had other answers, including some ambivalent ones.

NUANCED VIEW OF FORCES

If attitudes among Kashmiri youth varied with regard to the legitimacy of pelting stones and with respect to militancy, their opinions about different forces of the Indian state also differed. The survey showed a sharp difference in opinions regarding the police and the army. In the past, Kashmiris had often used the term 'army' to describe all armed forces—not distinguishing between the regular army and the BSF, for example. In an interview to the author, militant commander Burhan Wani's grandfather said: 'We used to call them all military. Only later, we learnt that this is Rashtriya Rifles and this is CRPF and so on.'[3]

He was talking of the 1990s, when anyone in uniform was seen as 'army'. The police was barely in action in the first half of that decade. A couple of decades later, however, many young Kashmiris distinguish between various forces. In classroom and campus interactions, I found a clear pattern of difference in opinions about the various forces. For example, I had a candid chat with a large room packed with more than 80 students of classes 11 and 12 at the Government Higher Secondary School in Baramulla in the third week of June 2010, after that summer's unrest had begun. The young men spoke candidly of barricading the '*seemunt pul*' (cement bridge) and pelting stones at anyone trying to cross.

They particularly targeted the CRPF and the police, they said, using strong language to criticize both forces. But they added that if an army lorry passed, they would open the way for them. Born around 1993 or 1994, they were perhaps too young to clearly remember the phase of fearsome repression by the army. Whatever their reasons, they were responding to the behaviour of those respective forces in the contemporary phase rather than the past. Later in the book, I will go into reasons for the sometimes visceral hatred against the police and the CRPF among the generation that became conscious of their world around 2007.

The questionnaire that documented the students' opinions a year after that classroom conversation in Baramulla made obvious a sharp differentiation. The questionnaire asked separate questions about the armed forces, including the two (police and CRPF) that many young demonstrators had confronted in 2010. Across the Valley at that stage, young people expressed the strongest criticism of the CRPF, followed by of the police, and least of the army.

In response to 'What do you think about the police?' one-fifth of the respondents called them good, and another fifth said they provided security. The largest number, 24.8 per cent, described them as bad, another 9 per cent referred to them as 'Indian dogs', 2.25 per cent as criminals, 5.26 per cent as killers, 3.75 per cent as terrorists, and another 3.75 per cent as corrupt. As against this, only 11.5 per cent described the CRPF as good and 16 per cent as providers of security. As many as 39 per cent described them as bad, 2.3 per cent referred to them as 'Indian dogs', 3.4 per cent as criminals, 0.5 per cent as killers, and 1.5 per cent as terrorists. In short, while around 40 per cent wrote positively about the police, only about 27 per cent were positive about the CRPF.

However, while far more students considered the CRPF, in comparison to the police, to be 'bad', it was evident from the survey that far more students were enraged about the police than about the CRPF, with more people using terms such as 'Indian dogs', criminals, killers, or terrorists for the police than for the CRPF (20 per cent for the former as against 8 per cent for the latter). Those figures point to a nuanced set of attitudes: while a larger proportion viewed the police positively (these might include relatives and neighbours of policemen and officers), far more of those who viewed them negatively were strongly agitated about them than about the CRPF. The high-pitched rage witnessed in 2010 and 2016 was evidently directed against the police more than the paramilitary force.

This owed much to those who had been recruited during the militancy and general chaos of the 1990s. Many of them had learnt to act with impunity in a situation in which laws, the judicial system, and, to an extent, the government at large were on the back foot. As Javid Mukhdoomi, the Inspector-General of Police cited in Chapter 1, 'Endings and Beginnings', noted, some officers had developed a 'bump him off' culture. In the lead-up to the 2008 uprising, and again during and after the 2010 uprising, many young Kashmiris experienced the police as an exploitative and vindictive force. We shall return to this later in the book.

To be sure, the police became far more professional after the militancy that had been incubating from around 2010 became tough to ignore by 2013, and impossible to ignore from 2015. Many of the officers and men who had been recruited in the new century became senior enough towards the end of the decade of flux examined in this book to make a difference to the way the police behaved. Some of them turned out to be more professional than had been common for half a century. In general, after 2016, the force seemed to become more professional than most police forces across India and neighbouring countries.

In contrast to responses to the police and the CRPF, 26.9 per cent of those who answered the same question about the army considered the army to be good, 25.64 per cent wrote that they provided security, 20.5 per cent that they were bad, 6.4 per cent that they were criminals, and 5.1 per cent that they were terrorists. A year after the stone-pelting demonstrations of 2010, 39 per cent wrote positively of the police only 27.5 per cent of the CRPF, but 52.5 per cent or a majority wrote positively of the army. Less than a third wrote of the army in negative terms. Not a single respondent called the army 'Indian dogs'.

In 2016, the army was far more active in operations to control the unrest, particularly in south Kashmir (and in Kupwara district from about April to August) than during the past more than a decade. In most places, it engaged in crowd control, pacification, or arrest operations along with police and CRPF men. I interacted with people in Srinagar, Baramulla, Kupwara, Tral, Anantnag, Qazigund, Shopian, Kulgam, and Pulwama during and after those agitations. My impression was that public anger still focused on the police rather than the army.

I also got the impression that there was greater variety and nuance in views about the police than there had been in 2010. Many Kashmiris praised the role of the police, particularly in places like Tral and Awantipora in July and August 2016, and in Srinagar in August and beyond—although most of them would have been afraid to defy the popular narrative by saying so publicly.

The need for insightful nuance holds true for much of what has been said about Kashmir over this decade of change, and even before. It had been clear throughout this decade that generalizations are inadequate. Flux has been constant. For those without a fixed perspective and agenda, there were nuances everywhere.

NOTES

1. A few of the findings of this survey have been published elsewhere. All the findings are the exclusive copyrighted intellectual property of the author. The permission of David Devadas must be obtained before they are republished or cited. The author must be credited if any of these survey findings are reported, republished, or cited.
2. Many students used the term 'other states' in their conversations with me. Around 2011, they still seemed to see themselves as part of India.
3. Author's interview of Burhan Wani's grandfather and other family members at their home near Tral, 10 August 2016.

5

Radical Shift

By 2017, almost 70 per cent of the population of the Valley was estimated to be below the age of thirty; about half was below the age of twenty. The teenagers and pre-teens who now comprised half the population of the place had been born around the turn of the millennium or thereafter. Generally, they had no direct memories of the militancy and counterinsurgency of the 1990s. A generation gap had emerged between them and those who were born around 1990.

As already noted in Chapter 1, 'Endings and Beginnings', and Chapter 2, 'Mass Rage', many of those who were born in the early years of the militancy which began in 1988 had become disillusioned with militancy as a method. By the time they became teenagers in the early years of the new century, they viewed it as futile. On the other hand, they saw hope around that time in Prime Minister Vajpayee's peace initiatives. But, by 2017, most of those who had been born near the beginning of that militancy were in their late twenties. They were already among the older half of the population. The mindsets of those who were teenagers in 2017 were very different to those who were teenagers in 2007.

As noted in Chapter 2, 'Mass Rage', most of those who had been on the streets during the uprisings of 2008 and 2010 did not take to the streets in 2016, after the first few days of that round of agitation. In those four months intense agitation across the Valley was run mainly by those who had been born around the turn of the millennium, or after. Those agitations differed sharply from the previous agitations of that decade of flux. For one thing, these demonstrations were concentrated in rural, not urban, areas. More important, the 2016 demonstrators backed and celebrated militants, in contrast to the 2010 demonstrations, which focused on opposing the killing of innocents. At one level, the demonstrators in 2010 had been demanding the rule of law and their right to life.

Another important difference between those born around 1990 and those born around the turn of the century was that, by the time they were teenagers, many in the later generation had given up on the state—quite often, on the very idea of a nation state. Many of them were fired by ideas of a caliphate and shariah law. Most of those who took up arms in the new militancy were of this generation. Several of the early guerrillas of this round of militancy were born in the second half of the 1990s. The much larger numbers who took up arms after the killing of Burhan Wani (on 8 July 2016) were often teenagers when they went underground. They had typically been born at the turn of the millennium, or thereafter.

BLINKERED SOCIAL APPROACHES

A trend towards conservatism became visible across many parts of the world as they got to their teens in the second decade of the new century. Political parties that espoused ethnic and religion-based exclusivism had gained substantial ground in several countries, including some European ones that had prided themselves as being bastions of liberal Humanism. The political systems in several countries too became less tolerant. The trend towards conservatism was also apparent in the Indian subcontinent. In Kashmir, the trend was more strongly evident among the millennial generation.

Kashmiri millennials were generally bright, inquisitive, full of aspirations. But, as noted in Chapter 3, 'Caged Childhood', the education system was in poor shape. Their minds were generally shaped by the factors that came into play around 2007 (mentioned in Chapter 1, 'Endings and

Beginnings'), including the internet. Narratives about the 'war on terror' and the global repression of Muslims were common. Televangelism was a major part of their childhood experience.

Around that year of change, uncompromising religiosity had become more common than before. Attendance at mosques increased noticeably. The turnout of young men, including teenagers, was particularly noticeable at taravi night prayers during Ramzan and aitakaf retreats. A great deal of money flowed to Kashmir around that time, much of it for the construction of mosques, from Saudi Arabia. Three mosques within a stone's throw of each other became commonplace in towns and villages across the Valley. These often subscribed to different sects, such as Jamaat-e-Islami and Ahle-Hadith. Many of the new mosques were not only large but were often set up lavishly with marble, wood panelling, and carpeting.

Mosque attendance had been high in certain phases during the past too, but religious praxis in Kashmir had often been liberal, even syncretistic. Social norms too were far more liberal and inclusive than in many other parts of India. This was particuarly true about gender relations. Albeit illiterate, middle-aged rural Kashmiri women had often presided over their homes from their kitchens, which doubled as the parlour.

RADICAL SHIFT

The shift to what may loosely be described as 'radical' thinking came dramatically to the fore in the spring of 2017, when 'Musa' burst to the fore as the radical face of Kashmir's militancy. On 12 May, an audio recording went viral on the internet.[1] It was soon being talked about right across Kashmir—and far beyond. It was the voice of Zakir Bhat, who was at the time designated as the 'divisional commander' of Hizb-ul Mujahideen for south Kashmir. Zakir had suc-ceeded Burhan a month after the latter was killed (ten months before that video went viral). Zakir had taken the nom de guerre 'Musa' in honour of Prophet Moses, who is celebrated for having delivered his people from slavery through miracles, and punished them for straying from God's path.

Musa's audio recording made it clear that the militants were fighting to establish an Islamist system based on shariah law. Describing voting and democracy as 'haraam' (unacceptable),[2] Musa expressed anger at those who described Kashmir's struggle as a 'political' one. He strongly rejected nationalism as the basis of the struggle—whether it was Kashmiri nationalism, Pakistani nationalism, or any other. Musa said that figures from organizations like the Hurriyat Conference must forthwith stop talking of the movement as 'political'.

That is not all. Musa announced that he would cut the throat of any 'leader' who called Kashmir's struggle a political one, and string them up in Lal Chowk—the centre of Srinagar. That part of his recording sent out shock waves. Hizb's handlers in Pakistan swung into action immediately. By the next day, Musa made an announcement dissociating himself from Hizb.

In particular, he clarified that he had not referred to Syed Ali Shah Geelani, the head of the Tehreek-e-Hurriyat. That clarification was vital for two reasons. One, Geelani had been the most steadily pro-Pakistan of the freedom movement's putative 'political' leaders for most of his life— certainly until that year of beginnings and endings, 2007. His desire that Kashmir should become a part of Pakistan was embedded in the fact that Pakistan was Islamic. He once told me that the second stage of his project, once Kashmir had joined Pakistan, was to make Pakistan more radically Islamist. Most pertinent in the context of Musa's message was the fact that Geelani had consistently held that the freedom struggle was based on religion—it was a struggle to establish Islam's dominance in Kashmir's politics, society, and culture. During an interview given in the late 1990s, he told me that the Quranic verse 'lukum deenukum waliya deen' does not mean 'to each, his religion'—as it has often been interpreted. Rather, he had held that the verse only referred to the right of a Muslim to practice his religion according to his tradition. Among the most prominent leaders of Kashmir's freedom struggle, Geelani's world view on this count was closest to the one Musa expressed. And he had at one time criticized just the phrase Musa opposed—political movement. Kashmir's was a religion-based movement, Geelani had then insisted.[3]

YOUNG MALE FANS

The thrust of Musa's audio recording was not new, but his angry ultimatums and threats riveted attention more sharply than earlier messages had. What shocked most people was the strong language he used to threaten the Hurriyat leaders who spoke of a 'political' movement—even those who had described it as religion-based in more candid phases. Musa had said much the same sort of thing about the objectives of Kashmir's movement in earlier messages, including a video recording in March 2017. In fact, Burhan's discourse in the video recordings he made in the summer of 2015 had been similar; only his style and language was characteristically far more palatable than Musa's. And Burhan had spoken with great deference over the telephone to the extremely narrow-vision Pakistani fundamentalist and promoter of jihad, Hafiz Sayeed.[4] Many of the new generation of militants, including Musa's rival as Burhan's successor, Sabzar Bhat, too subscribed to these ideas.

Far more important is the fact that it was popular across most males of that generation. Musa shot to popularity among Kashmiri teenagers for making that statement, despite its abrasive threats. When Musa appeared at Sabzar's funeral, his name was chanted amid querulous screams; the frenzy to touch his face, hair, and clothes raised a cloud of dust. In the days since his recording had gone viral, the general discourse among most young people was that Musa had said what was right. Until April 2017, Zakir Musa had been feared as a militant commander but was resented by many south Kashmir youth for some of his past choices; he was never loved like Burhan. But in May 2017, most teenaged males across Kashmir glorified Musa after he took his extremist Islamist line to a higher level. It was as if his message of 12 May had crossed a critical threshold—as if someone had hit a switch that brought to life a vast array of floodlights. The way his tirade sparked the minds of young Kashmiris showed just how powerful radical ideas had become. The discourse among some of the more politically conscious, including some scholars at Kashmir University, was that Musa had erred in saying this publicly—but he was right.

Several adult Kashmiris suspected that, since Musa's line suited the projection of the Kashmir movement that the government in New Delhi preferred, he might have been manipulated. Whether or not he had been, the fact was that Musa's extremely radical line was popular among a large proportion of teenaged males—even after he was reported to have joined Al Qaeda.

Older Kashmiris did not by and large share the sentiment. Even among the young, although a significant proportion of Kashmiri students and other teenagers did share Musa's views, not all young people did. In fact, some young men in their mid to late twenties were extremely uncomfortable with Musa's discourse. It filled some with dread about what lay ahead. Soon after Musa's recording went viral in May 2017, a couple of Kashmiris who focused on world affairs had even begun to talk of a future that might resemble what had occurred in parts of Syria—violence, chaos, even mass migration.

A large proportion of young women had reservations about Musa's views on the objectives of stone-pelting—even though they too had demonstrated rage. There was good reason for women, including those who hurled stones, to be uneasy—even resentful. In a recording released on 7 May, he had urged women to stay at home and remain veiled, and to leave stone-pelting and other public activities to men since 'your brothers are still alive'.[5]

Even more significant was the fact that some Kashmiri teenagers were now not only joining but becoming leading lights of such narrow-vision Islamist militant groups as Lashkar-e-Taiba and Jaish-e-Mohammad. These groups had been active in the Valley since 1992 and 2001 respectively, but had then comprised mainly Pakistani members. The few Kashmiri boys who had been associated with them were more or less limited to providing local liaison. Even when militancy was revived around

2010, most Kashmiri boys joined Hizb-ul Mujahideen. Burhan and Zakir, for example, were leading lights of Hizb—until Zakir left it after his viral recording in May 2017.

By contrast, 2018 was rung in with a militant attack at 2 a.m. on 31 December 2017, by teenaged Kashmiri militants of Jaish. One of them, Fardeen Ahmed Khanday, recorded a video message which was released after he died during the attack. It was meant to be a suicide attack, for the message began with: 'God willing, when this message reaches you, I will already be a guest of my Lord in his heaven.' Sixteen-year-old Fardeen had gone underground only in September that year. He was motivated by the idea of martyrdom, as were most of the teenagers who became militants around that time. In one interview, Musa laughed while saying 'they threaten us with death, but that is what we want'.

Overall, there was an obvious positive correlation between a younger age demographic and the absorption of narrow-vision Islamist ideas. Such ideas were more common among teenagers than among young adults—and, generally, least commonly accepted among older Kashmiris. But, as already pointed out, teenagers mattered more than any other age group. A demographic bulge had made their numbers large. They were the future. And it was precisely the age group that had been on the streets for close to four months following the killing of Musa's predecessor, Burhan. Many of them were eager to take up arms. A large number of school students in parts of Pulwama said in April 2016, a couple of months before Burhan was killed, that the only thing that prevented them from taking up arms as 'mujahids' was that guns were not available.[6]

Musa's statements forcefully and unambiguously brought to the fore several trends that had developed over the decade from 2007 to 2017. The first of these trends was a radical shift in the way young people by and large treated religion and its role in their social and political life. Generally, their practice of religion was far more devout than had been common in the past. The content of their religious beliefs was more orthodox. They generally rejected Sufi traditions and other practices that they considered syncretistic. For most of them, practices that flexibly included traditions that were not firmly rooted in the Quran and the practice of the Prophet Mohammed had to be rejected.

The second trend that Musa's statement reflected was a general rejection of liberal democracy as a legitimate system. Pull and push factors had combined to bring about this rejection over the decade. On the one hand, the romance of an Islamist regime based on shariah law and the traditions of the early caliphate pulled at their heart strings. On the other, the generation that had been born around the turn of the millennium had turned disgustedly away from the way they had experienced a supposedly liberal, democratic regime through the previous decade and more. (We will discuss this further in the next four chapters.)

Of course, a third trend that Musa brought to light was a generational shift, which has already been highlighted in Chapter 2, 'Mass Rage'. Musa was in his early twenties. Most of the 'commanders' were younger than twenty-five. Burhan had been only twenty when he was appointed the 'divisional commander' of Hizb, and became the face of Kashmir's militancy in 2015. And another twenty-year-old, Saddam Paddar, was among the biggest names in south Kashmir's militancy after Burhan's death.

GLOBAL INFLUENCES

During the decade since that year of endings and beginnings, the insistence on Islam's primacy which Musa's messages reflected had seeped into young minds through a barrage of messages via social media, televangelists, SMSs, and the discourse of some clerics. In most young minds, such ideas were not carefully thought through. They were rooted in the belief that Muslims were oppressed and degraded on a global scale. The world view underlying Musa's message reflected a contemporary reinvention of ideas that can be traced to the nineteenth-century poet, Altaf Husain Hali, and the nineteenth-century political activist, Jamaluddin

'Afghani', as also the eighteenth-century Saudi zealot, Mohammed ibn Abdul Wahab.

In the tradition of Hali and Afghani, many preachers held, and youths believed, that Muslims were in bad shape because they had strayed from the path shown by Allah through the Quran; they were being punished. If they strictly followed 'pure' Islam instead, eschewing corruptions, it would bring a golden age. It is important to keep in mind that Islam, and hence a system of justice and administration based on Islamic principles, was morally privileged in most young minds. To many Kashmiri students, shariah law seemed to signify an end to the pervasive corruption, self-centred ethics, and maladministration that they found around them. As with the Taliban in Afghanistan during the late 1990s, the logical next step would be to force all those around them to do the same, so that their entire society may be purged; Islam was, after all, a community religion. The next step after that would be to make it a global agenda.

Fundamentalist discourses of various sorts were vigorously pushed during and after that year of endings and beginnings. The proselytizing Tablighi Jamaat preached most widely. Bands of Tabligh volunteers visited different areas for three days, or forty days, to encourage people to live according to the example of the Prophet and the teachings of the Quran. Such bands were generally coordinated from madrasas. These were not officially recognized. Nor were they impeded. Indeed, at that stage, sections of the police went out of their way to help them. The army too took the view that they were okay since they were apolitical. Some Tabligh-affiliated Muftis ran shariah-based courts at their madrasas. They pressed women not to work, to wear burqas when they left their homes, and not to go out unaccompanied by a male member of their family.[7]

The most prominent of these was the Rahimiya madarsa at Bandipora, founded by the revered spiritual leader, Maulana Mohammed Rahmatullah. Its principal, Mufti Nazir, held that no book except the Quran was worth anything. His chief purpose for meeting non-Muslims was to convert them.[8] The Mufti functioned as a *qazi* (judge) too. In that role, he decided property and marital disputes.[9] He appeared to privilege men's versions with regard to marital disputes.

The pattern appeared to be the same at other madarsas. Some of these, particularly the Bilalia madarsa in Srinagar, organized annual *ijtima* assemblies during the years around 2007 and after. The intensity, style, and emotional appeals of speakers at these often resembled that of preachers at Christian Pentecostal congregations, and sometimes included healing. At these congregations, students were given prizes for the best recitals of the Quran by rote.

The Salafist movement, the Ahle-Hadith, too was vigorously active around 2007. Some leaders of the movement appeared to have the backing of top functionaries of the state around then, no doubt at least partly because those 'leaders' saw the Jamaat-e-Islami as backing to other political groups. The movement was very active in south Kashmir. Maulana Maqbool Akhrani ran a vast multi-storeyed mosque adjacent to Sher Bagh in Anantnag.[10] An entire floor was reserved for women. Well-equipped, multi-storeyed Ahle-Hadith mosques also came up in other parts of south Kashmir such as Shopian. Ironically, there had been so much opposition to the first Ahle-Hadith preachers who visited Kashmir in the 1870s that the maharaja had externed them from the state. The movement was first established in Kashmir in 1925 but had never had such wide success and popularity as in this phase, when it was encouraged by Saudi Arabia.

Akhrani's passionate sermons drew congregations of several thousand every Friday. Towards the latter part of the decade which witnessed the rapid growth of blinkered exclusivism, Akhrani was overtaken by far more fiery preachers—for example, Maulana Mushtaq Veeri, whose fans doted on him no less enthusiastically than a sports star's. In at least one sermon, a video recording of which was circulated on the internet, he praised Islamic State and its leader, Abu Bakar Al Baghdadi. 'Radicalism' spiralled during that decade so that, by 2017, Veeri was overshadowed by his own acolytes, such as Ashiq Salafi. Soon after Musa was forced to dissociate from Hizb,

Salafi addressed a congregation in Tral to publicly applaud Musa's Islamist, anti-democracy stand.

The Ahle-Hadith, the Tablighi Jamaat, and the long-established Jamaat-e-Islami had become undeclared rivals around that year of beginnings and endings, even as all three expanded their following considerably over the following decade. For a few years, leading lights of each held that theirs was the one true sect among the 73 splinters that the Prophet Mohammed had predicted.[11] Until about 2015, members of these sects sometimes disagreed openly in mosques over how the faithful ought to fold their hands during prayers.

Apart from fiery sermons from preachers such as Veeri, this generation received such ideas from televangelists and through a barrage of messages, mainly via internet telephony. The most popular televangelists during the decade were the Pakistani Dr Israr Ahmad, who was associated with Jamaat-e-Islami, and the Indian Dr Zakir Naik, whose discourses concentrated on comparing religions to show that Islam was superior. In the tradition of Jamaat-e-Islami founder Maulana Maududi's more politically radical phase, Dr Israr argued in support of establishing a state based explicitly on Islam. These and several other televangelists were extremely popular in Kashmir from around 2007. Many of the youths who dominated the streets in 2016 had grown up watching their discourses.

As discussed in Chapter 1, 'Endings and Beginnings', Kashmir had become a huge market for SIM cards, mobile internet usage, and handsets. Young people were bombarded with religion-based videos and other messages via social media, including WhatsApp groups. The various movements also used CDs, public meetings, and religious instruction at darasgahs and during *aitakaf* retreats when many youngsters fully immersed themselves for several days and nights into a meditative retreat in a mosque during the month of Ramzan. This sort of preaching, which became very popular among young men and boys, often focused on the victimhood of Muslims worldwide. That seemed to fit with the narratives they heard about an inherently Muslim Kashmir's repression at the hands of an essentially Hindu India, about their land being occupied and looted by non-Muslims, and of suffering great oppression because they were Muslims.

These messages reaffirmed the narratives and experience of repression and human rights abuse. More important, they placed these experiences and narratives in the context of a global trend—political, economic, and cultural aggression against Muslims en masse. Several trends dovetailed with, and gave added credibility to, this perception that Muslims in general were being oppressed by more powerful others. For example, perceptions about the victimhood of Muslims got a strong boost when Muslims were killed by beef vigilantes in various parts of India after 2014. The death of a Kashmiri teenager who had been sleeping in a truck that was burnt over this issue near Udhampur in the Jammu division of the state had a particularly strong impact in the Kashmir Valley. The boy was a helper on the truck, which was transporting apples. The truck was set on fire by a mob in that Hindu-dominated area, which targeted Kashmiri vehicles during a set of agitations over beef in October 2015.[12]

Classroom interactions with young Kashmiris in 2016 showed that beef vigilantism in various parts of India, and the lynching of Muslims, had made a huge impact. These incidents seemed to confirm in those young minds that Muslims could not live together with, or trust, non-Muslims. The young did not seem to focus on the Two-Nation Theory through which Pakistan was created.[13] Rather, they saw these events and trends as confirming the core message of some of the televangelist and other preachers they had heard, of videos that celebrated Islamic State, and the message of new, radical militant commanders such as Musa.

COUNTERINSURGENCY DISCOURSES

The preference for an Islamist system based on the shariah—even a caliphate—was deepened by these perceptions and narratives;

no doubt a caliphate seemed in teenaged minds to denote a divinely sanctioned, sacred, and therefore safe refuge in a world that seemed to hold hatred and danger for Muslims. As already stated in Chapter 2, 'Mass Rage', students frequently pointed to the narrative that bullets and pellets were used against demonstrators using stones in Kashmir, whereas water cannons were used against violent agitating arsonists in other states of India. During discussions in classrooms and elsewhere, they specifically pointed to the Jat agitation in Rajasthan and the Patel agitation in Gujarat. Students also pointed to the horrors of thunderous 'sound bombs' and of tear-gas shells burst outside their schools. However, in the summer of 2017, Director-General of Police S.P. Vaid said pellets had been used in those states too. 'I would love to use water cannons instead,' he said, 'but the water gets exhausted in five minutes and they would (then) burn the truck.'[14]

Administrative callousness and an overwhelming miasma of corruption contributed to the rejection of the existing system. We will explore in the following chapters the ways in which people often experienced the established system as exploitative and repressive. Young people easily bought into the idea that a system based on religious tenets would be just and equitable. One of the most vocal of the teenaged students in a Pulwama classroom that I visited in April 2016 said that society was corrupt—but equated corruption with any participation in the established system. In his world view, all those who worked for the government were '*mukhbir*' (the word means informer, but he seemed to use it to mean traitor). His logic seemed to be that those who participated in the established system were corrupted since they were motivated by greed for money. In many young minds, a system of governance sanctioned by religion seemed liked the logical alternative to a system steeped in mundane greed.

Students' disillusionment with democratic politics increased manifold in the years after the Valley-based PDP joined the Hindutva-based BJP to form a coalition government in the state early in 2015. Most Kashmiris, particularly in the PDP's south Kashmir stronghold, viewed that coalition as a betrayal. The BJP and its parent organization, the Rashtriya Swayamsevak Sangh (RSS), became a major focus of youth resentment. They associated the RSS, and by inference the state government, with such things as beef vigilantism by gangs who lynched Muslims in some parts of India. It therefore added substantially to young Kashmiris' anger, and their disillusionment with the entire system of democracy. And it boosted the idea that an Islamist system of governance was the desirable way forward.

One of the most striking trends of the decade following 2007 was that anger increased among young women too—albeit more slowly than among young men. By 2016, some young women too had begun to say they were willing to take up arms as 'mujahids'. In 2017, several women students of colleges in many parts of Kashmir threw stones outside their colleges. The survey discussed in Chapter 4, 'Varied Opinions', showed that the discourses, attitudes, and aspirations of young women were far more moderate than those of young men until about halfway through the decade following 2007. But by 2016 and 2017, the discourses of some young women too had become more radical than before.

UNDERMINING NATIONALISM

The sort of thinking Musa's recordings reflected was as dangerous for the stability of nation states such as Pakistan and Bangladesh as for India. It is easy to forget that Pakistan jailed the Jamaat-e-Islami founder Maulana Maududi during the 1950s—when the orthodox Islamist Maududi argued against a republican nation state.

The link between Jamaat-e-Islami and Hizb-ul Mujahideen, which Musa and Burhan commanded, was long and deep. When Hizb was launched in November 1989, it was more overtly Islamist than most of the other Kashmiri militant groups, but its founders included activists of both the Jamaat-e-Islami and the Salafi group, Ahle-Hadith. Using wily political stratagems under the guidance of Geelani and the ISI, activists of the Jamaat-e-Islami took over the group between March 1990 and October 1991. Despite the fact that those decisions of Pakistan's managers in the 1990s had later come home to roost (Islamist groups caused mayhem with certain terror attacks in Pakistan, including assassination attempts against President Musharraf in December 2003), Pakistan had plumped for the far more radically Islamist new generation of Kashmiri militants too—militants among whom Musa was the norm rather than an exception.

Some shrill Indian television anchors who described Musa's viral recordings in the spring of 2017 as having been dictated by Pakistan failed to see the extent to which those speeches were bad news for Pakistan. Those anchors also trained their verbal fire at leaders of Kashmir's freedom movement such as Geelani—again, missing the wood for the trees. For, not just Musa, most young Kashmiris, especially teenagers, had little regard for Geelani or any other 'political leader' of the freedom movement.

It was even easier to ignore older, and marginalized, sections of the population within Kashmir. Most adults did not share the sorts of aspirations and thinking that Musa represented. Even among teenagers who did, it was a mistake to presume that they had clearly thought through the repercussions of their romanticized ideas about religion, society, and politics. Conversations indicated that they quite often had a simple, comforting idea of a divinely ordained alternative order.

The survey discussed in Chapter 4, 'Varied Opinions', clearly showed that many young people did not have in-depth knowledge or insights about even their own religion, leave alone the world at large. They most often reacted on the basis of emotions and feelings rather than closely thought-through arguments. As discussed in Chapter 2, 'Mass Rage', their heartstrings were tugged powerfully by masterfully produced videos of Burhan, with tranquil verdant spaces full of nature, cricket, traditional spaces, and symbols of Islam and of empowerment. In addition, millennials were shaped by what they encountered on the internet, television, and through socializing with other young people—and educators—in schools, playgrounds, and mosques. Many of the videos they came across on the internet glorified the actions of Islamic State, often with subtle techniques that combined special effects with background recitations.

The radicalization of millennial youth discussed in this chapter was in any case only one of the processes that developed during the decade of flux from about 2007. On the other hand, there were significant factors within the system that simultaneously pushed young people away from the established status quo they had inherited. We will discuss some significant push factors in the next four chapters.

Many readers will surely prefer to focus on radicalization as the chief factor that pulled young Kashmiris towards agitation, the pelting of stones, and picking up guns. It was surely a major factor, particularly among those who picked up guns. However, it is vital to explore the complex roots of the terrible rage that drove people—not only hot-blooded youth, but middle-aged mothers too at certain points—to pelt stones. Any serious attempt to break out of the cycle of violence requires us to examine why people, including middle-aged women, rushed from nearby villages to support militants caught in an encounter with troops. This trend needs to be contrasted with the fact that, however much support people may have felt for militants during the 1990s, people without guns tended to rush away, if they could, from an encounter between militants and forces during that decade.

In discussing in the succeeding chapters the trends that caused rage, hopelessness, and despair to surge in the period after 2008 and 2010, we will see how an extended period of violence can so hollow out the system that instability tends to become self-perpetuating. This has become clearly visible in Iraq during this same decade, and in Afghanistan—twice in the past three decades. Whatever their causes may be, instability and militancy tend to weaken the protections that an established system is meant to afford, particularly to the poorest and most vulnerable in a society. More so in periods when hope (of the sort that Prime Minister Vajpayee's initiatives had generated among Kashmiris around 2003–04) is snuffed out, the extended vulnerability of people, mainly the weak and powerless, destroys faith in the established system, and hope for the future.

While the generation that was born in Kashmir around 1990 had hope and aspirations as they entered their teens, those who were born around the turn of the millennium became teenagers at a time when prospects seemed to them to be very bleak. It is important to boldly explore how and why this came about, with an open mind and a willingness to acknowledge mistakes—if one wishes to decrease further bloodshed.

NOTES

1. https://www.youtube.com/watch?v=7vviC60nLh4, accessed on 25 June 2017. https://www.theguardian.com/world/2017/may/22/kashmir-conflict-shifts-top-militant-fight-islam-independence-zakir-musa
2. https://www.youtube.com/watch?v=XIS1ul_YDTA
3. http://kashmirwatch.com/interview-of-syed-ali-shah-geelani-with-yoginder-sikand/, accessed on 5 June 2017.
4. https://www.youtube.com/watch?v=4olHh5F0oBE, accessed on 25 June 2017.
5. https://www.youtube.com/watch?v=G_-bQ5WHMsU, accessed on 25 June 2017.
6. Author's interactions with school students in April 2016.
7. The author spent several hours with Mufti Nazir at the Rahimiya madrasa in Bandipora, visited the Bilalia madrasa in Srinagar's Lal Bazar area, and attended the annual *ijtima* convention at the Bilalia madrasa in 2009 and 2010.
8. Mufti Nazir berated the author for researching a book instead of being converted.
9. In the presence of the author at the Rahimiya madarsa, Mufti Nazir heard a man's complaints about his wife. The Mufti appeared to be sympathetic. The wife was not present.
10. The author interviewed Maqbool Akhrani and toured the mosque during 2009.
11. Author's interviews with several leading clerics, including Mufti Nazir at the Rahimiya madrasa in Bandipora and Maulana Akhrani at his mosque in Anantnag.
12. http://indianexpress.com/article/india/india-news-india/trucker-injured-in-petrol-bomb-attack-in-udhampur-dies/
13. In many of his speeches during the early 1940s, the All-India Muslim League leader M.A. Jinnah had held that Hindus and Muslims were separate nations that could not live together, since Hindus worshipped the cow and Muslims ate beef.
14. Author's interview with Director-General of Police S.P. Vaid at the Police Headquarters in Srinagar on 20 June 2017.

6

Disillusionment with Politics

A particularly critical ending came about during the couple of years after that year of endings and beginnings, 2007. Young Kashmiris by and large lost faith in political leaders in 2008 and 2009. As with the endings of that year, the fact went generally unnoticed. At that stage, it was still the generation that had been born around 1990 who were teenagers. Over the past five years, they had developed hope and faith in some established leaders, even the electoral system and the goodwill of some established local, national, and international bodies. In particular, they drew hope from the negotiations between the leaders of India and Pakistan, and between leaders of Kashmir's 'separatist' movement and top Indian leaders, which got going in 2003.

That lasted till 2007. Then, in 2008, faith and trust in 'separatist' leaders took a serious knock in the minds of young people at large. When agitations began in May that year, groups of young people turned up at the front gates of those established 'leaders' asking them to lead their processions. Some of those leaders acknowledged that they had been taken aback, but had hurriedly joined up at the head of those processions. By the time those agitations gathered momentum in June, those 'leaders' had found their feet at the forefront. Over the past few years, key geopolitical powers had worked with three of the most prominent leaders, turning them into the collective public face of Kashmir's freedom movement: Syed Ali Shah Geelani, Mirwaiz Umar Farooq, and Yasin Malik. When those three were gathered on one platform at the height of those agitations, Geelani asked the vast gathering to acclaim him as the sole leader of the struggle. He was booed instead by a few of those gathered there.

For many young people, it was a moment of truth, a turning point. The Hurriyat Conference had been formed in 1993, under the influence of covert agencies, including but not only Pakistani. Syed Ali Shah Geelani had already taken over Kashmir's militancy for Pakistan, starting in January 1990. From 1993, he also took charge of ensuring that the Hurriyat Conference did not stray from the path desired by Pakistan.

That people generally did not respond to his call for acclamation was also an indication of what was coming. In 2010, Geelani only briefly got a decisive say after the far more blinkered Masarat Alam, who had been a commander of the pan-Islamic Hizbullah in the 1990s, was arrested and jailed. Even during his brief public prominence, Geelani was publicly criticized after he asked for a lull in agitations so that students could write their exams. Through a substantial part of the 2010 agitations, Alam had taken on a dictator's role from underground locations. In 2016, young people did not even approach any established 'leaders' to lead their demonstrations.

Those leaders remained safely ensconced behind security inside their homes in 2016, under what the government called 'house arrest'. That of course only ceded ground to young men like Musa to dictate the nature, agenda, and objectives of the movement. Only the managers of the Indian state seemed to think that those Hurriyat and other leaders of the freedom movement were still relevant. A delegation of members of India's Parliament visited Srinagar to engage them in talks in the first week of September 2016. Some members of the delegation went to each of the three presumed leaders' homes, but in vain. All three knew better than those MPs and India's intelligence agencies that they could not talk. The most liberal of them, Mirwaiz Umar Farooq, had said in November 2015 that the government must engage him urgently. He had acknowledged then that he and other similar 'leaders' had little influence with the current generation of boys, and feared that the situation in Kashmir could descend into a vicious cycle of destruction.[1]

When I conducted an extensive survey of Kashmiri youth in 2011 (described in Chapter 4, 'Varied Opinions'), the largest number of students still named Geelani as the best leader for Kashmir. That was particularly true of those who had been born around 1990. Some of those who had been born in the mid-1990s did not have as much regard for him. By 2016, most adults still held him in high regard, but school students often referred to him as 'Geelani' in classroom conversations, without any honorific prefix or suffix. Generally speaking, they did not seem to have much regard for him—or indeed for any established leader.

In 2016, when I interacted with a large room full of college students in Pulwama, the epicentre of protests and defiance by then, the only response to my question, 'Who is your hero?' was 'the Prophet'. When I asked who their hero was in the contemporary world, the students responded with silence. When I specifically asked about Mr Geelani and Mirwaiz Umar Farooq, the presumed leaders of the freedom movement, the students said that neither was a hero to them.[2]

The survey described in Chapter 4, 'Varied Opinions', showed that many young Kashmiris considered the entire spectrum of leadership, whether supposedly 'mainstream' or 'separatist', as one lot. To some extent, there was indeed an overlap. It seemed in 2017 that influential leaders of the ruling PDP were in close touch with the Geelani-led faction of 'separatists'—to the extent that a public statement from Geelani allowed the state government to get the controversial Goods and Services Tax (GST) passed by the state assembly. And, a few weeks later, there was an altercation at Srinagar airport when senior police officers of the state tried to prevent the National Investigating Authority (NIA) from taking Geelani's son-in-law to Delhi after arresting him in the course of investigations into terror funding.

That year (2017) also brought out different facets of National Conference leader Farooq Abdullah, whom many had considered unshakably Indian. Indeed, when he had been the state chief minister from 1996 to 2002, he had defended the Special Operations Group (SOG) of the police. He first acknowledged to the *Business Standard* in April 2000 that 'they are going berserk and will pay a heavy price for it',[3] and added that SOG men were Kashmiris and would have to live among their people. But then, he tempered that judgement, saying that 'there are a few black sheep, but overall it is doing a yeoman's service. ... You don't want to demoralize the entire force'.[4]

That sounded mature and responsible then, but was a far cry from some of the positions he publicly took when he was in opposition in 2017. Then, he turned smoothly into a backer of 'azadi' demonstrators. Having taken back the presidentship of his 'mainstream' party by then, Farooq Abdullah was in position to return to the much-coveted chief minister's chair. He seemed oblivious to the fact that the anger that was manifest after 2007 stemmed in part from the horrific behaviour of the forces when he was, as chief minister, responsible for coordinating and controlling them. Nor did he seem to introspect on the fact that the killing of innocents that had fuelled the 2010 agitations, the daily killings during those demonstrations, and the humiliations by the police SOG which drove boys like Burhan to a fresh militancy, had occurred under his party's rule. None of that seemed to matter to him—or to the movers and shakers in New Delhi who dealt with and patronized him.

As the turnout, and the violence, at the by-election through which he was elected to the Lok Sabha on 9 April 2017 demonstrated, more and more Kashmiris, particularly young people, were angry with double-faced behaviour patterns. They generally turned away from politicians whom they saw as taking advantage of the system while they had power, and then adopting whatever rhetoric and positioning they thought might be required to win votes and regain power. People complained that many politicians used their power to oppress the poor and unconnected, as well as supporters of their opponents. When they were out of power, the same persons tended to glibly criticize the oppression, exploitation, corruption, and cynicism of those who now ran the state. Some of those who used the levers of power to oppress others and aggrandize themselves cynically calculated that taking populist 'separatist' positions would make people less critical of their own roles as oppressors. Too often, the calculation worked. One of the most striking findings of the survey described in Chapter 4, 'Varied Opinions', was that the sons of highly placed functionaries of the state, established (and meant to be functioning) under Indian law, were the bitterest critics of the system. These included the sons of men who had held very powerful offices, in the bureaucracy, police, and politics. Perhaps the single most trenchant critic of Indian oppression and 'colonization' I met was a student who was then pursuing a prestigious course of study in the West. The son of a leading minister, he had been raised in a virtual fortress, surrounded by walls and barbed wire fences guarded by bunkers of paramilitary forces. He later became a powerful member of the state government. He was not the only one who sat in power and promoted the colonization narrative. One of the most powerful figures in government, a point man for New Delhi, disparaged a prominent rival leader of his own party among his constituents as 'an army (backed) man'.

No wonder young Kashmiris had already lost faith in the entire political class when that young man was indulging in that hypocrisy. If young people lost faith in 'separatist' leaders when they publicly engaged in ego battles during the agitations of 2008, they lost faith in 'mainstream' leaders, and the system of governance which nourished them, during the months soon after the agitations of 2008 ended in October that year. That loss of faith could be pegged to some extent to the responses—and non-responses—of the state after the bodies of two young women were found in a stream in Shopian on 30 May 2009. A series of shifting positions taken by the police, the state government, inquiries instituted by it, and premier Indian investigative agencies such as the Central Bureau of Investigation left people generally cynical. Kashmiris by and large were convinced that the two women were raped and murdered by men of one or other of the armed forces. Three security forces' camps were located near the spot where their bodies had been found. The women had been missing since the previous evening.

For many young Kashmiris, the general elections to elect a new Legislative Assembly for the state the previous winter had been a sort of test. Some stated publicly at the time that they were giving the established system a 'last chance'[5] and that, if their hopes and trust were dashed, they might turn more decidedly away from the established system. When the relatively young Omar Abdullah was installed as chief minister after those elections in January 2009, many observers saw him as a youthful, earnest, well-spoken reason for hope. His behaviour around the extraordinarily challenging situation in Shopian a few months later dimmed that hope to a large extent. His inability to handle the uprising of 2010 put paid to what little hope remained.

VALIDATING THE MAINSTREAM

That hope had built up since 2003. For, while he engaged with 'separatist leaders', Vajpayee did even more to revive public confidence in mainstream politics. First, he caused free and fair elections for a new state assembly in 2002, monitored by large numbers of foreign observers with open access. Second, he did not interfere when the two largest parties that emerged from those elections negotiated power-sharing arrangements in a coalition. And third, he supported Mufti Mohammad Sayeed, who emerged as chief minister after those negotiations, which were conducted mainly between Sayeed and Congress leader Manmohan Singh in Srinagar.

Those election results were unexpected: several times over the previous weeks, Vajpayee's National Security Advisor Brajesh Mishra had told A.S. Dulat, who was by then the Prime Minister's Advisor on Kashmir, that he hoped Omar Abdullah was going to be the chief minister.[6] But, as chief minister from 2002 to 2005, Mufti Sayeed revived a general sense that the government was for the people. There was hope of better economic prospects too. The opening of a large number of new colleges and universities initially reinforced that hope in the minds of young Kashmiris. More important, there was for a while a greater sense of security than before—a sense of faith in the rule of law, that one could turn to those in power, and one's elected representatives, for the redressal of grievances. That was remarkable, for people had been cynical about mainstream politics even before militancy began in 1988.[7] In fact, the ham-handed rigging of the 1987 assembly elections was often cited by analysts as having triggered the turn towards militancy.

At the height of militancy in the early 1990s, there had been no space for politics at all. Mainstream politicians had to keep their heads down during the first half of the 1990s, when guns, grenades, and bombs could appear anytime, anywhere in the Valley, and 'mainstream' politicians were easy targets. Many grass-roots political workers were attacked, killed, or humiliated. A very large number did not dare to sleep at home for years. A few migrated to places like Jammu. In an atmosphere in which religious organizations like Jamaat-e-Islami had a lot of clout, Communist workers (including labour rights activists) who were labelled anti-religion had a particularly bad time.

Workers of the National Conference, the major mainstream party, were forced under threat to place advertisements in local newspapers dissociating themselves from the party and expressing regret for ever having participated in politics. Many of these activists readily bounced back when the armed forces got the upper hand around 1995, and elections were organized in 1996.[8] Kashmiris generally took that in their stride, for they had already since at least the 1980s viewed political activists as power brokers who channelled the crumbs of government largesse to their favourites, keeping the loaves for themselves, or to be sold for profit. Since the rigging of elections had been the norm since the beginning, democracy was often seen as a high-sounding word for a system of institutionalized corruption, an organized bazaar of patronage.

The hope that was generated in 2003–04 dimmed after 2009–10. By the time the next round of assembly elections came around in 2014, there was a burst of enthusiasm and hope again. The stage for the 2014 elections was set by a terrible phase of floods, mainly in south Kashmir. The Valley was overwhelmed by the flood waters, which rose to the second floors of houses in many areas in early September. The devastation continued into October. Once more, people at large were terribly disappointed by the government. In the view of most common Kashmiris, rescue, relief, and rehabilitation were all messy, tacky, and inadequate. Still, many Kashmiris hoped that the Government of India had decided to wait until after the elections to give the state a massive package of funding for rehabilitation through the new state government.

A major strand of the election campaign was the BJP's high profile. The party of right-wing Hindutva-based Indian nationalism seemed to be determined to win a majority in the new assembly. That gave an edge to the rest of the campaign; many Kashmiris focused on trying to prevent a scenario in which the party of Hindutva would dominate their Muslim-majority state. The BJP finally failed to win a single seat in the Valley—not even close. But it won 25 seats in the new assembly from other parts of the state. The PDP, the major opposition party in the Valley, won 28, the largest number in the new assembly. As soon as the results were announced, BJP President Amit Shah made it clear that the BJP would sit on the ruling side of the house, either leading the government, participating in a coalition, or backing the party in government without participating in the coalition ministry.

Over the next few weeks, the two parties engaged in negotiations on how they might form a coalition. Mufti Sayeed, the leader of the PDP, made it clear that he thought the coalition to be a logical alliance of the party which had won the majority of seats from the Jammu division, and his party, which had won the majority of seats from the Valley. His party's arguments essentialized the two parties to not only their region-based but also religion-based identities.

When the two parties agreed an 'agenda for alliance', it seemed like a dream document for the PDP. The BJP not only agreed to put aside all those of its longstanding objectives (such as doing away with special constitutional guarantees of a 'special status' for the state) which made Kashmiris uneasy, the BJP even agreed to adopt parts of the PDP's agenda that many observers had considered anathema for the BJP—such as engaging with 'separatists' and with Pakistan. Many Kashmiris were pleased with the document, and hoped that, now that it was part of the coalition government of the state, the BJP government in New Delhi would hand out a large package for post-flood rehabilitation in Kashmir.

Almost immediately after the new state government took office, however, it became obvious that the two parties had very different interpretations of how their 'agenda for alliance' was to be implemented. The BJP adopted what was perceived as a 'hard' line—generally inflexible. Nor was there any sign of the massive funds that many in Kashmir had expected.

Through the rest of that year, 2015, people in Kashmir got the impression that pro-BJP activists were trying to push forward the objectives that the BJP had formally agreed to leave aside for the moment. The special status of the state was challenged in court, and a court in Jammu ordered the implementation of the ban on beef. The slaughter of cows and the sale and consumption of beef had been punishable offences in the state since the nineteenth century, but those laws had remained a dead letter for several decades.

If Mufti Sayeed had hoped that he, and the Kashmir issue, could be a bridge to bring the governments of India and Pakistan to a negotiating table, the government in New Delhi was evidently averse to ceding any such role to him. It did not keep its coalition partner in Kashmir in the loop when it covertly moved towards a rapprochement from at least October that year (which led up to an unannounced visit by Indian Prime Minister Narendra Modi to Pakistani Prime Minister Nawaz Sharif in December). In fact, when Modi visited Kashmir in early November, he snubbed Mufti at a public meeting, saying he did not need advice from anyone on Kashmir.

Whatever hope people at large in Kashmir had had from political processes until then had already turned to bitter disappointment and rejection. Young people in particular had come to reject not just this particular dispensation but the entire system under which it functioned. While the state was generally seen as having failed to show goodwill, empathy, generosity, and purposefulness during and after the floods, Islamist organizations like the Jamaat-e-Islami had quietly made a great impact. Activists of its youth wing, the Islami Jamiat-e-Tulaba, worked hard in south Kashmir to rescue the stranded, and provide relief and help.

It was during the year following the floods that the political system and the idea of democratic functioning seemed to lose its charm. The idea of democracy which Vajpayee—and Mufti, while he was chief minister until 2005—had given credibility had already begun to dim by that year of endings and beginnings. Those who had been born around 1990 were becoming disillusioned as they grew up. And that idea never touched the millennial generation. They were little children when Vajpayee was in power. The hope that phase had generated was over by the time they came to their teens. The radical ideas that had been circulating over the previous few years clicked into young minds as a suitable alternative.

LOSS OF FAITH

Perhaps the most potent cause for youth to turn to political and religious radicalism—and to intertwine demonstrations with militancy—was the loss of faith in 'leaders', a delegitimization which cut across the artificial dividing line between 'mainstream' and 'separatist' leadership. It was an extremely dangerous trend. For, a society without faith in purposeful and effective leaders is amenable to the most radical, hate-filled, and nihilistic ideas; the attitudes reflected in Musa's recording in May 2017 stemmed partly from this delegitimization.

During my interactions over the previous couple of years, teenagers had shown disdain for most 'leaders', irrespective of whether they were meant to be 'mainstream' or 'separatist'. Many of them showed great respect for long-bearded religious scholars, mainly televangelists, but not for political leaders of any sort. That also held true of many of those in their twenties. This meant a majority of the population.

The reasons for their disdain are not difficult to see. By the time 2007 came around, young Kashmiris were cynical about the wealth of an entire slew of their supposedly 'secessionist' as well as 'mainstream' 'leaders'. Shabir Shah, for example, had been the towering icon of Kashmir's aspirations since he had first torn and burnt the Bharatiya Jana Sangh[9] flag at Lal Chowk as a fourteen-year-old in 1968. He remained an icon until he was released from jail in 1995,[10] but his popularity plummeted within a couple of years as a range of people questioned the sources of his wealth. By 2017, cynicism about leaders in general had in many cases turned to disgust.

Quite early during the previous decade of rising rage, it had become fashionable for young Kashmiris to express disenchantment with politics. Facebook had become extremely popular around then, and phrases such as 'I hate politics' or 'dirty business' were commonly to be seen in the space for 'political views' on the profile of almost every young Kashmiri. Since Kashmiris by and large had been impressed by the effectiveness of the 2002 assembly elections to change an unpopular government, the decline of faith in electoral politics from around 2007 was tragic.

PLAYING WITH FIRE

The games of smoke and mirrors of some prominent intelligence agents played a great role to cause the delegitimization and consequent marginalization of leaders. A major part of the task that various intelligence operatives set themselves was to buy over, and manipulate the activities of, a range of political leaders. They felt the need to control all 'leaders' in a 'conflict zone' such as Kashmir, whether 'mainstream' or 'separatist'. They did not seem to realize—or care—that, if their games delegitimized the system under which those 'leaders' functioned, it would promote radical alternatives, further damage social cohesion, and spur more conflict and chaos.

They happily played with fire, trying to purchase several of the state's (or incumbent government's) opponents, whether these were militants, politicians, or street-level troublemakers. Their cash flows were vast—and only loosely accounted. Some of those in charge of disbursing cash would complain plaintively that other agents pocketed some of those funds. In fact, if Kashmir's prodigious grapevine was to be believed, a lot of hands were in several tills. At least three prominent 'secessionists' got property in a plush south Delhi colony. At least one other owned a fine hotel in the popular holiday resort, Pehalgam. Several Kashmiri leaders invested in property in Bangalore and other Indian cities.

There was no dearth of anti-India 'leaders' happy to build palatial houses—with paramilitary bunkers providing security and pelf at their gates—while they promoted the 'cause' at international conferences. Since these militants, politicians, activists, or opinion makers that various agencies influenced were meant to be leading wars against the state, they could not of course call a halt to their wars. But their agency 'handlers' tried to influence the contours of these wars, to calibrate opposition. So, along with payouts, these intelligence agents gave advice on what to say or do. That advice was not always motivated by the national interest. At times, the events those operatives manipulated might promote their or their mentors' individual careers, or their political masters' agendas. The net result was that they kept the issue alive, and facilitated the processes through which it was passed from one generation to the next.

For the most part, they ignored changes on the ground, between generations, different social milieus, or places within Kashmir. Once they invested in a 'leader', they tended to remain invested, whether or not that 'leader' continued to have any influence. If they noticed that their own patronage had undermined that 'leader', they were quite happy. They did not focus on the vacuum in leadership that might result. Many such operatives were simply blind to the potential consequences of their blithely handing out money. Others were chuffed about the power and importance they enjoyed. Some might have been happy to see the conflict kept alive.

This was a recipe for permanent chaos, for the war was to continue, only change its dimensions. It was perennially possible to find incentive-takers (in cash) and makers of promises. On the other hand, in case it was true that some of those who disbursed incentives kept portions for themselves, they too would not want the disbursing to stop.

That hypocritical give and take provoked anger in the minds of young militants and their teenaged backers. That anger extended to the modernist ideas of nationalism which those agents and politicians supposedly espoused. By 2017, overkill during the past decade about turnouts of voters had ended up delegitimizing not just voting but democracy itself among several youths. In combination with the cynical, self-serving unresponsiveness of those who took power, it made the entire system of democracy seem like just a propaganda exercise. Young minds were influenced by far more potent narratives than those that Indian intelligence agents employed.

On the other hand, some of the 'leaders' who were the chief focus of those agents were not just objects of a tug of war between Indian and Pakistani agents. Major global powers also pulled their strings. In fact, if the grapevine was to be believed, some of Kashmir's most high profile 'separatists'—ones with a narrow-vision religious bent of mind at that— could arrange a visa even for countries considered the most difficult to enter. One such was said to have called the embassy of an extremely powerful country to say he was sending a student for a visa the next day; the boy got his visa.

Amid this brazen commodification of leadership, people became increasingly dismayed and enraged. Those 'leaders' and intelligence operatives tended to see ordinary people as an amorphous blob in the background, not as insightful, sensible assessors of the games being played.

They miscalculated. Particularly in an age of hyper-visibility and communication, the people at large should always have been sharply in focus.

Dealing with the secessionists openly, as Vajpayee did in 2003–04, turned out to be far more sensible. For, it put them on the backfoot without Vajpayee even wanting to. This happened in two ways. One, they turned out to be terribly divided within. The cracks which had been papered over as long as the government of India had ignored them emerged when they had to respond to the government's efforts to engage them. Two, those who did engage turned out to have no agenda. When they were asked to give a paper to the Home Ministry on the basis of which discussions could be held, they had to turn to a London-based activist to put together a paper.

As it turned out, they only had a few meetings over tea with Vajpayee, his Home Minister, L.K. Advani, and Vajpayee's successor, Manmohan Singh. Rather than present a thought-out charter or vision, some of those 'leaders' made petty requests to their leading intelligence handlers. Around the middle of that decade, the wives, sons, brothers, and other associates of several 'leaders' got jobs, admissions, loans, land, buildings, and visas.

The Modi government initially tried to marginalize these 'leaders' when it came to power in 2014, but then did a policy flip-flop.[11] A scandal emerged in March 2017 over the fact that a government-run establishment employed Geelani's grandson in a plum post at the height of the 2016 uprising—during a week when Geelani had called for a shutdown. Such shutdown calls ended soon after. That may have suited those who thought in terms of short-term 'normalcy' and 'law and order'. But, to the extent that such moves undermined the credibility of those supposed 'leaders' of the Kashmir movement, they pushed many young Kashmiris to turn to religious idealism. The millennial generation moved farther down the road towards radical ideas.

Policymakers seemed to be oblivious to this trend. From the spring of 2017, what little remained of the reputations of Kashmir's 'leaders' continued to be undermined. In May that year, a government document leaked to a television channel revealed what was already well known in Kashmir—that Pakistan funded insurgency in Kashmir. A petty businessman based in

Srinagar's Maharaja Bazar[12] was the conduit for Pakistani funding to Shabir Shah. A set of sting recordings by a rival television channel proved during the same month that Pakistan funded Hurriyat leaders to the tune of hundreds of crores of rupees (around a hundred million dollars) for each season of unrest in Kashmir. Demonstrations were instigated and various sorts of government buildings were burnt to create 'chaos', the Kashmir region president of the Geelani-led Hurriyat faction[13] revealed during one of those stings.

Their reputations were further undermined by a series of searches by India's National Investigation Agency on 4 and 5 June 2017 at the houses of various Hurriyat leaders and other Kashmiri businessmen suspected of funding the insurgency in Kashmir. That was a direct follow-up on the sting operations.[14] Many in Kashmir thought those searches were selective. They suspected that several other leading figures in both 'separatist' and 'mainstream' camps, including powerful figures in the government, had been involved. The right time for comprehensive investigations would have been the period leading up to that year of endings and beginnings, 2007, when people in Kashmir were by and large disillusioned with militancy and agitations. Such searches could have changed public attitudes within Kashmir at that stage, when the factors that formed rage and a new militancy over the next decade had just come into play. People generally wanted peace and stability then, and a resolution of the issues that had been hanging fire. They wanted a functioning, responsive system. They had not yet turned to fundamentalist ideas, but young people were beginning to receive such ideas by then. It was a critical juncture.

The attitudes and aspirations of people had changed radically by 2017. The millennials who had been at the forefront of the 2016 uprising had developed a seemingly unstoppable momentum. They already had no regard for, or trust in, the 'leaders' whose homes were searched. In fact, as these sting revelations and searches finished what little credibility the various 'leaders' of Kashmir's movement still had, many of the youth became more enamoured of the sort of pan-Islamist shariah-based regime Musa espoused.

COUNTERPRODUCTIVE STRATEGY

Cash flows had contributed to undermining those 'leaders'—and popularizing the 'pure' and 'sacred' option that Musa's messages represented. With the occasional exception of men like Fazl Haq Qureshi,[15] the lifestyles, properties, and vehicles of a wide range of leaders indicated that they had prospered during the insurgency. If the strategy was (as it was around the turn of the millennium) to smooth the way towards a negotiated settlement with money and perquisites, policymakers ought to have realized how fraught with danger the process was if it did not result in a generally accepted settlement between India and Pakistan. Without that, and possibly even if that process had remained on track, the business of handing out money, perquisites, and other benefits within Kashmir was flawed for several reasons. For one thing, the perception that their 'leaders' had been bought over made it likely that Kashmiris by and large would, for that reason alone, reject any settlement these 'leaders' agreed. Regardless of its merits, such a settlement would be seen as a betrayal simply because of the rewards it would be seen to have brought to its negotiators.

Even if there were no evidence of payouts, most of those 'leaders' would have found it very difficult to compromise on the maximalist positions they had taken in the past. Too many militants and other Kashmiris had died after the first few months of 1990 for their families and neighbours to accept such compromises from the very leaders who had projected themselves as the flag-bearers of that movement. In fact, many common Kashmiris complained that vast numbers of the poor had been killed, while these 'leaders' had lost nothing; they had sent their own sons abroad, never to fight in the militancy.

A third flaw had crept in unnoticed by 2017. This was that it neglected generational change. Naeem Khan spoke plaintively of a '35-year record of service' after the sting operation in May 2017 exposed his hand in organizing Pakistan-funded arson and violence,[16] but those who had been born in the 1990s and after did not care what he had done in the twentieth century; for them, that was history. Yet, oblivious to vanished reputations, and other pitfalls of covert negotiations accompanied by monetary and other sweet-eners, those intelligence operatives kept at it.

If Geelani was about the only leader with credibility by the time a new generation of Kashmiris erupted, largely leaderless, on to the streets in 2008 and 2010, it was largely because of his perceived intransigence in the face of intelligence operatives' efforts to lure him. In a world in which image mattered far more than fact, the majority of Kashmiris viewed him as the only prominent leader who had stood firm since the insurgency began. He was generally perceived as one who had not compromised, although his positions in fact had shifted. He had even described the JKLF's militancy as 'afra-tafri' (hooliganism) in 1989, before accepting the ISI's request to take charge of the militant movement through Hizb early in 1990. During the decade after 2007, his earlier strong espousal of Kashmir's merger with Pakistan had given way to a more ambiguous 'azadi barai Islam' (freedom-filled Islam) for a while, and then to an ambiguous 'azadi'.

Since he nevertheless retained the image of incorruptibility, he man-aged to restore calm in 2008 and again in 2010. All those other putative 'leaders' who were perceived to have been kept happy by those agents were in no position to help to pacify rage. By 2016, no 'leader' at all outside the ranks of militancy seemed to have any influence with teenagers across Kashmir. The bitterness of disappointment, and their sense of betrayal, had generated far greater loathing than earlier generations had felt.

The vacuum in leadership that had developed during the decade after 2007 had made young people turn to alternative forms of government and political organization.

Islamic State did not have an organizational presence in Kashmir, but the ways in which the hearts and minds of the millennial generation had developed made the ground fertile for even that level of extremism. The fact that adults by and large did not share such narrow-vision attitudes hardly mattered any more. The delegitimization of political leaders of various hues had combined with a demographic bulge to bring such extremists as Musa to the forefront. The popularity of his rhetoric among young Kashmiris was a sobering indicator of the extent to which radical ideas had gained ground in the space created by various kinds of frustration and enraged despair during the decade since that year of endings and beginnings.

NOTES

1. Author's interview with Mirwaiz Umar Farooq at his residence at Nagin in November 2015.
2. Author's interaction with students of Pulwama Degree College in April 2016.
3. David Devadas, 'Anti-Terror Force Excites Revulsion', *Business Standard*, New Delhi, 11 April 2000.
4. David Devadas, 'Anti-Terror Force Excites Revulsion', *Business Standard*, New Delhi, 11 April 2000.
5. Author's interviews with several voters across the Valley during November and December 2008.
6. Author's interview with A.S. Dulat in the Gymkhana Club in New Delhi on 6 January 2016.
7. The first three grenade blasts took place in Srinagar on 31 July 1988.
8. Lok Sabha elections were held in June, and assembly elections in September–October 1996.
9. The Bharatiya Jana Sangh was the precursor of the BJP. Rejection of any special status for the state of Jammu and Kashmir was its chief plank from the time it was formed in 1951.
10. Shabir Shah was arrested from a truck en route to Jammu (from where he was said to be planning to cross the border to Sialkot) in the winter of 1989–90.
11. http://www.firstpost.com/india/kashmir-unrest-handing-out-freebies-to-seces-sionist-leaders-only-damages-the-governments-image-3317668.html, accessed on 22 June 2017.
12. Mehmood Sagar. See David Devadas, *In Search of a Future* (New Delhi: Penguin Books, 2007), pp. 131–32.
13. Naeem Khan.
14. Author's interview with Varun Sindhu Kul Kaumudi, Additional Director-General of the NIA, at his office in New Delhi on 12 June 2017. Kaumudi led the team that went to Srinagar to conduct the searches ten days earlier.
15. A founder of the Hurriyat Conference, Fazl Haq Qureshi was shot and critically injured by militants in December 2009. In July 2000, Hizb-ul Mujahideen deputy chief commander Majid Dar had nominated him to negotiate with the Government of India.
16. Author's conversation with Naeem Khan at his office in Jawahar Nagar, Srinagar, a few days after the sting was telecast.

7

Law Subverted

Burhan Wani, the iconic hero of Kashmiri youth in 2015–16, became a militant after he was slapped and abused by policemen of the SOG in 2010. He felt humiliated. Zubair Bashir Turey returned to militancy in 2017, saying that he had been harassed beyond endurance by the police.[1] In the first week of January 2018, Mannan Bashir Wani, a PhD scholar of the Aligarh Muslim University, became a militant. He stated on Facebook that he was angry over being questioned crassly by an SOG policeman some time earlier. He too felt humiliated, although the questions he said he was asked were inane: Why do you have long hair? Why isn't your beard trimmed? Why do you wear a shawl at your age?[2] No doubt the intimidation in the tone and attitude of the questioner mattered more than the content of the questions. Responses to the survey discussed in Chapter 4, 'Varied Opinions', also showed that a large section of Kashmiri youth felt deep rage against the police. The survey showed that, although a larger section were angry with the paramilitary CRPF, rage against the police force ran deeper among those (about 60 per cent of the young respondents) who felt it.

Even minor incidents could set off extreme reactions because there was a deep well of disgust and resentment against excesses, corruption, and fudging which people had experienced at the hands of the police. This had accumulated in society over a long period, and it often took only a relatively minor incident to drive a young person over the edge. In fact, the rage that had been manifest through stone-pelting in 2008 and 2010 had tapped into this deep well of resentment. Once the 2008 agitations had been sparked, that deep well of rage exploded, emerging like lava from a volcano.

And it was through those agitations that both public unrest and militancy passed to a new generation—after a gap in the middle of the first decade of the twenty-first century. Until 2008, most of the millennial youth had little idea about the 1990s, but were dramatically introduced to resistance against the state through the agitations that year, and the vigorous narratives that followed. It is striking that, despite the determined memorializing that had occurred since 2008, the 'stone-pelter' boys who manned barricades in 2010 allowed army vehicles to pass. Lt General Naresh Marwah, who was Corps Commander in the Valley that year, said there was not a single attack on the army itself during the prolonged uprising that year.[3] The truth of that statement was apparent on the ground that year.

The great irony of the concentration of rage against the police, especially the SOG, is that it led boys to become militants when even the SOG's behaviour was generally much less cruel than sections of it had been during the second half of the 1990s. In fact, the police force had only come back into form in those years, having lain low between 1990 and 1995. Constables were recruited in large numbers during the second half of the decade, but very few commissioned officers to lead them were directly recruited from within the state during the 1990s—apart from the few who were posted from 1994 onwards to the Jammu and Kashmir cadre from the all-India IPS (Indian Police Service). As the size of the force, and its responsibilities, grew rapidly after 2000, promotions galloped. The very few officers who had been inducted during the 1980s and 1990s had to be promoted fast to fill vacancies, including the very many new vacancies that were created as the force expanded fast. By 2018, there were no less than eighteen officers of the rank of Director-General or Additional Director-General in the state cadre.

Movement up the ladder of promotions was more dramatic lower down the scale, among junior and non-commissioned officers. Among some officers, 'kills' and 'captures' began to play the sort of role that they had in the army during the late 1990s: officers and units sometimes competed to notch up higher numbers. That is how the sort of 'bump-him-off culture', to which Javid Mukhdoomi referred,[4] took root. The system of rewards and promotions was one reason cynical attitudes remained in some sections of the police, even though many of the officers who were recruited in the new century were comparatively professional.

As the new militancy emerged, many in the police force responded with professionalism, even under severe stress and in very dangerous circumstances. Indeed, it became one of the more professional police forces in South Asia. Yet, several bad apples remained. So did some of the distortions that had entered the system during the war-like situation in the 1990s. To a large extent, the damage had already been done. Rage had been generated, mainly from 2006, when the mismatch between militancy and the apparatus of counterinsurgency was obvious to residents of Kashmir. It grew strongest in the generation of the 1990s—those, ironically, who had been willing to settle down to peace in the middle of the first decade of the new century. Many of the millennials who channelled that rage into a new militancy simply rejected the entire system of democracy, lock, stock, and barrel.

SYSTEMIC DISTORTIONS

In this chapter, we will examine some of those distortions, and some of the abuses to which they led, and then take a look at the comparatively minor humiliations that so enraged the generations which were born during the time of violence, and had been immunized to violence and fear. These youth were by and large far more defiant, and easily provoked, than the previous generation. So, although there were much fewer human rights abuses than in the 1990s, the threshold of acceptance had decreased far more steeply. Policymakers and planners did not seem to realize that levels of aspiration are very significant as contexts for the growth of frustrations.

Unmindful of generational change, they focused on projecting 'normalcy' at this stage. To most of those in government, that word meant changes in the statistics of militant attacks, curfews, tourists, etc. Kashmiris by and large, particularly those beyond the networks of power and influence (networks that included established 'separatists'), focused on their own experience rather than on graphs and statistics. To them, 'normalcy' meant lawful rights in their everyday lives; my surveys showed that many of them craved rights almost like an imagined promised land. It was part of the reason why a divinely sanctioned regime based on shariah seemed so attractive to many of them; it seemed to promise a perfect world.

For the moment, many young Kashmiris perceived their lived reality as being a little like the rule of the jungle—might is right. Among millennials, this impression was partly shaped by the narratives they heard from 2008 onwards about not only the situation of Kashmir, but about the nature of the state, and the counterinsurgency apparatus. Much of that was about what had emerged in the 1990s.

EARLY BREAKDOWN

The rule of law was among the early casualties of the insurgency. This happened in two ways. One, the government almost collapsed in January 1990. The police force was on the back foot until at least 1992, and very few other functionaries of the state went out among the people—or even to their offices. It was the autumn of 1990 before the arms of the state could begin to take control of the major part of even Srinagar city.[5] A year later, most offices in the city were functional and people had begun to come to some of them.[6] But it was only after September 1992 that the state was able to control places like Sopore in north Kashmir.

From 1990 to 1992 (and to some extent thereafter), the writ of militants ran in large parts of the Valley. Many Kashmiri militants extorted money under the threat of the gun, even on occasion indulged in outright loot. This loot ranged from daylight robbery of petty businessmen—some of these were given a receipt for a donation to 'the cause'—to forcing a boy on the street to part with an expensive new pair of sneakers, a leather jacket, or a motorcycle. Many of those who owned a car in enviable condition kept the vehicle garaged for months at a stretch, even years, for fear that a militant would demand it. Many Kashmiri militants took advantage of young women in the houses in which they took shelter. Some of them forced marriages.

Militants used torture too at times. Apart from soldiers whom they captured, their main targets were those whom they accused of being 'mukhbir' or informers. At times, particularly during early 1990, these were Kashmiri Pandits (Hindus) but, in the next couple of years, they sometimes vented their cruel fury on anyone they labelled a 'mukhbir'. Militants' methods were at times brutally violent, including dragging a victim tied to the back of a car, gouging out eyes and other kinds of dismemberment, rape, and painful torture. As with the forces, their objectives too were punishment, revenge, and to strike terror in the minds of those they considered a threat.

Rural Kashmir witnessed the worst of militant excesses, mainly in 1991–93, since militants had a much freer run in rural areas at that stage. Although most people would not say it openly, this is one of the reasons—albeit a subliminal one—for the consistently and significantly higher turnout of voters in rural than in urban areas. However, in the years thereafter, the excesses of mercenaries and of police SOG were at least as horrifying as those of militants had been during that short period.

As the government struggled desperately to regain control, the second aspect of the breakdown of the rule of law came to the fore. Rights were formally suspended and armed forces given extraordinary powers. Ironically, this happened after the peak of enthusiasm for insurgency in 1990 had already passed. The Governor declared parts of the state 'disturbed' in 1991, thus giving the armed forces emergency powers. Taking a page from similar laws it had imposed on insurgent states in India's north-east since the 1950s, India's Parliament also enacted an Armed Forces Special Powers Act for Jammu and Kashmir. Under this law, eight districts of the state were initially declared disturbed. In 2001, when suicide attacks were in full swing, twelve districts were declared disturbed, and then every district in the state. In 'disturbed areas', the army and paramilitary forces were authorized to enter any premises, search any person or place, detain and interrogate anyone they suspected of being an insurgent, and kill anyone who resisted or tried to flee.

There were various patterns to what many in the forces called 'kills'. To begin with, the large majority of those killed were militants who were captured and killed on the spot—or in a jungle or other isolated location after they had been interrogated. The catch-and-kill procedure had begun quite early, when prosecution and judicial processes had more or less broken down. Sometimes a captive died during interrogation. Without the due process of law, innocent citizens too were sometimes killed. Sometimes, they were wrongly identified by forces' 'spotters' or other informants—either through a genuine mistake or owing to a rivalry or other malevolent motive.

When large numbers of troops were inducted from 1994 on, the proportion of innocent citizens who got killed increased. But the misuse of counterinsurgency, including torture and threats to life, limb, property, and social standing—at least partly for extortion—began as early as 1990. It had happened even in the family of one of the most prominent young leaders of the generation that grew up during the period of violence, Waheed ur Rehman Para.[7] When he was a little boy, his paternal uncle, a school teacher, was picked up in that early phase, and only released after two lakh rupees were said to have changed hands.[8] His neighbours said that the original demand was for ten lakh rupees, which was scaled down to two lakh rupees after tense negotiations.

That uncle was tortured, according to his relatives and neighbours, hung upside down, tied to a chair. He was apparently questioned about whether militants took shelter in his home. This could have resulted from misinformation from resentful opponents; there was a lot of that. Para says that for the first fortnight he was missing, his family had had no idea where the teacher was. This happened despite the fact that the teacher's father, Haji

Abdul Rehman, was one of the staunchest Indian nationalists in Kashmir. Long before the militancy began, he would sit outside his house on India's Republic Day and Independence Day every year and distribute sweets to anyone passing that way. For decades, he had been associated with Mufti Mohammad Sayeed, who had been a leader of the Congress party before he became India's Home Minister during 1990.

DIFFERENT STAGES

The trend of 'picking up' anyone and locking up, torturing, or killing them began in the BSF, which was at the forefront of early counterinsurgency, along with the CRPF and the army. The codenames for the BSF's catch-and-kill methods around 1991 were Operation Eagle and Operation Tiger. E. Rammohan, who became the Inspector-General in charge of the BSF in Kashmir in 1993, put a stop to that, but it continued in various forces—only more discreetly.

The second stage came in the mid-1990s, when some human rights activists, journalists, and others involved in exposing cruel lawlessness were also targeted. The most high profile of these was Jaleel Andrabi. A leading lawyer who fought against human rights abuse, Andrabi had strongly argued before the high court that those detained in the state should not be lodged in jails outside the state. According to statements of key witnesses, Andrabi's car was stopped on the road in March 1996 and an army officer and some others took him away. His body was found floating in the river a few days later. Some witnesses named Major Avtar Singh of the Indian Army in the murder of Andrabi and some others. A Special Investigating Team of the police reported this to the court.[9] Questions were raised about the transfer of judges who had made critical observations and ordered investigations,[10] and about the Government of India's reluctance to extradite Avtar Singh from California, where he went to live (and later apparently committed suicide).

By about 1997, the Kashmiri people had largely come to fear counter-insurgency measures as vicious instruments of humiliation, extortion, and arbitrary violation. Local mercenaries employed by the forces sometimes used the arbitrary tactics available to the forces—search, detention, torture, and execution—to blackmail people. The object of that blackmail was generally money, but extended to sexual favours, vehicles, and the settlement of disputes the way someone with a connection to a force wanted. Just as they had when they were militants, many of the mercenaries threw their weight around among other Kashmiris—only this time, their extortion, loot, rape, and other forms of molestation had the backing of the armed forces.

In some areas, the local Rashtriya Rifles or BSF commander was only vaguely aware of what the mercenaries working with his unit were up to, but, at times, an officer directly blackmailed or looted a citizen. Waheed Para experienced this in 2005, when he was in his late teens. A BSF officer accused him of being a militant, dramatically holding a pistol to his head, and then tortured him mentally until he broke down. He was released after a minister in the state government intervened, but the swaggering officer threatened, while letting him go, that he would 'discover' weapons from the car and then blow up that car with the boy in it. The boy was studying in Class 11 when he became a victim of such torture and threats. The reason was greed; that officer wanted the boy's new black Indigo car.

When he finally loaned the officer his car, it was spotted in Gulmarg with the officer, his Kashmiri security man, and young women. The car was returned to him after a week.[11]

Officers such as this, and some of the mercenary groups through which some of the forces operated, had enough of a free rein to behave like dacoits in a B grade Bollywood film. The future youth leader had good reason to take that officer's threats seriously. Such things had happened. The public execution of a teenager who had refused to give up his motorcycle was embedded in the collective memory of Safapora residents. Waseem Jan, a fifteen-year-old schoolboy, rode a new RX 100 Yamaha motorcycle one morning in January 1996 to buy mutton. At the shop, a bunch of Ikhwani thugs demanded the bike. The boy asked why they were eyeing what was not theirs. For his gumption, people of the neighbourhood said, he received a burst of automatic gunfire in his chest.[12]

Unless they were well connected, the victims of mercenaries could not even complain to the authorities; for the record, those gunmen were taken to be militants. They were supposed to be insurgents against the state, rather than paid operatives of the state. And it was apparently easy for them to manipulate records to show that their victim had been a militant and had attacked them before they killed him.

When the forces got used to catch-and-kill executions—and that giddily exciting power, the power over life and death—some among them clung to it even when judicial and prosecutorial systems were back in place. According to a former militant, a senior police officer shot a person at the gate of a court compound. He was emerging after the court had just ordered his release. The officer who killed him may have argued in his defence that ready-to-hand justice was better than court procedures when the state was dealing with insurgency or terrorism. But when officers subvert the law, they get used to it. That officer was later caught for tampering with evidence in the murder of a young man who was part of the charmed network of influence, and had had nothing to do with insurgency.

The system struggled to revert to lawful functioning during the second half of the 1990s, but it was not easy. Justice Bashir Ahmed Khan, former chief justice of the Jammu and Kashmir High Court, said he had to struggle to restore the sanctity of habeas corpus orders in that phase, during which he was a judge of the high court.[13] When a series of orders had been ignored, and a superintendent of police had ignored summons, Khan ordered an army colonel to arrest the superintendent of police and produce him before the court. If that colonel too had not respected the court, the court might have had to give up. However, since the colonel showed his intention to take the order seriously, the superintendent of police was in court that afternoon, with the missing person.

TRAUMA AND EXTORTION

Despite all the images from Iraq, Syria, and elsewhere over the past several years, it is difficult to imagine how badly the rule of law can collapse in a war zone, unless one experiences it. In order to establish terror among their victims, mercenary gangs occasionally staged horrific public executions. Their terror tactics succeeded only too well. Residents of Safapora vividly recalled an execution at the centre of their village many years after it took place in November 1995. Mohammed Sidiq Hajam was blindfolded, they said, and encircled by a gang of Ikhwan mercenaries. Then, laughing and mocking him, they took potshots at him, shooting him in the legs and hands as he crawled in the mud, grovelling and desperately stuffing mud in his mouth to stop himself from screaming from pain. None of the villagers who witnessed this dared protest. For the next few years, they would remain in terror, giving in to the extortion of the Ikhwanis.[14]

Extortion was commonplace. Mohammed Murtaza was the head of a middle school on the outskirts of Safapora. He was abducted one afternoon and taken to an empty park nearby; Ikhwan mercenaries demanded fifty thousand rupees to let him go. After some negotiations, Murtaza managed to get away from them five hours after he was abducted—after, according to some residents of the area, twenty thousand rupees were paid as ransom.[15]

A mercenary who liked to call himself a 'chief commander' would round up eight to ten residents almost every Saturday—when many government employees would return to the village for the weekend. He would lock them up in a cowshed in his village, while his father collected a ransom for the release of each. Safapora residents add that the tall, fair mercenary would often send his men to summon one or other woman who had caught his eye, to his lair in a nearby hamlet.[16]

RAMBO-STYLE OPERATIONS

The Ikhwan gangs and SOGs of the police were at their barbarous worst around 1997–99. They went after militants, tortured and sometimes killed them. Members of the SOGs were given commando training, extra increments, equipment, facilities, perquisites, and other incentives. More important for their careers, they received much faster promotions than other policemen and officers. Many of them competed to notch up more 'kills' and encounters. Many of them took almost limitless power for themselves. Within a couple of years after the SOGs were formed in the mid-1990s, some of them had begun to participate in excesses of various kinds.

Particularly at that stage, many of the policemen in this outfit fancied themselves as some sort of Rambo characters. With black bandanas wrapped around their heads and high boots worn over their pants, some of them would lean rambunctiously, whooping as they stood in open jeeps speeding down roads, brandishing automatic weapons.[17] These modifications in their uniforms, and the way they carried their weapons, all pandered to their macho egos. They were policemen, but their respect for the law and standard operating procedures matched their respect for their prescribed uniforms.

Anyone could be their victim. Safapora residents recalled another horror story; it involved the men of the SOG camp near their village. One night, militants attacked that camp. They said that, the next morning, SOG men pulled Ali Mohammed Sheikh, who lived next to the camp, out of his house, made him stand on a pile of firewood outside a baker's oven, and triggered the explosives they had placed in the stack. The explosion blew Sheikh to pieces. Sheikh had had nothing to do with the attack on the camp the previous night, but the policemen had made a point: the entire village would live in terror of the consequences of another attack on that camp.

A militant group had carried out exactly the same sort of execution in Downtown Srinagar during the early 1990s. The man who was blown to bits then was suspected of being an 'informer'. But that event, which was meant to terrify potential collaborators from within the militancy, did not embed itself in the collective memory of the community, like the murder of Sheikh did.

After a while, the citizens of that village learnt to live in terror even of complaining about their misfortunes. Neighbours and relatives recounted what happened to Abdul Khaliq, a highly respected Numberdar or designated village elder at Safapora. Khaliq used to complain to the authorities about abuse of power by the SOG men and others. One day in March 1998, neighbours say that two SOG men picked him up from the market. They tortured him mercilessly and electrocuted him with 400 volt shocks through wires clipped to his thumbs. Then, they left him unconscious on his doorstep.

Relatives say the family had gone to Srinagar that day. When they returned, they found a throng outside their house. They added that Khaliq only survived the ordeal after the army officer in charge of the local unit, Colonel Khushal Singh Thakur, rushed to his rescue upon being informed. They also added that one of the policemen who had taken Khaliq for torture that day subsequently rose from constable to sub-inspector in a decade—repeatedly promoted, out of turn, for 'kills'. That pattern of promotions-for-kills was commonplace. In 2010, that trend plugged into many others to wrench that scream of defiant rage which vented itself as mobs of stone-pelting boys.

Many Kashmiris came to perceive the SOG as a network of gangsters in uniform. Under the cover of counterinsurgency, some among them would abduct, loot, molest, torture, even kill citizens against whom they had an animus. The cause of animus could be as trivial as someone having honked at their vehicle in traffic.[18] Their vengeance could be horrific. In the summer of 1999, Kashmiris were agog with stories of how SOG policemen had killed three young men who were part of a wedding party near Hazratbal. *Business Standard* reported that 'a DSP [deputy superintendent of police] of this group is absconding, wanted across the country for involvement in abduction, robbery and murder of three boys picked up from a wedding procession near Hazratbal last July'.[19] In the summer of 2000, people around Sonwar, adjacent to Srinagar's cantonment, spoke in horror about a former militant whom SOG men had beaten up repeatedly. Three times, according to neighbours, that man's legs had been broken. Each time his legs healed, they returned to break them.

The Rambo-style macho behaviour of these 'operations' units was restrained after they were integrated with police stations in 2003 but, in the experience of many common Kashmiris, blackmail for extortion and the extra-legal settlement of disputes continued, only a little more discreetly. In fact, integrating 'operations' into police stations infected many others in those police stations with the greed, extortion, and blackmail which had once been practiced by militants, had entered army operations through Ikhwan, and the police force through the SOGs. The police became more emboldened to treat ordinary citizens who were not linked with the network of influence with abusive, aggressive contempt.

While he was engaged in research for his PhD, Dr Lateef went to get his car registration renewed. Accompanied by two friends who were medical doctors, he arrived at the office of the concerned authority at Humhama near Srinagar's airport. The policeman at the gate told him the office had closed and rudely shut the gate with an abuse involving Lateef's sister. Pricked, Lateef pushed the gate open and demanded why the policeman had abused him. Lateef says he was dragged in to the compound by his t-shirt and pummelled by several policemen with the butts of their rifles. 'I was crying,' says Lateef, 'but they would not stop'. He adds, 'I would like to shake the hand of an army man. I would like to shake the hand of a BSF man. I would like to shake the hand of a CRP man. But I would not like to spit at a JKP man'. That sentiment is a pointer to the causes of rage—often minor in themselves, but adding to each other—that emerged in stone-pelting. Each force generated some rage, but essentially it was about the breakdown of law and order, and the due processes of lawful functioning.

FUDGED RECORDS

One of the most pernicious effects of the period of violence was that it became commonplace to manipulate records. This made it extremely difficult for ordinary citizens to assert rights or get justice. So remorseless was the practice that the police sometimes did it even with elected representatives. By 2010, the year of stone-pelting, the government had been touting 'normalcy' for a while. But, even that year, Abdul Rashid, an independent member of the Jammu and Kashmir legislative assembly, experienced police perfidy. Rashid, who was generally known in his constituency as 'Engineer', was more in touch with the poor than most politicians. So, that summer, the relatives of one Ghulam Hasan Kumar, who had once been a 'battalion commander' of Hizb, told Rashid that Kumar had been summoned to the police station. Kumar had been arrested around 2004, and had later been released.

'Engineer' said, 'I took him to the police station in my bullet-proof car'—the secure vehicle that the state provided for the legislator's protection. He said the policemen there said they only wanted to check some things and Kumar would soon be released. When Kumar's family went to Rashid five days later, asking when he would be released, 'Engineer' phoned the superintendent of police. The superintendent called back to say that Kumar was at a police counterinsurgency facility that Kashmiris generally know as 'Cargo'. From that generally dreaded facility, 'Engineer' discovered that Kumar was actually at the Parimpora police station. When he went there, 'Engineer' was told that policemen from that station had caught Kumar from the prominent 'HMT crossing'. They showed 'Engineer' a First Information Report that said he had been caught at that spot with a Lashkar letter pad and two hand grenades. 'I personally handed him over to the police station', 'Engineer' repeated while recounting this story, his voice rising in agitation.[20]

'Engineer' took the case to senior police officers and politicians but got nowhere. So, when the Prime Minister of India, Manmohan Singh, was to visit Srinagar, 'Engineer' gathered a couple of hundred supporters to demonstrate about several such cases, including Kumar's. 'Engineer' says his supporters slipped surreptitiously into Srinagar, to avoid detention, and he too went 'underground'. When they came out on the roads on the morning of the prime minister's visit, he says the legislator and his fellow-activists were beaten and dragged to the police station next to 'Cargo'—not to the local station. That night, says 'Engineer', the police released Kumar.

Although the previous insurgency had ended, and the new one had not yet begun, even elected representatives found themselves flailing in a surreal world in which the rule of law was subject to manipulations and falsified records. The worst part of this surreal world was that a variety of forces and agencies, of various countries, tried to suborn or buy over anyone who raised a bold voice on behalf of the poor who were beyond the network of influence and power. So, men like 'Engineer', who might have begun as courageous grass-roots activists, were at some point or other sought to be lured with money, property, and other attractions. Most accepted, some from more than one side. In that surreal world, it was tough to figure out which power or agency backed a public activist or outfit—or how many powers simultaneously thought they did.

In that surreal world, 'disturbed area', and the special powers and methods that went it, had become the overarching frame not only for intelligence agencies but for police work too. When two newly recruited (IPS) police officers on training were discussing what had gone wrong when the chief minister's car had got stuck in a traffic jam on the Boulevard beside the Dal Lake the previous day, the officer from another state stated the steps he thought should have been taken. His colleague from Kashmir promptly replied: 'No, no. You can't do that. This is a disturbed area.'[21] To him, the steps required to clear a traffic jam also hinged on the framework of 'disturbed area'. The young officer who hailed from another state looked nonplussed. This was in 2009, when militancy had ended, and a new one had not yet begun. (That officer from another state proved exceptionally effective in dealing with the uprising of 2016.)

As mentioned in Chapter 1, 'Endings and Beginnings', officers who had been recruited and learned policing during those terribly disturbed years had risen to key positions by 2007. It turned out that a few among them were not above manipulating events, trends, and statistics. Whether they were conscious of it or simply went along with the flow, their manipulations ensured that the conflict continued, at least on paper. So the apparatus of counterinsurgency remained in place even when most people in Kashmir were convinced that the militancy which began in 1988 had ended. To many people, particularly the young, this apparatus now seemed more and more illegitimate. It was particularly irksome to those of the millennial youth who were imbued with a desire for a divinely sanctioned system of governance and law.

WEBS OF POWER

At times, the patronage of powerful police officers allowed others too to repress citizens who were beyond the web of influence. At times, the security police guards provided to persons in authority ensured that those they were assigned to guard could break the law and bend the rules. In the summer of 2012, the security men of a minister in the state government battered a traffic policeman who tried to stop the minister's car and security escort from driving past a red traffic signal. When the media asked him why he allowed his security staff to assault the traffic policeman, the minister was blasé. He could not see what his security men were doing with the traffic policeman behind his car, he said.

Of course, the misuse of security men as the personal mafia goons of politicians and others with power had become shamefully common across India by this stage. Security cover had become a symbol of status and pelf since the late 1980s. During the 1990s, it became an instrument of bullying domination, of breaking the rules, and getting one's way. The breakdown of the rule of law and the special powers in force in Kashmir made security posses there that much more lethal. It plugged into the other factors that infuriated young people of the already traumatized generation that had been born amid violence—enough for some of them to undertake a new militancy.

Also more dangerous than in other states was the fact that the special laws in force in Jammu and Kashmir gave those personal security goons of politicians the right to kill, as long as they could fudge the records. The year before that traffic policeman was assaulted, I had been battered by the security men of another functionary of the state. I was assaulted on the road, dragged into a police vehicle, and then further assaulted in the local police station, while being accused of being a terrorist. They asked where my pistol was, and said I would be killed and my body would disappear.

Those security men—or their boss—thought my car had not given way fast enough to their boss's convoy of vehicles. It was the behaviour pattern employed by army trucks and other vehicles in the mid-1990s. Drivers of vehicles who did not get off the highways and other roads fast enough were likely to be beaten and their cars damaged. Army men in those trucks would routinely hit the roof of a vehicle they passed with a long stick, if it had not got far enough off the road to avoid the stick. Among the cars hit in this manner in 1994 was a white Ambassador car (the sort of vehicle that normally transported government officials) carrying the state's Security Advisor to the Governor and the Additional Chief Secretary (Home).[22]

A few days after the assault on me became a public scandal, the chief minister, Omar Abdullah, invited me to his office. He told me this sort of assault occurred commonly on the route of that particular vehicle. The chief minister said that he had to handle the fall-out each time, but there was nothing he could do to stop it. Since he was an honourable functionary of the state, the chief minister said, 'I cannot take away his security'.

As the home minister of the state, the chief minister was directly responsible for ensuring the security of citizens. Some Kashmiris saw the public at large as being caught in a web of oppressors who colluded with each other's abuse of authority. So deep was the general impression that the powerful could do as they please that many Kashmiris became extremely suspicious when, in the late summer of 2011, a political activist of the ruling party died after he had visited the chief minister. According to the grapevine, he had had a disagreement with the party bosses over a division of spoils from the seemingly all-encompassing system of corruption. The police had been called in to handle him and, according to the police version, he died of a sudden heart attack. Srinagar was abuzz with talk of how he could not walk when he was brought out of the chief minister's residence. The chief minister stated that his visitor had been fine when he left his presence.[23]

The subversion of the rule of law meant that those within the network of power also had to adjust to the special powers of the police. A senior legislator, who had earlier been a minister, said candidly that he could not travel to any part of his constituency unless the police station house officer allowed him.[24] 'If he says there is a security threat, and he can't ensure security, I simply can't go', he said, asking to remain off the record. His remark had troubling implications, but the sad truth was that the impunity with which sections of the forces, particularly of the state police force, behaved was made possible because most legislators accepted it.

RESISTING ACCOUNTABILITY

By that time, the business of accusing someone of terrorism, militancy, stone-pelting, or anti-national activities could be used to suppress all kinds of protests, including those that had nothing to do with 'separatist' sentiments—such as protests against corruption. The law was at times manipulated to suppress common people into accepting the ways in which the subverted system functioned in various departments of government. Things seemed to be designed to allow corrupt, inefficient, and cynical elements in the administration to make money, and shirk responsibilities, without being held accountable.

In March 2011, for example, the Ministry of Rural Development in New Delhi sent a team to investigate complaints that money had been fraudulently disbursed under the National Rural Employment Guarantee Scheme. Some activists had written to the Home Ministry in Delhi, and the Home Secretary had forwarded the complaint to the rural development ministry. On the morning the team from New Delhi arrived, the police locked up an activist who had led the complainants in his village Wagam near Chadoora. His companion activist, Muzaffar Bhat,[25] the one who had written to Delhi, spent the day trying to get his colleague released. Frantic, he went from one police officer to another. Bhat was familiar with the force, since one of his close relatives was a police officer, but he could only get the activist released around 4 p.m. The team from Delhi was on its way to the airport by then, to return to Delhi. They had held a public hearing in the village but no one reported wrongdoing. According to Bhat, villagers had been intimidated into silence after the lead activist's detention.[26]

Preventing the mechanisms of accountability from operating transparently was essential to the success of the farce that large parts of Kashmir's administration had become. 'Normality' in Kashmir was largely a hollowed-out veneer displayed to the world, while common people were prevented by the apparatus of counterinsurgency from saying that the Emperor had no clothes.

Over time, records had sometimes been fudged in various departments in this state, not just the police. Early in the new century, a very senior doctor in the government's health service asserted that although the National Rural Health Mission had excellent documentation regarding its functioning in the state, there was little sign of it on the ground. It was the same with the Rehbar-e-Sehat scheme for bare-foot medical assistance, he said.[27]

For fudged documentation to be accepted as real, it was essential that no one checked or questioned its authenticity. So, the intolerance of protest, and of the assertion of dignity and of rights, became such a vital part of the system that it was almost a reflex. The explanation that was most easily given, and which few dared question, was that protest was a form of insurgency and so had to be put down with a firm hand. Projecting this was easy, since Kashmiris reflexively shouted slogans for 'azadi' while protesting anything from electricity meters to high prices. Tragically, the frustrations generated by the repression of protests of various kinds contributed to creating a new militancy in the second decade of the twenty-first century.

Activism on developmental and other local issues could have let common people give vent to their frustrations over at least their everyday concerns. Instead, these frustrations added to alienation, disgust with the 'democratic' system, and hence fresh militancy. Many of those who ruled the roost no doubt realized that activism would empower common people, and that this could end self-serving, systematized subversion of the law. Perhaps some of those who operated the levers of authority really did not care whether they functioned under the aegis of India, Pakistan, or any other dispensation, so long as they were not held to account.

The saddest aspect of their self-serving priorities was that it negated the tremendous commitment, back-breaking hard work, and sacrifices of many dedicated and courageous policemen and officers. Their corruption and exploitation turned even those who served professionally, and with empathy, into targets of resentment and hate. Indeed, it delegitimized the entire system in young minds, and therefore all those who worked for that system.

NEW CRIMINALIZATION

A critical point was reached around 2006–07. Things could have moved towards a more peaceful future if the counterinsurgency apparatus had been reduced around then, in tandem with the reduced militancy. More important for peacemaking would have been forward movement on Prime Minister Vajpayee's (1998–2004) various initiatives—with Kashmiri leaders, militants, and people, and also with Pakistan and the rest of South Asia. Instead, disillusionment slipped in during 2006–07, and rage erupted in 2008.

The uprising of 2008 petered out gradually that autumn. On the other hand, the uprising of 2010 came to an abrupt end after a fire at a police facility became the reason for a prolonged and very severe curfew. The arrest of Masarat Alam, who dictated the uprising, and statements from Syed Ali Shah Geelani, who had been in custody in a VIP house, contributed to it subsiding.

Tragically, the police turned the term 'stone-pelter' into a new category of criminal. Over the next several months, some sections of the police locked up a large number of boys, particularly in Anantnag, the centre of south Kashmir. That trend seemed to peak in February 2011. Perhaps someone in the corridors of power decided that preventive/repressive action was required in light of the 'Arab Spring' uprisings that had taken place in Egypt and parts of West Asia since December.

Several boys complained of torture and various kinds of abuse—from verbal to sexual—while they were in custody. Some showed burns, cuts, welts, and other wounds. Many of the boys were released after a few days without being formally charged. There were whispers of money having changed hands along with written guarantees of good behaviour. Their treatment in those police stations contributed to stoking rage in not only the minds of those boys, but also several boys among their relatives and neighbours. Some of these took up arms over the next few years.

The abuse of power over the past couple of decades, the fabrication of records, and lack of accountability, had all made it possible for some sections of the police force to use the threat of categorizing a boy as a 'stone-pelter' to intimidate or blackmail boys who had had nothing to do with militancy—or even with protest demonstrations. Ironically, the very powers that had been forged to suppress the previous militancy generated a new militancy. During that period around 2010–12, Kashmiri boys were full of harrowing experiences.

On the day after Eid-ul Fitr in September 2010, a polytechnic student was sitting in a car near a park in the heart of Srinagar. He was waiting for his friend, who was across the road. Just then, one of three boys on a passing motorcycle grabbed at the dupatta (scarf) of a passing girl. She screamed. Realizing there might be trouble, the student who was across ran to the car. Just then, a police jeep screeched to a halt beside the car. The police officer in the jeep had heard a girl scream. His men pulled the boys out of the car, beating and kicking them (to many, this was normal police procedure for anyone who did not look as if they might be connected to power). Despite their protests of innocence, they were dragged to a police station, beaten further, and told their names would be added to the list of 'stone-pelters'. While they were being pummelled, kicked, and mocked, a policeman told one of the boys he would be sodomized that night.[28]

Another pattern of police behaviour that was most irksome to the young was the interference by some police men and officers in relations between men and women. Not only was their interference sleazy, it was in most cases illegal. Policemen would harass and extort money from young couples who might be walking near their school or college, sitting in a park, restaurant, internet café, or vehicle. Generally, the policemen's questions reflected a Taliban-like mindset, even though many of the policemen had illicit relationships too. The couple was likely to be asked whether they were related to each other. If they said they were cousins, they were asked how. Then they would be asked for their fathers' phone numbers.

Some elements in the police played on the respectability, ego, and social standing of common people. In a conservative society in cultural flux, in which most fathers would castigate even their adult children over an unsupervised relationship, very few girls or boys would want a parent to be informed of their friendship with someone from the opposite sex. So, they would generally bribe the policeman to let them go. If a young man could not pay his way out of the situation, he and his family could be subjected to humiliation and public shame.

Police interference in matters of the heart sometimes involved group rivalries. One student used to escort his girlfriend home by bus on most afternoons. Boys in her locality, some of whom she had spurned, resented him. One day, they set up a ruckus as the girl alighted near her home, accusing the duo of behaving indecently in public. They hit the boy and dragged him to the nearby police station. There, he was beaten and kicked by the police, mocked for his long hair, locked up for the night without any paperwork, and told he would be imprisoned for two years under the draconian PSA.[29]

In 2010, policemen even turned up to harass couples sitting under the trees in Chinar Bagh within the campus of Kashmir University. There was speculation that they used satellite imaging, installed at huge cost for counterinsurgency, to spot couples under trees or behind bushes. More important than the waste of resources meant to counter insurgency was the issue of the state's cultural ideology. The crass and sleazy greed of some policemen and officers pushed Kashmiri society towards a Taliban-like mindset regarding what was permissible and what was immoral. This sort of prudery was often a calculated attempt to prove that the policemen and officers were 'good Muslims' even if they participated in oppression or extortion.

Moral policing had become common in most states across India but, in Kashmir, it could lead more directly to violent responses, and to geopolitical unrest. For, one way for a young man whose reputation the police had undermined among his relatives and neighbours to gain respectability was to take up a gun against the state. To be known as a mujahid was a sure-fire way to restore social standing. In fact, such was the matrix of the place, and the time, that both sides—extortionist oppressors and their victims—could end up promoting the world view of religious exclusivism, and violence too. Elements in a police force mandated to uphold the law and constitution of a secular democracy founded on liberal principles implemented rules that they imagined to be properly religious. Perhaps it was a metaphor of those ironies that, just around the time when the children of that period of violence pelted stones in rage against the injustices of (among other things) the police force, the grandest mosque in Kashmir, with marble, and in-built aquariums, came up in Srinagar's police lines.

NOTES

1. https://www.google.co.in/?client=safari&channel=mac_bm&gws_rd=cr&dcr=0&ei=7-FeWpOZIoa98QWi_55w, accessed on 17 January 2018.
2. In a Facebook post, Mannan had attributed his decision to become militant to this sort of questioning.
3. Author's interview with Lt General Naresh Marwah (retd.) at National Disaster Management Authority headquarters.
4. See Chapter 1, 'Endings and Beginnings'.

5. Author's interview with Lt General (Retd) M.A. Zaki in Hyderabad on 17 December 2001.

6. Estimate of the Director-General of Police, J.N. Saksena, from interview with author in 2001.

7. Para became the Youth President of the People's Democratic Party in 2013.

8. Author's interview with Waheed ur Rehman Para at Tahab village in July 2011.

9. Hartosh Singh Bal, 'The Man Who Knew Too Much', http://www.openthemaga-zine. com/article/india/the-man-who-knows-too-much.

10. Hartosh Singh Bal, 'The Man Who Knew Too Much', http://www.openthemaga-zine. com/article/india/the-man-who-knows-too-much.

11. Author's interviews with Waheed ur Rehman Para and his neighbours at Tahab village in July 2011.

12. Author's interviews with citizens of Safapora, including school teachers and university lecturers.

13. Author's conversation with Justice (Retd) B.A. Khan.

14. Author's interviews with residents of Safapora, including school teachers.

15. Author's interviews with the schoolmaster and other residents of Safapora.

16. Author's interviews with residents of Safapora, including school teachers.

17. The author was witness to this.

18. The author witnessed the fury and threats of a jeep full of SOG men, led by a DSP, when two young men in a vehicle behind them honked at their jeep at the gate of the Dak Bungalow in Kishtwar in August 2010.

19. David Devadas, 'Anti-Terror Force Excites Revulsion', *Business Standard*, New Delhi, 11 April 2000.

20. Abdul Rashid's interview with the author at the author's rented residence in Srinagar.

21. This conversation took place in the author's presence.

22. Author's interview with Lt General (Retd) M.A. Zaki.

23. 38. http://indiatoday.intoday.in/story/jammu-and-kashmir-custody-death-omarabdullah/1/153885.html.

24. An MLA's off-the-record interview to the author at the MLA's residence in his constituency.

25. Muzaffar Bhat, who made a name as an activist for the Right to Information in Kashmir, contested the 2014 Lok Sabha elections as an Aam Aadmi Party candidate.

26. Author's interview with Muzaffar Bhat.

27. Author's off-the-record interview with a doctor who has headed a department at the Government Medical College, Srinagar, and been Medical Superintendent of a government hospital.

28. Author's interview with the two students.

29. Author's off-the-record interview with the young man in Srinagar.

new militancy emerged, although it was led and dominated by Pakistanis. Some top Lashkar commanders in this phase, such as Abu Qasim and Abu Dujana, lived long periods in Kashmir and settled in with families. So their cadres too were much more easily at home in Kashmiri homes than Lashkar cadres had been during the earlier period of militancy. Widespread resentment and anger in Kashmir was the key to their welcome in homes. It was the oxygen that sustained the new militancy.

That they were welcome in homes meant that their requirement of foreign funds for their daily needs was much reduced. But it was evident that they had no shortage of funds. Villagers said that, when they passed through an area, they generally handed money to overground workers to buy them food, beverages, and other requirements. Soon after the Government of India demonetized high denomination currency notes in November 2016, Lashkar militants looted a couple of bank ATMs in south Kashmir of crisp new notes worth hundreds of thousands of rupees. By the summer of 2017, businessmen were being asked to keep aside a few thousand rupees for militants.

On the other hand, the vast network of the overground coordinators of agitations in different corners of the Valley were generally well-funded. In most places, these organizers could easily mobilize hordes of angry boys to pelt stones once they got a demonstration started. It was those initial instigators—who often melted away once a sufficiently large mob had gathered—who could require pay. In 2009 and 2010, Shopian in southwest Kashmir was apparently kept on the boil by one teenager, Zubair Turey. When the police locked him up, following complaints from merchants' associations, the town remained calm for a few years, even when other parts of the Valley were disturbed. Merchants and town elders were unwilling to say anything about the boy's activism on the record, particularly after Turey became a militant in May 2017. But they seemed sure that he had disbursed money to at least some of the boys he mobilized to pelt stones. 'Why else would it have become so calm after he was locked up?' a prominent civic activist asked. He added that many of the boys in those mobs had been from relatively poor families. Indeed, calm in Shopian was remarkable, for it had been most restive during the early years of the century—and even during Kashmir's uprising in 1931.[1]

Since over-invoicing and other trade-related channels of funding had risen in importance compared with the 1990s, businessmen of various sorts could keep money flowing to such local coordinators as Turey. By the time agitations erupted in every corner of the Valley in 2016, the coordinators were generally much older than Turey had been in 2010. While there is no denying the very real rage that was manifest among Kashmiri youth—and others, including women—across the Valley, it was less intense than in 2010, broadly speaking. The agitations were sustained through concerted coordination. Many of the coordinators in 2016 were activists of the Jamaat-e-Islami. Some were activists of 'mainstream' parties. And some were salaried employees of the government—off work owing to the extended shutdown.

Links across the 'mainstream' and 'separatist' categories ran deep. According to the grapevine in Kashmir, some Hurriyat leaders made money by arranging for stone-pelting or other demonstrations at politically strategic times or places. Certain 'mainstream' candidates owed their electoral victories to disruptive agitations that prevented voters from reaching booths in strongholds of their opponents. It was a sordid situation. Vast amounts of cash were available from the sea of corruption that had filled Kashmir, particularly over the three decades since 1987.

SALARIES AND LOOT

Pakistan not only paid various 'leaders' of the Hurriyat groups, factions, and splinters to instigate turmoil, but also monthly salaries. One Europe-based figure who knew this circle well claimed that a prominent Hurriyat 'leader' acknowledged this at a wedding feast. The Europe-based figure said that, when he ribbed the 'leader' about getting four lakh rupees a month from Pakistan, the 'leader' swore that Pakistan sent him 'only' three lakh rupees (close to five thousand dollars) as monthly salary. Many of those 'leaders' built luxurious houses, and owned SUVs and other cars. Some of them not only owned property in Kashmir, but also in Delhi and other places.

Each of the different groups and factions had an office in Pakistan's capital. The main task of the officer in charge was to channel funds to their bosses in Kashmir. A large part of their task was to lobby with the ISI. They tried to show what their particular organization, or splinter outfit, was doing to promote unrest and other kinds of activities to promote the 'movement'. The purpose: to keep the funds flowing and, to the extent possible, to increase the allocations granted to their particular outfit.

Apart from money for activities that could promote their cause, they also channelled money for relief. These were amounts meant for victims of human rights abuse or the families of those killed as militants. Much of the 'relief' money which these 'leaders' received for disbursal was raised at mosques in places like Pakistan and the Gulf after heart-rending accounts of massacres and other atrocities on oppressed Muslims. A sordid aspect of the self-serving priorities of some of them was that very little of the money sent for that sort of relief reached the intended beneficiaries. There was talk of how, for example, a most prominent 'leader' of the freedom movement handed a five hundred rupee note (about eight US dollars) to the destitute widow of a militant who went to him for help—and told her she ought to find a new husband to take care of her and her children.

Some non-governmental organizations (NGOs) too misused the funding they received—from both, indeed various, sides. Some of those who had worked as staff at an NGO that specialized in organizing dialogues complained of the boss's tight control and a lack of transparency in accounting. That NGO was publicly funded by a major diplomatic grouping, and covertly by an intelligence agency. A few activists were hard-nosed enough to target the funds of genuine activists. Those who ran a prominent rights-based NGO that often spoke of genocide persuaded a brave human rights activist to join them, and then bought a plot of land with money that a Dutch charity had sent her to aid her activism. That land was right beside a highway along which several new colonies of mansions came up during the decade since that year of endings and beginnings; the price of land there soared.

BENIGN NEGLECT

For long, agents of the Indian state had watched all this benignly. Some of those agents had even competed with their Pakistani counterparts to keep those 'leaders' happy. Some of them doled out amounts, and ensured that those 'leaders' and their relatives got jobs, loans, properties, admissions, and security. By the time India's National Investigation Agency launched a massive probe into the wealth of these 'leaders'—searching various properties not only in Srinagar and Jammu but also in Delhi and Haryana on 3 and 4 June 2017—it was already too late to stop the violence that was in the works. Significantly, though, there were no protests or allegations that the government was unjustly targeting the 'leaders' of the freedom struggle. Rather, most Kashmiris were pleased, and hoped the looters would get their just desserts. Those who were happy included most of the angry youth who had pelted stones and backed militancy.

Their rage was partly fueled by the fact that those who were counted as 'separatist leaders' not only received benefits from foreign powers but also in many cases from agents of the Indian state. This has been revealed in detail in several books, including my own work *In Search of a Future: The Story of Kashmir* published in 2007. One of the reasons the earlier militancy was not allowed to end in that year of endings and beginnings was that these 'secessionist leaders' were in such an extremely lucrative situation. An even bigger reason was the lucrative benefits the conflict economy brought to very large sections of those who ran the state—the so-called 'mainstream'. This chapter takes a look at how the 'mainstream' actors who were meant to control militancy and insurgency also sometimes benefitted from the conflict economy, and so developed stakes in continued conflict.

At one level, this was far more dangerous. For, the only way the conflict economy, and its benefits for all sides, could continue was if insurgency continued—or at least the illusion of continued militancy was maintained even after militancy barely existed. The generations that came of age around this time were more often than not victims of this jungle economy.

On the other hand, the lure of lucre in the cesspool of loot that Kashmir had become was a major incentive for various forces[2] to continue to operate there. The humiliation, anger, and frustration caused by continued deployment generated a vicious cycle. For, expressions of that anger and frustration were portrayed as proof of continued insurgency, and therefore reason for continued deployment.

Many police officers, politicians, and various kinds of government employees accumulated wealth far greater than their salaries would have permitted. The wealth of a range of Hurriyat and other secessionist leaders too had obviously ballooned. Some officers of the army and paramilitary forces accumulated wealth disproportionate to their incomes. All this wealth was often visible in luxurious bungalows and on display at wedding celebrations. The lavishness of the weddings hosted by several of those who had headed the state police force was particularly astounding. Garish displays of wealth were not limited to those in the top ranks. According to the Srinagar grapevine, one government clerk bought 52 quintals of meat so that wazwan[3] feasting continued for a week when his daughter got married.

It seemed that the Indian government was pleased to preside benignly over this engulfing black economy. Until investigations finally kicked in during the summer of 2017, most of those who accumulated vast wealth appeared quite confident that they would not be investigated by taxation authorities. It is said that when a top leader of a Kashmiri political party was asked to pay income tax after investing Rs 1,200 crore in Bangalore, Rs 380 crore was duly paid. Apparently, nobody wanted to know from where the invested amount (more than USD 180 million) had come. The state of Jammu and Kashmir was meant to have an Accountability Commission but, for most of the decade of change, the Commission did not have any member.

India appeared to be the investment choice not only of those working for the Indian state, but those working against it too. They too invested in property and other assets in Delhi and other parts of India. Sudhir Bloeria, a former Chief Secretary of the state, observed that 'none of these [Hurriyat and other secessionist leaders], Geelani onwards, has invested a single penny in Pakistan, all in India'.[4]

MULTIPLE TENTACLES

Corruption had already reached extraordinary levels during the 1980s, before the insurgency began. In fact, it was in 1987, the very year when preparations for the militancy began, that wedding planners and Kashmir's construction industry first noticed conspicuous consumption and the garish display of wealth in Srinagar.[5] Once militancy began, vast amounts of cash were sent from Pakistan. It was often carried across the LoC in bags by militants who had been trained there. Kathmandu had become an alternate route by the middle of the 1990s: Kashmiris would fly from Pakistan to Nepal and, since a passport was not required to cross the border between Nepal and India, could reach Kashmir relatively easily overland. That allowed them to carry larger bags, containing more cash. Pakistan sometimes sent high-value insurgents via Dhaka or Dubai, with false passports and other documents.

The place was awash with cash during those years. When a militant was killed in an encounter, the family with which he had taken shelter would often keep the cash they found among his things. Kashmiris in the 1990s would commonly talk of families that at one point did not own a bicycle, but then got three cars. Not all those cars were bought. Some were just taken. For, while the instruments of the state were in disarray, loot and extortion became common. Anyone with a gun could demand what he pleased. New vehicles were highly desired. Those with guns could access motor dealers' records. In this light, many of those who bought vehicles did not want to register them as new purchases. So, Kashmir became a huge market for cars stolen across north India from the mid-1990s until the beginning of the new century. That further boosted the cash economy.

Around the turn of the century, construction became Kashmir's largest industry, as people built plush mansions, splurging hundreds of thousands in cash on curtains or wall-to-wall carpets alone. Mansions with a dozen rooms across three floors, often used by only three or four inhabitants, became common. In the foothills beyond the saffron fields near Pampore, eight cement factories came up in an industrial zone at Khrew—a result of an industrial policy under which New Delhi granted vast amounts of subsidy. During the second half of the 1990s and into the new century, people competed to serve more and more lavish wazwan feasts at weddings. For a couple of years, it was the fashion to serve 30 or 40 dishes. Ostentatious display of wealth reached a point where, briefly, a few hosts had begun to stuff gold coins into the Gushtaba meatballs that are traditionally the last course.

Sections of the police force, and some officers and men in the paramilitary forces, churned this black economy. For some of them too, extortion had become a major industry in this frightful economy. Many citizens who were detained (or their guardians or relatives) were forced to pay the police to release them—unless they were lucky enough to have a relative or friend in the network with influence. Rates were sometimes fixed. So, during the winter of 2010–11, some Kashmiri parents claimed that they had paid the police to get custody of their sons, who had been detained for 'stone-pelting' the previous summer. The going rate, according to them, was around Rs 20,000. In 2016, when several thousand more were detained, the rate was said to have risen to between Rs 30,000 and Rs 50,000. Lt General D.S. Hooda, who was the commander-in-chief of the Northern Army Command from 2014 to 2016, told a national security seminar at the beginning of June 2017 that people had at times sold land to pay off the police in order to get their sons released.[6] Some of those who were detained in 2010–11 became militants over the next few years. Some of those detained in 2016 did too.

The army and other forces brought more money into the economy, through supply, construction and equipment contracts, apart from the money that soldiers spent from their salaries. From the mid-1990s, the Indian government stepped up aid to the state, for development and reconstruction—for example, of the very large number of schools that had been destroyed by militants. Many Kashmiris suspected that a vast proportion of that money was siphoned off through corruption. In addition, large amounts were disbursed as secret funds, so that police, army and paramilitary forces could pay for information. Funds were also sanctioned to pay for mercenaries—very many of whom also extorted money from people at large.

The targets of their extortion were very often persons who had once been militants, had become disillusioned, and were trying to rebuild 'normal' lives. Of course, they targeted mainly the poor and unconnected among former militants. Those who had wealth and influence found it relatively easier to protect themselves and their families in this jungle of corruption and exploitation. Others were sometimes forced to sell land, cattle, or other property. It was an exploitative, extortionate economy run by men with guns of one sort or another.

RISK TO NATIONAL SECURITY

For a while, corruption had hollowed out the operations of the Jammu and Kashmir police to the extent that a few members of the force were apparently willing to certify non-involvement in militancy as easily as they might label someone a terrorist. All that was needed in some instances was the right price. Social and political activist Tanveer Hussain Khan,[7] even claimed that a bona fide Non-Involvement Certificate could be got in one week by paying Rs 2,000.[8] This certificate was one of the bizarre documents the state government had introduced during the insurgency. It certified that the holder had never participated in insurgency. The certificate was required to get employment, a passport, and much else.

Khan's claim shows that, for some officers, the certificate was only another channel for corruption. The file was required to pass through various police departments, including the local station, the CID intelligence wing, and the counter-insurgency CIK wing before the District Magistrate finally signed the certificate. When Khan sought the file in the office of the superintendent of police a few months after, he found there was no record of it there. The duly stamped and signed certificate had been issued, but the investigations which were supposed to precede its issuance had apparently not been done.

No doubt the corollary was also true: one who did not pay for a certificate might not get it, even if he had never had anything to do with militancy. Without the certificate, he would be presumed under the rules in force to have been a part of the militancy. Hence, he would be denied a job, a passport, and the services of the government—while one who had been involved with militancy might obtain a certificate of non-involvement for the right price. Since questions were rarely asked in the extraordinary circumstances of counterinsurgency, law enforcers sometimes used or dispensed with laws as they pleased. To too many of them, laws and rules had become no more than instruments for extortion and suppression. They treated this as the system.

It did not seem to bother them that this 'system' alienated and angered young Kashmiris, many of whom saw the cynical manipulation of the law as a strategy of 'India'. In fact, some Kashmiris in the police force boasted that the alienation they caused was their very convoluted contribution to Kashmir's 'movement' against India. When a senior Delhi-based Kashmiri journalist complained that policemen had broken the windowpanes of vehicles outside the graveyard during his father's funeral, the police officer in charge of the district put his arm around his shoulder and whispered: 'If we don't do even this much, what will happen to *azadi*?' The journalist was a close relative of a senior Hurriyat leader. The officer was counted as a star of counterinsurgency operations.

In the bargain, such police officers not only ensured that the insurgency economy remained well stoked, they managed to get promotions, extra allowances, and secret funds from those who ran the state from New Delhi—to combat protests that were at times sparked by anger over such deliberate provocations. These sections were not above using the special powers they had been given to counter insurgency as tools for extortion and extraordinary pelf.

PERQUISITES AND SPOILS

Counterinsurgency had also given them extra office and domestic staff. The Union government had given the Jammu and Kashmir Police funds to employ Special Police Officers (SPOs) at a salary of Rs 3,000, then Rs 5,000, and then Rs 6,000 a month. These SPOs were meant to be the eyes and ears of the police in the field, bringing back information about insurgency to the police station to which they were attached. In 2010, about 30,000 SPOs supplemented the 70,000-strong regular police. By 2017, the total number in the force had ballooned to around 120,000—up by 40 per cent during the decade since that year of endings and beginnings, when the militancy that began in 1988 had more or less ended.

A large proportion of the SPOs were actually deployed as household help at the homes of police officers, their relatives, friends, and patrons, including politicians. Apart from cooking, cleaning, and gardening, some fetched children from school or shopped for the kitchen.

Some policemen and officers described a schema for the division of spoils. Under this schema, they said, the corrupt and cynical could potentially exploit their special powers in such a way that those posted in police stations could extort from those without access to the networks of influence, while some officers of the rank of Superintendent and above could siphon some of the 'source funds' they controlled, in cash. They explained that, for those who were cynical and corrupt, it was relatively easy to get recipients to sign for more than they received in a situation that involved secret sources or activists, and which prevented accountability. These secret funds were meant to pay directly for information and to reward members of the force who combatted insurgents with extraordinary courage. A certain amount was allocated to each senior police officer in the field, to disburse at his discretion.

It was sometimes alleged that much of it was not actually used for the purposes for which it was meant. A constable, on the condition of anonymity, complained that 'we go into an encounter, putting our lives in danger to kill militants. Then the SP (superintendent of police) hands Rs 2,000 or, in very rare cases, Rs 5,000 for us to share among all those who went into the encounter'. He raised uncomfortable questions about the rest of the reward amount, which was often a couple of hundred thousand rupees.

In the neat division of spoils of which they spoke sotto voce, officers posted as Station House Officers sometimes said they did not need to share income from corruption in police stations with senior officers—who, they said, were generally satisfied with the ways in which they disbursed unaudited secret funds. Of course, while extorting or settling disputes extra-judicially, police stations needed to be careful that their victims were not connected to a senior police officer, or to any of those officers' patrons among politicians, the bureaucracy, the media, or other powerful institutions. Corrupt sections of the police force needed to keep people in all these categories happy, so that nobody spoilt their party.

They managed this shrewdly. Many politicians, media persons, and others wanted security. Apart from the pelf it gave them, it provided extra hands around the house, for those security men sometimes doubled as drivers or household help. For the police, providing security gave even greater leverage than posting an SPO or two for domestic help. For example, when a former director-general of police publicly criticized the police force in the autumn of 2008, the incumbent director-general is said to have sent him a brand new bulletproof vehicle. The criticism stopped. A couple of years later, the police apparently bought a Range Rover SUV for the chief minister at what many Kashmiris considered to be astronomical cost. The chief minister liked elan. Conscious of the security the police force provided, and the pelf its top officers could provide through such vehicles, few ministers thought fit to check the force's excesses against ordinary citizens.

Many Kashmiris believed there was a cozy symbiosis between politicians, bureaucrats, and the police: I-scratch-your-back-you-scratch-mine.

A third level of potential corruption in the police force involved those who were senior enough to award contracts to purchase equipment. Vast sums were spent to purchase vehicles, uniforms, shields, computers, and monitoring and other equipment, as well as for construction or recon-struction—much more in the course of counterinsurgency that in 'normal' times. According to Srinagar's grapevine, some officers negotiated deals for the purchase of equipment, ranging from vehicles to shoelaces, with particular keenness. The sometimes poor quality of such purchases could affect efficiency. There was talk about particular contracts for the purchase of closed-circuit television cameras, bulletproof jackets, and data conver-sion systems for police computers—which did not function efficiently.

Police constables spoke of corruption in their recruitment and postings too. A posting near one's home or to a highly valued police station could be valuable, they said. It would surely be an exaggeration to call the entire Jammu and Kashmir police force corrupt, and there were certainly degrees of cor-ruption. However, in the first week of April 2011, a dozen officers who had recently been promoted to the rank of deputy superintendent insisted that only two senior officers in the force (one Inspector-General and one who had recently retired with the rank of Director-General, both of whom hailed from the Jammu region of the state) were incorruptible. They said so during a classroom discussion in which I interacted with them at the Sher-e-Kashmir Police Academy at Udhampur. Prodded, they named another two officers of the Indian Police Service.[9] They insisted that these were the only honest officers in the entire force, but they must surely have forgotten many others.

YOUTH ALIENATION

To most young people, the corruption and self-serving pelf of various sorts of Hurriyat 'leaders' was disgusting but did not directly affect them. Since corruption in the police force was often entwined with repression, assault, detention, or false cases, it was the most potent cause for the alienation, disgust, and hatred of the new generation of Kashmiris. It was also a major reason why many of them turned passionately to zealous piety. A sancti-fied alternative would surely be better than one they perceived as being run by, and on behalf of, 'kafir' oppressors whose rule had been illegitimate from the start, according to the narratives that surrounded them. Anger focused most fiercely on corruption in the police force from around 2007, when the fearless generation born around 1990 began to come of age. Not only had special counterinsurgency powers facilitated the corruption of the police force by then, allowing it to rise to unprecedented levels, those powers allowed some of them to extort from citizens almost at will. The cigarettes that Burhan Wani had been told to bring for special operations policemen represented just a sliver at the tip of the iceberg of extortion.

In such an unstable, volatile, and conflicted place as Kashmir, that sort of micro-corruption could pile up to cause the wholesale rejection of a system by a generation, as became obvious in 2016. Young Armaan[10] experienced that sort of micro-extortion during that year of endings and beginnings, 2007, when he was in his mid-teens. Supremely excited over his new motor-cycle, Armaan took his mother for a ride on the pillion. She wanted to visit a relative, and it was an opportunity for him to show off his motorcycle. At a crossing on the outskirts of Srinagar, a paramilitary lorry came round a bend at high speed and Armaan's motorcycle was knocked over. Since his mother was bleeding, his first concern was to get her to hospital. An hour later, two policemen came to the hospital, having heard of the accident. They were ostensibly there to investigate but demanded her gold earrings, asserting th   boy had a driving lice   ensibly as evidence, b   )y's father got a court

Policemen in various parts of the world are corrupt. Street-side and pavement vendors, stall owners, and others pay a monthly, weekly, or daily amount to local policemen, and let them pick up some of their wares for free. This is common knowledge in various cities across the globe. But, amid the vile subversion of the rule of law in Kashmir, the pressure to pay policemen was occasionally so unbearably intense that one autorickshaw driver in Srinagar set fire to his auto in frustration one day. He had not earned enough to pay the fee which the policeman took to allow the man to park his vehicle in the lane outside his home at night—but the policeman would not budge. And it was reported that, one night, a street vendor in Batmaloo knifed a policeman who had harassed him for his daily fee on a day when he had not earned enough to pay.

'Nobody can win a dispute (such as over property or marital relations) with a family that has a policeman', remarked a social worker of south Kashmir.[11] He said that a Station House Officer in a nearby city telephoned well-off citizens to ask for a loan. Nobody refused. None of them saw their money again. By then, law enforcement as an instrument of blackmail was taken to be the norm. Nobody was safe. The young were the most vulnerable. One Sunday in March 2011, a volunteer among some of the young men who ran a medical aid camp in a south Kashmir town every weekend asked a visitor not to break the queue. The man said he was a policeman, as if that gave him the right to break the queue. When the volunteer still insisted that he take his turn, the man threatened revenge. A few days later, that volunteer's name was on a list of 'stone-pelters' at the local police station. At that time, 'stone-pelting' was a dreaded crime in Kashmir. A very large number of boys on such lists had been locked up a few weeks earlier, in the wake of the 'Arab Spring' in Cairo and elsewhere.

Gradually, the arbitrary application of legal provisions, combined with corruption, had turned much of the police into a set-up that many Kashmiris tried to avoid—unless they had access to the charmed network of influence. By the end of the first decade of the twenty-first century, some Kashmiris preferred to settle disputes with the help of community elders and preachers than to take disputes to the police. Consequently, organizations like the Jamaat-e-Islami gained societal leverage. So it became easier for Jamaat-e-Islami activists to play a leading role to organize the uprising of 2016 in south Kashmir.

Some Kashmiris remarked wryly that there was a time when the police would take money from one who was accused of a crime, now they often took money from both the accused and the accuser. When, after a road accident on the outskirts of Srinagar in the autumn of 2007, both sides agreed to settle the matter among them, the police turned up and insisted that they must register a case. When both sides said they did not want to, the policemen are said to have taken Rs 600 from the one at fault and Rs 500 from the one whose vehicle had been hit—just to allow both to settle the matter between them.[12]

SPREAD LIKE A CANCER

Corruption in security forces is more crucial than in other departments, for it can allow extortion through cruelty and force. The way common people experienced corruption was a major cause for the rage of those young Kashmiris who had, around 2007, only wanted to get on with 'normal' lives. The rage that was expressed through stone-pelting in 2010, led to the alienation of many of those who were still children then—extending at times to support for, or participation in, a new militancy. As they grew up, those children experienced corruption wherever they turned. It had become ubiquitous. Kashmiris were full of tales of corruption in public works contracts, recruitment, passing university examinations, and the purchase of equipment, including life-saving equipment at hospitals.

Corruption seemed to have been normalized in every facet of life, from driving a vehicle past the state's main border checkpoint to buying equipment at some of the state's premier hospitals. Corruption is not, of course, the chief focus of this book. Nor was corruption new during this time of violence. Kashmir's ancient history, Kalhana's Rajtarangini, records horrifying corruption more than a thousand years ago.[13] Corruption had been given free rein since the mid-1950s—as a political strategy to keep Kashmiris happy. According to some Kashmiris, corruption had risen to new heights after 1975. During the time of jungle law during the 1990s, it had had even freer rein, for there had been little scope to enforce accountability even if someone had wanted.

What is relevant here is that, when the veneer of normalcy returned after 1997, aspirations for clean and responsive governance rose—and Kashmiris were frustrated. To many Kashmiris, corruption seemed to have become the norm even more than it had been in the 1980s. The government of Farooq Abdullah, which took office in 1996, began by backing a bold accountability bureau, but that effort fell by the wayside by the end of 1997. It had made little impact. Aspirations rose again in the middle of the next decade, this time for long-term solutions and peace, but frustration set in again around that year of endings and beginnings. Tanveer Hussain Khan, who contested for the Anantnag seat in the Lok Sabha in 2014, observed in 2011 that: 'The mindset that has developed in the last 20 years is that we go to the market to buy vegetables, we go to a government department to buy the service we need. People don't know their rights.'[14] Things only got worse after 2007. Until 2009, Transparency International had consistently rated Jammu and Kashmir as the second most corrupt state in India for several years. After that, the state moved ahead of Bihar to be rated the most corrupt in India. Yet, so normalized had corruption become by this time that nobody seemed to focus on the violently disruptive potential of this squalid 'first position'.

INCENTIVES FOR DEPLOYMENT

Opportunities for corruption was one of the reasons why significant sections of each of the counterinsurgency forces resisted reduction in their deployment—or their special powers, and the relative lack of accountability—even after militancy decreased substantially in the middle of the first decade of the twenty-first century. And it was among the factors that generated rage from around that year of endings and beginnings. It was a Catch-22; insistence on the continued operation of the apparatus of counterinsurgency, even after the 1990s' militancy had declined, was a major cause for the support the new militancy received in the second decade of the century—which then required increased deployment of the counterinsurgency apparatus.

Several straws in Kashmir's winds had indicated that several senior officers of many of the deployed security forces did not want their involvement in Kashmir to end. Already by the mid-1990s, key army officers had held that, given the orders, they could finish militancy in six months.[15] But they were never given a deadline.

There are times when extraordinary situations develop their own inertia. The economic benefits and the balance of power in the new status quo cause resistance against efforts to restore things to the way they were. Soon after 2007, some unit commanders in the field said they could not see any reason for their continued deployment.[16] But some other officers were so convinced of the permanence of their presence in Kashmir, and their special powers there, that they took umbrage at suggestions that army deployment be thinned. When the prime minister of India spoke of reducing the army's presence in Kashmir, a senior army officer stated publicly that the prime minister should consult the army before making such statements—exactly the sort of overbearing position that several analysts have come to expect from the Pakistan Army.

GOODWILL INITIATIVE

By the new century, the army had begun to participate in far more than counterinsurgency operations. It was running schools, building bus shelters, equipping computer centres, and handing out heaters, irons, and other appliances to common people. This was part of the Winning Hearts and Minds (WHAM) programme it had adopted in the late 1990s. This initiative began when the government in New Delhi was most earnestly trying to initiate negotiations with Pakistan and build peace—just before militancy picked up with renewed vigour after General Musharraf took over Pakistan's government in a military coup in October 1999.

This WHAM initiative was called Sadbhavana, meaning goodwill. Billions of rupees (hundreds of millions of dollars) were granted to the project, through which army units sought to make friends and influence people in the vicinity of their camps. They built schools, medical centres, gymnasiums, and university classrooms, and distributed kitchen utensils, heating and other household gadgets. It was a patriarchal—one could say patronizing—top-down model of development, which undermined the basics of democratic accountability. For, if the work at some of those public facilities was shoddy, villagers could not complain. The army had done them a favour and the government, which was responsible for providing and maintaining such facilities, could wash its hands off it.

The worst aspect of this became crystal clear in 2016—that the colossal sums that had been spent for goodwill did no good to the army when it actually had to operate in a war-like situation. In fact, some of the goodwill programmes may actually have been counterproductive—such as the tours of India for which the army took students and groups of clerics. Those tours were meant to showcase India's diversity but, in the unsettled, traumatized world of Kashmir, those who returned from such tours sometimes felt compelled to stave off rumours that they had been recruited as informers. Some of them did so by adopting a radical, adversarial discourse—which created ill-will rather than goodwill. There was particularly sharp opposition to the army taking groups of women students for such tours.

Many of the Army Goodwill Schools were efficiently run, but negative perceptions about some of the other goodwill programmes outweighed the overall benefits. Ultimately, perceptions and local narratives matter a great deal, if the objective is to generate goodwill. Some Kashmiris complained that they experienced the implementation of this 'Operation Sadbhavana' as corruption. At Safapora, which had suffered so much at the hands of Ikhwan hoodlums, a unit of the army adopted a high school for girls, undertaking to install fans, equipment, and facilities. The version of a schoolmaster there was that army men turned up one morning and drew lines with chalk in the school yard, photographed it, and asked him to sign a paper saying they had constructed a basketball court. He did not know how much money was claimed for that basketball court. He claimed that, on another day, they turned up with three large bundles of cable. The schoolmaster alleged that they sold this, virtually setting up shop outside the school all day, at cut-rate prices to whoever needed some cable. He said that the cable was shown as having been used for electrification of the school. He further claimed that, to repair one commode in the school toilet, two trucks of sand, and perhaps 50 bags of cement were brought—and sold. Such claims could be false or exaggerated, but figuring out the veracity of each claim is less important than to understand the discourses they generated locally. For, those discourses determined whether such programmes actually generated goodwill or not. The Sadbhavana programme began just when the millennial generation was born; it was gradually expanded as they grew up. Discourses among their elders regarding corruption and shoddy functioning contributed to shaping their viewpoints.

At some places, a visitor might hear bizarre stories about Sadbhavana gifts. At one village in the vicinity of Rajouri, for instance, villagers said that household appliances that poor families had been given in front of senior officers and the media were taken back a couple of days later, ostensibly for some glitches to be fixed. The appliances never returned.[17]

In a scathing editorial on 4 December 2010, the daily *Kashmir Images* commented:

It is the absence of Sadbhavana (goodwill) among the people of Kashmir that army deployed here has felt the need for 'Operation Sadbhavana' to 'win over the goodwill of general public'. But besides this, there is also a lot of money involved in running this operation. So there are material interests as well; because more money expended on anything means more commissions and kickbacks and opportunities to pilfer money into private coffers.[18]

As it gained confidence after suppressing the rage of the youth in the period after 2010, the police force decided that it too should engage in winning hearts and minds. When he was Chief Minister (2009–14), Omar Abdullah was also the state's home minister, and so was directly in charge of the police. He introduced a Civic Action Programme through which the police force was meant to win the goodwill of the public. Since the chief target was the youth, programmes such as computer training workshops and drug rehabilitation centres were conducted under this scheme. For this initiative, the chief minister made available budgetary allocations from other government departments which remained unutilized at the end of a financial year. This was a neat mechanism. Without making specific budgetary allocations, which could be debated and scrutinized, the scheme bypassed the basic mechanism of democracy—legislative control over expenditure.

It was projected as a way to utilize funds that would otherwise have lapsed. Of course, governmental apathy, inefficiency, and cynicism would determine how much remained unutilized. Such moves that further undermined the mandated system of legislative control, transparency, and accountability were symptomatic of the self-serving cynicism that so enraged the generation that had grown up amid violence—enough to make many millennials reject democracy altogether.

After the uprisings of 2008 and 2010, it had become extremely urgent for policymakers to investigate rumours of corruption in various security forces and the organs of administration. For, corruption hollows out a system. If there was truth to this sort of talk, it would prolong the instability and violence. It would not only allow loot to go on, it would allow human rights abuse to continue. It generated rage, which plugged into other factors to shape a new militancy.

NOTES

1. David Devadas, *In Search of a Future: The Story of Kashmir* (New Delhi: Penguin Books, 2007).
2. These forces included the Special Operations Groups of the Jammu and Kashmir Police.
3. The traditional Kashmiri feast of many courses, served on a platter at which four guests eat together.
4. Author's interview with Sudhir Bloeria at his residence in Jammu in November 2009.
5. Author's interviews with three of the most prominent wazas (organizers of Kashmir's wazwan feasts) in Wazapora, Srinagar on 28 September 2002.
6. http://timesofindia.indiatimes.com/city/chandigarh/everyone-in-valley-not-a-stone-pelter/articleshow/58970407.cms?utm_source=toimobile&utm_medium=Facebook&utm_campaign=referral&from=mdr, accessed on 5 June 2017.
7. Khan lost to Mehbooba Mufti, President of the People's Democratic Party.
8. Author's interview with Tanveer Hussain Khan at the author's residence in Srinagar in May 2010.
9. The author had a discussion with these promoted officers when he was asked to give them a lecture at the state police academy at Udhampur.
10. Name changed at the student's request.
11. Off-the-record interview with the author.
12. Wherever identities have been withheld in this chapter, the victims are well-known to, and trusted by, the author.
13. R.S. Pandit (tr.), *Kalhana's Rajatarangini: The Saga of the Kings of Kashmir* (New Delhi: Sahitya Akademi, 1968).
14. Author's interview with Tanveer Hussein Khan in Srinagar in May 2010.
15. David Devadas, *In Search of a Future: The Story of Kashmir* (New Delhi: Penguin Books, 2007).
16. Author's off-the-record conversations with unit commanding officers.
17. Author's interviews with residents of the village in April 2011.
18. *Kashmir Images*, 4 December 2010.

9

Smoke and Mirrors

The irony we have examined in this book is that the generation that had been children during the 1990s had, broadly speaking, become cynical, even disgusted, with militancy (and, quite often, even its objectives) by around 2007—as discussed in Chapter 1, 'Endings and Beginnings'. It had been a great opportunity to restore the situation in Kashmir to even keel, with a suitable change in the system that people at large in the state might consider an honourable solution. A decade later, that opportunity appeared to have been lost—not just for a solution within the context of a particular nation state, but even, for many teenagers, within the ambit of nation states, or democracy. But if there was any glimmer of hope for a resolution, it was vital for policymakers to understand what went wrong soon after 2007.

The extraordinary intense rage young people displayed in 2010 was caused to a large extent by the continuation of an environment of militarization, fear, and the suspension of rights after militancy was as good as over. That rage focused most sharply that year on the killing of innocents.

Let us examine how the targeting of innocents came about. The breakdown of law and order discussed in Chapter 7, 'Law Subverted', provided the context—and opportunities. The conflict economy discussed in

Chapter 8, 'Conflict Economy', gave the incentive. The falsification of records had become so commonplace that most Kashmiris gradually became cynical about the official versions of any counterinsurgency 'encounter'. G.K. Pillai, who had been the Home Secretary of India in 2010–11, publicly acknowledged in 2016 that outfits within the government sometimes caused the killing of citizens whom they considered to be potential threats. He said that this happened in many countries, and was acceptable as long as there were procedural checks. These deaths were sometimes shown as unsolved crimes or as suicides. That statement seemed to confirm what many Kashmiris had believed about the killing of persons like the human rights activist Jaleel Andrabi.

The word 'encounter' had already acquired an ominous ring for most Kashmiris. Some of them raised questions about any 'encounter' between militants and the armed forces, asking whether the encounter had been staged. Several reasons had generated this miasma of suspicion. It had begun with the need to cover tracks when a soldier or mercenary killed someone in the course of torture, extortion, or the imposition of ego-inflamed will. By the time militancy was winding down in the new century, some Kashmiris suspected another reason: that some of the forces actually engineered incidents of militancy in order to project a need for continued deployment—and the continuation of the conflict economy.

Some of the events narrated in this chapter might seem incredible or exaggerated. They might even perhaps seem motivated. They are certainly horrifying. However, they are based on strong evidence. And there are many more such events and narratives in Kashmir. For, these narratives are only a small part of the wide range of narratives that have together fanned the rage that burns in the minds of young Kashmiris. If one wants to understand their anger, and their actions, it is imperative to be aware of the narratives that have formed them. Further, it is imperative to bring such things to an end, for they severely compromise the national interest.

SUSPICIOUS ATTACK

It was difficult, of course, to establish that an attack was fraudulent, but an incident occasionally gave credence to suspicion. One such incident took place on 13 September 2004 at Cheeni Chowk in the heart of downtown Anantnag. Cheeni Chowk is a bustling commercial area of narrow streets jammed with pedestrian and motor traffic. On that Monday morning, a shopkeeper started walking from his shop to the nearby branch of the J&K Bank. He was going to deposit cash. He did not notice a man following him. When the shopkeeper had reached near a prominent bunker of the para-military CRPF, the man who had been following him grabbed his money and mobile phone. When the shopkeeper resisted, his assailant drew two grenades from his clothes and brandished them. Those in the crowd who could see the grenades panicked, shouted warnings, and ran. The assailant ran too—straight into the CRPF bunker.

According to a newspaper report on the incident the next morning, the assailant was quickly ushered into the bunker when he showed the CRPF man at the bunker entrance his identity card. That newspaper's reporter and photographer went to Cheeni Chowk a few minutes later. A crowd had surrounded the bunker, yelling slogans and demanding that the man with grenades be handed over to them. The officer and men in the bunker refused, but seemed distressed. They were finding it difficult to argue with the citizens' point that they should not be protecting a militant. The crowd was demanding that if the person was a militant, he be handed over to them and they would punish him on the spot. Indeed, some in that mob said they would kill him. By this time, the crowd was probably focused as much on challenging the CRPF men as on punishing the assailant. For, it seemed to them that the men in the bunker were protecting the militant. The normal response of security forces would have been to kick, pummel, and beat a presumed militant as soon as they caught him. Not only were these security men not doing that, they were preventing the mob from doing it.

The reporter persuaded some of the crowd to offer the harassed-looking officer in charge of the bunker a via media. The people would be satisfied if the reporter and photographer were allowed into the bunker to speak with the man with the grenades. The officer agreed, and the newspaper team was able to speak with the assailant, and photograph him and his identity card. The reporter's perspective was clear. The man had been a 'government gunman', his report stated. The assailant's name was Bashir Ahmad and he had earlier worked with the Jammu and Kashmir Light Infantry, an army regiment. The report further stated: 'He was reportedly also involved in a number of cases including smuggling of drugs.' The newspaper also quoted CNS (Current News Service) news service, which stated that 'the accused was … working for the troops of 3 Rashtriya Rifles, CNS said. Police has filed a case against him.' The newspaper reporter, Hilal Bhat, confirmed that the identity card he saw had been issued by the 3 Rashtriya Rifles unit.

Bhat's experience through the rest of the day was a revelation. He did not report this at the time but later said that, after meeting the assailant in the bunker, he went directly to the residence of the Superintendent of Police at Anantnag. As he was approaching the gate, he said, he saw an army officer arrive in a convoy of three vehicles. The policeman on guard at the gate told Bhat he could not go in, since an important meeting was being held. When Bhat insisted that the policeman show the officer his press card, the superintendent invited him in. He was sitting with an army Major, said Bhat. When Bhat told the superintendent of police what had just happened, the army officer asked Bhat to identify himself. After he did, Bhat says, the army officer said nothing more. However, Bhat claimed, the police searched for him for a couple of weeks after the report was published the next morning. He did not stay at home or go to his normal haunts during those tense days. Then, one day, he went straight into the superintendent's office. The officer seemed surprised to see him but let him go with a warning that he must check with the officer before publishing any such report in future.[1]

Bhat's report had stated, with a photograph graphically corroborating the fact, that the local police had mounted a baton charge to disperse the citizens who had surrounded the bunker. 'In the second half of the day,' the newspaper reported, 'police along with personnel of Special Operations Group cane charged the people in which many people were reportedly injured. Scores of tear gas shells were also fired to disperse the angry mob. The area was sanitized of protesters and the accused government gunman was whisked away in a police vehicle.'

That the CRPF picket protected the man with grenades from the crowd, and the police drove them away, confirmed the suspicion in the minds of many local people that agents of the forces were by this phase responsible for some of the attacks that appeared to be by militants. The newspaper reported that a civilian in Cheeni Chowk had commented: 'Our fears that grenades were being thrown by government agents to malign the name of militants came true'. The report added: 'Eight persons were killed and scores wounded in grenade attacks carried out by unidentified persons in busy marketplaces in the past few months.'

Since, by this time, one of the purposes of many of those who controlled the forces was to ensure continued deployment, the target audience of any games of smoke and mirrors would have been decision makers in Delhi. However, if there were indeed any games of smoke and mirrors, they had a greater impact within Kashmir. People there came to perceive that normalcy, the rule of law, and democracy were being denied to them, and this fuelled their rage. This was a large part of the rage that erupted in 2008 and 2010; the transfer of land to a shrine board in 2008 was perceived as a threat to geographical identity, but it also tapped into a deeply, even subconsciously, felt threat to physical identity—the de facto denial of the right to life.

So caught up in their entrenched perceptions and agendas were many of those in power that they failed to see that the focus of rage evolved. As explained in Chapter 2, 'Mass Rage', it was about a perceived threat to ethnic identity in 2008. In 2010, it was explicitly over the impunity with which those not involved in militancy were sometimes killed. By 2016, it had melded with militancy and determination to secede.

TOO MANY GUNS

A major reason for this spiralling rage was the perception that the counterinsurgency apparatus, which was experienced as restrictive, threatening,
and humiliating, had remained after insurgency was over. It had turned
the place into a cocoon for arbitrary death and destruction. The fact is that
pumping large numbers of arms into a society can result in an uncontrolled
mess; it willy-nilly undermines the functioning of the established system.
Quite soon after militancy surged in 1990, there were so many armaments
of various sorts in Kashmir that it was easy for sharp operators on various
sides to snitch a few secretly aside.

A clandestine market, and secret stocks, of weapons may have
emerged quite early on. In an interview to the *Times of India*, Ghulam
Mohammed Sofi, the respected (late) founder editor of the *Srinagar
Times*, said:

> In 1992 there was a 'cordon and search' operation carried out in Chest
> Diseases Hospital, Srinagar. In our presence seven rifles and a lot of
> ammunition was recovered during the raid. The next day we were
> shocked to note that the authorities announced recovery of just one
> rifle and some ammunition. You can draw your conclusions for the rest.
> Some of the present day politicians are the products of militancy. The
> present state government has been fully supported by the Congress and
> other parties in the national interest. Some people in the government
> are aware that with the waning of militancy, their own power too will
> wane. This is true of Pakistan too. Some people in that country see their
> survival and prosperity in the continuation of Kashmir conflict.[2]

For years, there had been rumours of gun-running between some members of the forces and militants. General Zaki acknowledged that he first
heard rumours around 1992[3]—that only some of the guns captured from a
militant or a hideout being recorded. The rest of the weapons, it was whispered, were sold at high prices. Some could be re-used, when convenient,

for example, to show fresh recoveries of arms or militants—to add to an officer's tally. It was not possible to investigate such rumours in the heat of frenetic countermilitancy operations in the early 1990s. That allowed such trends to become entrenched. It is possible that, during later phases, some of the rest of the weapons were used in encounters that might be staged in order to show that militancy continued. Among other officers, a Senior Superintendent of Police was in jail, accused of having staged encounters.[4]

By around that year of beginnings and endings, such operators may have become more blasé than before. One wide-eyed Kashmiri journalist even said he was offered a large sum to carry a cache of guns in his car from a canton-ment to a jungle. He said he was told that all he had to do was dump them at a designated spot.[5] A computer sales and service store owner who sold hard-ware and software to the forces (often inflating prices, since he said he had to grease so many palms to get payments released) also claimed that a Subedar Major had proposed to give him five Kalashnikov rifles to dump in the forest. He was to telephone the Subedar Major after a week or two with information about where the guns were, he said, and he would be paid Rs 25,000 per gun.[6] A police officer was investigated for gun-running but, after no evidence was found against him, became one of the state's top-most police officers.

GENERAL CYNICISM

By the time the grenade incident occurred in 2004, many Kashmiris had begun to view just about every militant attack with suspicion. The genera-tion that grew up during this time of violence was just becoming politically conscious when that sort of cynicism was most widespread. They read about such incidents in local newspapers.

Unless a militant group claimed responsibility for an attack, Kashmiri journalists who reported such events preferred to use the ambiguous term 'unidentified gunman' to describe one who threw a grenade, detonated a bomb, fired a gun, or lit a fire. They often had a shrewd idea of who might be behind such attacks. For, since the early 1990s, most Kashmiri reporters had access not only to the spokespersons of different security forces but also to militant commanders or their spokespersons. They could check over the telephone. 'Chief commanders' of some outfits called a few of them directly, even from Pakistan. Others had attended 'underground' press conferences or been escorted to a 'safe' spot (which might be a deserted park in a militant-dominated area such as Kokernag in the mid-1990s, or a deserted street in a downtown area) where a militant commander would meet them. Alternately, a militant spokesperson would claim responsibility through a statement to one of the several news agencies that had sprung up in Kashmir.

Quite often, however, doubts remained unclarified. The general impression was that a terrible part of the Kashmir story had been reduced to games of shadows, smoke, and mirrors. In the long term, this did great damage to the Indian state—and severely damaged the Indian nation. The net result of any games of smoke and mirrors that might be in play was that instability continued in Kashmir—and rage was fuelled. For, once rumours about such things began to spread among Kashmiris, they spread like wild fire. Even coincidences, events that occurred in the natural course, or perfectly innocent statements, were suspected to be part of some monstrous conspiracy by 'India' to fool or undermine 'us'.

The India-versus-us perception was ironical as it did not strike most Kashmiris that the people of India and, to an extent, the Indian government too were being fooled by any games of smoke and mirrors—indeed, that that might be the chief purpose.

UNHEALTHY COMPETITION

By and large, Kashmiris had been suspicious about reported encounters since the 1990s. In fact, families of a militant would celebrate if the capture of their relative was reported in a newspaper. For, once his capture had been reported, he was more likely to remain alive, even if only to face a long jail sentence. Early in the new century, a few units eager to notch up higher tallies of 'kills' occasionally targeted citizens whose families were unlikely to be able to reach the halls of justice. A senior police officer revealed that some men from Bihar who had come to Jammu for labour some years earlier were taken to Poonch, killed and declared to have been foreign militants.

Such rumours gained credence after five bodies were exhumed from graves in Ganderbal in the early summer of 2007, that year of endings and beginnings. The murders were discovered when it came to light that Abdul Rehman Paddar, a local carpenter, had been killed by the SOG in Ganderbal and buried. The forces, including the army and the SOG, had initially claimed that they had buried the body of a foreign militant who had been killed in a gunfight. When the fraud was discovered, five police officers associated with the SOG in Ganderbal were arrested. They included H.R. Parihar, the senior superintendent of police.

The army was reported to have been involved with the SOG in joint operations to notch up these 'kills', but the army did not permit the prosecution of their men. Nor did it agree to the district court's suggestion that court martial proceedings be initiated against them. The backing they received from their bosses indicated that those bosses were not shocked by the revelation that common people, unconnected with militancy, had been killed and labelled as militants. A report in the Chennai-based *Frontline* magazine noted:[7]

> For the most part, the media have cast the killings as the work of a small group of rogue midlevel police officers acting through subordinates in the ranks. Documents available with Frontline, however, demonstrate that at least three separate Indian Army units in Jammu and Kashmir participated in the murders. Official reports filed by officers of the 5 Rashtriya Rifles, the 13 Rashtriya Rifles and the 24 Rashtriya Rifles made it appear as though the victims were terrorists killed in legitimate counter-insurgency operations.

Frontline reported that the army's 13 Rashtriya Rifles unit and the SOG at Sumbal had falsely claimed in a First Information Report (FIR) that a Karachi-based terrorist code-named Abu Zahid was killed in an operation. The magazine reported that the FIR, filed by the army on 5 October 2006, had also claimed that an assault rifle and a wireless set were recovered. The truth, according to the magazine, was that the man the army and the SOG had killed was a cleric from Banihal called Shaukat Khan. Khan had been reported missing from Srinagar shortly before his death—from the Zadibal area in the north of the city.

The magazine noted, 'All the Ganderbal victims were desperately poor and therefore voiceless'. It also said:

> ... but such incidents, while rare, are far from unknown. For instance, 12 Army personnel, including the 18 Rashtriya Rifles' then-commanding officer Colonel R. Pandey, are facing criminal proceedings for having murdered four labourers at Devsar-Lolab in April 2004 and for having passed them off as terrorists. The murders would have passed undetected had not an anguished member of the unit written a letter to the parents of one of the victims.

It appeared to many Kashmiris that arbitrary murder, whether or not for blood money, was accepted. A passionate article by Anuradha Bhasin Jamwal, Executive Editor of *Kashmir Times*, reflected the horror that was felt within Kashmir over such murders in 2007:

> From Kashmir's hot-bed of graves—Ganderbal, one story after another begins to churn out—all morbid and repulsive tales of what happened to a bunch of innocent men. Tales go beyond the confines of Ganderbal and emerge from across the Valley, even from other parts of the state. These are gory sagas of healthy young men, who had nothing to do with militancy or counter insurgency, who disappeared mysteriously and how their families have moved from pillar to post searching for them, lodging reports but only to be told that the whereabouts cannot be known.

Some have finally found their sons buried in obscure grave-yards, laid to rest with the tag of foreign militant. Many others continue to wait. Many languish in jails, branded as terrorists.

CAUSE FOR RAGE

The horrors about which the *Frontline* correspondent wrote failed to stir the Indian government or, for that matter, even the general public opinion across India. That the Indian government and people remained largely unmoved by such occurrences in Kashmir was one of the causes of the rage that found its way into the stone-pelting of 2008, 2010, and 2016, and the new militancy.

One of the incidents that sparked anger in 2010 was similar to the Ganderbal fake encounters. Some of the victims at Ganderbal, which is in the northeast of the Kashmir Valley, had been brought there from around Kokernag in the south—a hundred kilometres from Ganderbal. In 2010, the victims were from quite near where they were murdered, in north Kashmir. That they were not taken far away to be killed indicates a decreased fear of getting caught. Again, the three young men who were killed were from very poor families, and cash rewards were apparently the chief reason.

To explain Parihar's motives for the Ganderbal murders, *Frontline* had reported that:

> According to investigators, the murder conspiracy was most likely conceived in late 2005, as pressure mounted on Parihar to show results—or risk losing his lucrative district posting, which some local newspapers have alleged he used to facilitate timber-smuggling operations along with local legislators. Officers of the SOG went along with the scheme because of the rewards available for each terrorist killed. Parihar roped in Army officers who wanted promotions to execute the actual killings and to provide the weapons that would make the murders appear legitimate. It is unclear whether the Army knew that the men it was killing were innocent—but either way, the killings amounted to cold-blooded murder.

Frontline gave the army personnel involved in those murders the benefit of the doubt in 2007, but the army officers involved in the murders of 2010 would have had to be thoroughly incompetent not to have known that their victims were local unemployed youth, not involved in militancy. Those boys were taken to the Machil camp by mercenaries working with that army unit on the promise that they would get work. Instead, they were killed, buried, and declared to be foreign militants. An inquiry ordered by the Corps headquarters found nine army personnel, including three officers, guilty.

Army Headquarters refused to order a court martial after receiving that indictment report from the Corps headquarters. This indicates a deeply disturbing acceptance, at an institutional level, of the murder of innocents. Very senior functionaries of government pushed hard for a court martial. N.N. Vohra, the Governor of the state, met Defence Minister A.K. Antony thrice to urge it. But under the then chief of army staff, General V.K. Singh, the army did not move to punish the guilty. A court martial was finally convened in early 2014. By the end of that year, it had found the accused guilty. Six army personnel were sentenced to life imprisonment.

UNMARKED GRAVES

The Ganderbal and Machil cases are the most high-profile and well-documented cases of citizens who had nothing to do with militancy being killed for blood money. They gave credence to allegations that some among the thousands who had been buried in unmarked graves in Kashmir were innocent citizens who had been killed and branded as terrorists for rewards. This became a vital part of the narratives that fanned the rage of the millennial generation, which had not experienced the militancy that petered out by 2007.

An independent investigation documented 2,700 graves containing more than 2,900 bodies. It said that 2,373 of these were unidentified bodies. The graves the group investigated were in districts of the Valley close to the LoC. In August 2011, the findings got the stamp of authority. The Jammu and Kashmir State Human Rights Commission released a report: after a three-year investigation, the Commission had found 2,156 unidentified bodies at 38 locations. That year, the Commission expanded the scope of the investigation, ordering the state government to investigate 3,800 other graves in the Poonch and Rajouri districts (which are also near the LoC). The State Human Rights Commission's report followed after reports from Amnesty International in 2008, the Srinagar-based Association of the Parents of Disappeared Persons (APDP), and other human rights bodies.

Army and other government authorities have argued that these are the graves of those killed during encounters between militants and armed forces. They acknowledge that some of these contain two or three bodies. No doubt, many of those graves do contain bodies of militants who were slain while fighting and were not carrying papers which could identify them. Others may contain the bodies of Kashmiris killed near the LoC while they were on their way to get training and arms, or returning. However, some other graves may also contain the bodies of Kashmiri citizens who were killed in cold blood.

But, despite the evidence from Machil and Ganderbal that at least some of the citizens who had been killed were not involved in militancy, and could not be described as 'collateral damage' of counterinsurgency operations, the security forces stoutly resisted stronger checks on operations. At a public debate on the subject at the National Law School, Bangalore, in the first week of January 2013, very highly respected retired army officers argued that since army officers had 'a sacred duty' to their men, they could not accept supervisory checks by any authority outside the army.

Teachers could also argue that their sacred duty to their students prevents them from accepting accountability to such government bodies as the University Grants Commission, a board of secondary education, or the Ministry for Human Resource Development. But that sort of argument undermines the core principles of democracy that date from the Magna

Carta. For the army, such an argument also ignores the constitutional injunction that the President of India shall be the commander-in-chief of the armed forces, an injunction which—read with the stipulation that the President shall act according to the advice of the council of ministers, which must have the confidence of the house of representatives—clearly places the armed forces under the supervision of Parliament and the government of the day and, finally, the people.

INTENSE PRESSURE

Let us briefly examine how the stage was set for the killing of innocents. The proxy war into which Pakistan had turned the Kashmir insurgency in the second half of the 1990s had put extreme pressure on the army units deployed in Kashmir. The Lashkar and Harkat men who dominated militancy at that stage were well trained, highly motivated, and had the advantages of undercover mobility, stealth, and surprise timing. After the counterinsurgency grid was expanded in 1994, the brass in both the army's Rashtriya Rifles and the paramilitary BSF put pressure on their units in the field to pull out all stops in their efforts to combat these foreign militants. They were told to notch up 'encounters', 'kills', and weapon 'recoveries', as if on a scoreboard in a vast gladiatorial arena. When unit commanders gathered at the Corps headquarters, officers with fewer 'kills' to show from their areas were humiliated before officers with bigger numbers. Some officers speak of a veritable race during those periods, to build one's record of anti-militancy successes.

So, more so during that period than before, cash rewards, medals, citations, and promotions became the currency of counterinsurgency. Units in the field competed for 'unit citations', which were awarded on the basis of 'kills' and 'catches' notched up—gauging performance on the basis of how many each unit had killed. This happened mainly in the mid and late 1990s, soon after the army had been inducted in very large numbers.

To the credit of the commanders who headed operations in Kashmir, and their political bosses in New Delhi, this emphasis on competing for 'kills' was replaced by concern for collateral damage and sensitivity to people who might be caught in the crossfire at the very peak of a phase of suicide attacks (1999–2001), when the army suffered maximum casualties. In fact, Kashmiri perceptions about the army and the attitudes of the government changed substantially when Prime Minister Vajpayee ordered a unilateral ceasefire through the month of Ramzan on 19 November 2000.[8]

Some of the most respected officers who had held command in Kashmir disapproved of unit citations as a method of assessing field success. When he was the Northern Army Commander-in-Chief from 2014 to 2016, Lt General D.S. Hooda told an army commanders' conference that the army ought to review the system of unit citations. 'It's not good,' he remarked about the system, pointing out that 'kills' and 'catches' were rewarded since these were quantifiable, but the army had to find a way to measure answers to the question: 'Have you ensured peace in your area?'[9]

Another highly respected professional who was against 'kills' and unit citations as measures of efficiency was Lieutenant General M.A. Zaki. 'It is wrong', he observed flatly about unit citations.[10] Zaki was appointed Corps Commander in Kashmir in October 1989, when militancy first erupted. In that most challenging phase, he risked his life by personally engaging militants in the field. A militant bullet grazed his forehead as he personally led an attack on a militant hideout—which his subordinates had initially lacked the courage to engage. He had arrived at the spot to find that the soldiers there had not dared approach the militants' hideout, which was on higher ground. So, he began to crawl towards it himself.

Such courageous leadership is rare. Under some of Zaki's successors, unit commanders in the field faced the prospect of ridicule and a sense of failure. So, if their unit's statistics did not compare favourably, some unit commanders looked for ways to increase the number of 'kills'. Since there was no dearth of militants in the Valley until the early years of the new century, they could 'catch' and 'kill' more of them by redoubling efforts. They sometimes targeted former militants who tried to go back to a normal life. Often targeted and harassed by Ikhwan and SOG men, these were easy targets for extortion.

The numbers of militants in the field gradually decreased when Prime Minister Vajpayee's steadfast efforts to make peace began to bear fruit in the new century. However, the security forces were generally chary of calling it over, even after 2007. In a situation in which the law had been subverted, and the fudging of paperwork was commonplace, the continued desire to show 'encounters' and 'kills' occasionally led to the sort of murders that occurred at Ganderbal and Machil. Especially when mercenaries and other Kashmiris who volunteered help were willing to do the dirty work—at least of identifying and corralling the quarry—some officers were apparently willing to murder innocent citizens from the more backward parts of Kashmir to add to their tally of 'kills'.

It was during the first decade of the twenty-first century—just when some in the forces were desperate to show encounters and 'kills', since there were relatively few militants around—that the new, relatively fearless generation of Kashmiris became conscious of the world around them. To some extent, the killing of 'innocents' became a part of this generation's understanding of what security forces were doing in Kashmir. It tied in with narratives of genocide against Muslims, and made some youths more receptive to religion-based arguments against secular, democratic systems.

BOUNTY INCENTIVES

There was pressure on the forces to show 'kills' from two directions. On the one hand, officers in charge of units faced the stick of ridicule and poor ratings on their career records. On the other, carrots were put out for them to notch up 'kills'. Apart from unit citations, the government had sanctioned monetary rewards for those who killed militants in encounters. There was a standard reward for any Pakistani militant, and also for others who had been specifically designated as terrorists. The lure of this blood money sometimes led to actual militants who were captured alive being killed after the encounter. At other times, it led to the murder of ordinary citizens, generally poor, who had no connection to militancy but were shown on record to have been militants. In many such cases, the record would show that the militant had been Pakistani, so that reward money could be claimed.

By 2007, the police had graded militants and set different levels of bounty on their heads. That led to the most cynical sort of manipulation. For, according to the grapevine, some officers had been known to wait and watch until the bounty on a particular militant had increased substantially before they killed him in an encounter. That was really cynical, for of course, the man had to engage in more terror activities for the bounty to be hiked. This could only happen of course in periods when the forces felt comfortably in control of the situation—such as around 2007. So cynical were those who indulged in such games that they did not seem deterred, leave alone horrified, at the result of the games, even after the rage of the new generation became evident in 2008 and 2010.

The officers and men who were in the field when the situation spun out of control had to reap the whirlwind that that cynicism had sown.

A BAD EXAMPLE

During a quarter-century of counterinsurgency in Kashmir, the Indian Army had willy-nilly had to watch the Pakistan Army very closely. From at least the 1980s, when General Zia-ul Haq had ruled Pakistan, the Pakistan Army had had the last word on matters of national security, and closely controlled sensitive areas of the country. It ran some of Pakistan's basic services and infrastructure, and owned some of the best tracts of land. A massive chunk of Pakistan's budget was at the army's disposal, and the army decided how it was run and what it required and acquired. Without even realizing it, some officers and men of the Indian Army must have absorbed lessons from what they saw across the LoC.

Pakistan's army had long been exposed to the temptations of corruption when they ran public services, business corporations, and government departments during and after periods of martial law. Running covert wars in Afghanistan and Kashmir for more than a quarter-century had vastly increased those opportunities. Former militants reported that, from quite early in the Kashmir operations, some Pakistan Army officers had got them to sign for more weapons than were actually handed to them.

A FEW BAD APPLES

Incidents of corruption and of murders such as at Machil were unforgiveable in any case. Historically, they were particularly tragic since, motivated by greed and an institutional determination to remain deployed, those murders generated rage in a generation that had largely forgotten the excesses of the 1990s. The result of that corruption and those murders was to keep the conflict, the conflict economy, the 'disturbed' situation and its special laws, in place. That caused rage in the new, fearless generation, over perceptions of humiliation and of being caged. And that caused some of them to take up arms in a fresh round of militancy.

One reason this was tragic was that the army had for the most part ceased to alienate by the time the murder of innocents sparked rage in 2010. That is why, even though the murders at Machil were among the sparks that lit the fires of rebellion in 2010, the boys on the streets did not attack the army that year. In fact, as has been noted in Chapter 2, 'Mass Rage', bands of stone-pelters who prevented public movement that year would commonly let army vehicles pass. As was clearly shown by the survey described in Chapter 4, 'Varied Opinions', the majority of young Kashmiris still thought positively about the army in 2011. The large majority despised some of the paramilitary forces, and the police too. Although attitudes began to change as the army came back into action from 2015, anecdotal evidence showed that there was a large measure of respect for the army even in 2017. Partly as a side effect of Sadbhavana interactions, and a high profile public relations exercise the year after the Machil killings, fear of the army had reduced considerably since the 1990s. On the other hand, a fearless generation had emerged. One result of those twin factors was that, when militancy returned and the army began to combat it again, youths took to pelting stones at the army, particularly during operations. In fact, they resisted the army so vigorously in places like Pulwama that, for a while in 2016–17, it was tough to lay cordons in parts of that district. That did not last, however. The army placed new camps across areas where militancy was clearly visible, and a new spiral of violence was well underway in 2017 and after.

The situation appeared to be moving inexorbly back to the horrific hate and violence of the 1990s, partly as a result of inertia, and tragically mistaken policies, in the years since around 2007.

NOTES

1. Author's interview with Hilal Bhat, who reported that incident in *Greater Kashmir*, at the author's rented residence in Srinagar.
2. http://www.jammu-kashmir.com/archives/archives1997/97november19c.html, accessed on 25 June 2017.
3. Author's interview with Zeneral Zaki at his son's residence in Delhi in April 2013.
4. http://indiatoday.intoday.in/story/kashmir-fake-enconters-has-perturbed-the-valley2007/1/155645.html.
5. Off-the-record interview with the author at the author's rented residence in Srinagar in May 2009.
6. Off-the-record interview with the author in Anantnag.
7. Praveen Swami, 'Terror in Uniform', *Frontline*, Volume 24, Issue 03, 10-23 February 2007, http://www.frontline.in/static/html/fl2403/stories/20070223002310900.htm, accessed on 20 June 2017.
8. http://www.thehindu.com/2000/11/20/stories/01200001.htm, accessed on 25 June 2017.
9. Author's interview with Lt General D.S. Hooda at the office of the General Officer Commanding-in-Chief, at Udhampur, on 7 November 2016.
10. Author's interview with Lt General M.A. Zaki at Mayur Vihar in March 2016.

10

Hateful Polarization

A major reason why the cynical opportunism around the sordid conflict economy could keep going was that policymakers too easily bought into two-dimensional, superficial descriptions of the situation in Kashmir. Even if observers focused on Kashmiri youth, they tended to view them as an amorphous, unchanging mass. They were glorified as heroic fighers by some, condemned as criminal troublemakers by others. Some of the first category of observers were committed to the idea of freedom. Some of the latter were Islamophobic. Both these viewpoints would not acknowledge shades of grey, or changes over time.

It did not suit either category to acknowledge that, around the middle of the first decade of the twenty-first century, many young Kashmiris were willing to settle down to peace with dignity, opportunities, rights and an honourable settlement. In fact, both sorts largely ignored the place at the time, and later angrily denied that such a phase had ever existed. The tragic result was that both sorts of polarized views together seemed to have brought their pre-determined world view into being by around 2017. At least, the situation had by then become actually more polarized, the way both sorts of extremes imagined, than it had been in 2007.

Our survey (discussed in Chapter 4, 'Varied Opinions') confirmed that society, opinions, and aspirations in Kashmir were actually in flux early in that decade—as much, if not more, than anywhere else. Those opinions and aspirations changed from time to time, sometimes with great swiftness and intensity. They also varied across different parts of the Valley, and across different age groups, classes, and milieus. If the influence of religion differed across time, place, age, gender, class, and milieu, so did attitudes towards the different armed forces. The term 'azadi' too appeared to signify different things to different young people, at least midway through that decade of change—and the experience of both militancy and counterinsurgency differed across time and place, even from person to person.

But, notwithstanding these facts, a sharp, black-and-white binary had developed about Kashmir during the decade after 2007. To some extent, that binary was artificially, but vigorously, manufactured—in television studios, publishing houses, university campuses, and elsewhere. An extraordinarily complex situation had been reduced to a two-dimensional polarity. Kashmir was seen as the site of a war between 'the people'—viewed as undifferentiated—and 'the forces', which too were seen as singular and undifferentiated across time or particular force or officer or soldier. These forces were seen as 'India'. In that light, the sharp two-dimensional binary was 'the people of Kashmir' versus 'India'—or 'Kashmir' versus 'Indian forces'. At times, particularly in the third quarter of 2008, it was reduced to a Muslims versus Hindus, or a Jammu versus Kashmir, binary.

It was of a piece with various sorts of exclusionary binaries that were gaining salience in different parts of the world. Each reduced the 'other' to a two-dimensional caricature, that could more easily be promoted as an object of hate.

To many, these various binaries were interchangeable—variations on the same theme. It all boiled down to 'us against them'. Like crowds watching a high-pitched wrestling match, those who saw Kashmir in this sort of polarized way saw one side as the hero, for whom they cheered raucously, and the other side as the enemy that must be defeated. The intensity with which that sort of binary was felt at times made it almost seem as if the hysteria on both sides was being artificially generated—just like at those high-stakes wrestling matches that are staged for the entertainment of television audiences.

In the manner of the most loutish football fans, some of those who viewed Kashmir as a binary fight were intolerant of a differing viewpoint. Their rejection was often rude and violative. Indeed, some of them reacted with greater fury against a viewpoint on Kashmir that was not reductionist and binary than against those on the other side of their preferred binary. They could understand the latter, but nuance was intolerable. Indeed, they revelled in the opposite viewpoint, taking it as validation of their own. For, the uncompromising new crop of Indian nationalists and the promoters of the narrative of Kashmiri victimhood agreed on one thing. Both appeared to be convinced that all Kashmiris wanted independence, that none wanted to be part of India. Various kinds of data and the evidence of mass protests were adduced to prove this—by both sides.

The new crop of Indian nationalists—those influenced by Hindutva activists, for instance—seemed to be convinced that Kashmiris must be kept under tight control, on the presumption that all Kashmiris were determined to secede from India. The promoters of the independence narrative, including those Indian activists, academics, and journalists who backed Kashmir's narratives for independence, were even more determined that all Kashmiris wanted to be free of India. In their narrative, those who did not share their view were presented as paid agents of the Indian state. This was ironic, for it was, in fact, often the other way round. Some of those who shouted loudest in the competitive clamour to dominate, control, influence, or represent Kashmir's freedom movement were often agents of one or other state power, most often but not necessarily Pakistani or Indian. Sometimes, they were connected with the agencies of several states—successively or even simultaneously. Agents of the most wily Indian intelligence operatives had been among the leading lights of the militancy since the first half of 1990—even a quarter century before.

The vast majority of those who developed strong views on Kashmir after 2008 had no idea that their sentiments and values were being manipulated, and that the net result of their accepting the black-and-white, polarized narrative was the continuation of the conflict economy. During the decade of swift change after that insurgency ended, agents of even wilier operatives of the state sometimes took other roles, some as propagandists and other kinds of activists. Propaganda, after all, had become a major method of insurgency from around that time. All kinds of agencies wanted to control the most influential voices, particularly those that shouted against them. Some calculated that they could play one leader against another, or temper the discourse of one or other.

Both liked the undifferentiated term 'stone-pelter', only one side saw these as disruptive, paid rebels, and the other side saw them as part of a heroic resistance against an evil state. Both viewpoints insisted furiously that nothing changed about the phenomenon of pelting stones, or about the generations engaged in it, or about their motivations. Niether seemed willing to accept the differences between the uprisings of 2008, 2010, and 2016 discussed in Chapter 2, 'Mass Rage', or the other kinds of changes that occurred during this decade.

It was from about 2008 that these binary perspectives had developed. Kashmir had not generally been projected or perceived in that simplistic way until the previous year. Indeed, until the India–Pakistan peace process got going in 2004, it had rather been viewed as an extraordinarily complex situation. Perceptive analysts had spoken of it as a set of issues, rather than a flatly two-dimensional binary fight. Abdul Ghani Bhat, one of the three who had chaired the Hurriyat Conference during the decade (1993–2003) it remained united, had often observed in the early years of the new century that the Kashmir issue was such a complex knot that it needed to be gently, patiently massaged between light fingers until it loosened sufficiently to be untangled. The Kashmiri leader Maulana Masoodi used to say the same thing in earlier decades.

FROM SYMPATHY TO HATE

The processes through which a certain world view becomes widely accepted are often complex and invisible. So it was with the development of this sharp, two-dimensional binary. There were several reasons why that binary emerged around 2008. In Kashmir, the good-versus-evil view of 'India', 'Jammu', or 'the forces' against 'us' (the Kashmiri people) emerged around the agitations in both the Kashmir Valley and the Jammu area that year. It was vigorously promoted in local newspapers, academia, books, and documentaries. A similar binary developed across India following a shocking attack by militants from Pakistan at the end of November that year in Mumbai. Soon, Indians largely viewed unrest and violence in Kashmir through the prism of Pakistan, which was now viewed far more widely than before as an implacable enemy.

In fact, the terribly turbulent unrest in Kashmir that summer had wrenched the country's focus back on to Kashmir. For, by the time militancy tapered off by 2007, interest in Kashmir had petered out around India. For the previous couple of years, people had generally been more interested in the 'peace process' between India and Pakistan, and even that had only been on the edges of most people's consciousness. Tourists had begun to flock to Kashmir by the hundreds of thousand every summer, and the discourse was all about not just peace, but normalcy.

Mufti Mohammad Sayeed's successes as chief minister from 2002 to 2005, to give traumatized Kashmiris what he called a 'healing touch', were quiet achievements. Outside Kashmir, they went largely unnoticed. Equally, nobody noticed when anger and frustration over continued humiliation and harassment by the counterinsurgency apparatus (even after there seemed to be barely any militancy left) started rising in the couple of years thereafter. So, when it found a vent in resentment over the transfer of land to a shrine board in 2008, the fury that erupted on the streets took most observers by surprise. Since they did not expect it, most analysts had no idea what to make of it. All that was clear was that it was far too strong to be only about the lease of a plot of land.

There was tremendous solicitousness among leading Indian analysts at that stage. A couple of editors wrote in late August 2008 that Kashmiris should be given the right to self-determination and to secede from India, since that was what they seemed to want. Swaminathan A. Aiyar argued in his Sunday column in *The Times of India*: 'We promised Kashmiris a plebiscite six decades ago. Let us hold one now ... Let Kashmiris decide the outcome, not the politicians and armies of India and Pakistan.'[1] Vir Sanghvi, then the Editorial Director of *Hindustan Times*, wrote: 'If you believe in democracy, then giving Kashmiris the right to self-determination is the correct thing to do. And even if you don't, surely we will be better off being rid of this constant, painful strain on our resources, our lives, and our honour as a nation?'[2]

In fact, so strong was the sympathy in India's national media that one of the major complaints of the counter-agitators in Jammu during July and August of 2008 was that the media was biased against them. Such was the environment then that the media generally referred to anyone who criticized Kashmiris as a narrow-minded chauvinist.

All that changed over the next five years. In fact, the turnaround came just a few months later. In the last week of November 2008, highly trained and armed Pakistani terrorists landed on the Mumbai coast, attacked the city's two most plush hotels, a synagogue, and seven other high-profile targets, causing mayhem across a large area. They attacked the wealthiest part of India's financial, film, and entertainment capital, the most cosmopolitan city of South Asia. Several police officers were among the 166 persons killed in those attacks. The Pakistan-based Lashkar-e-Taiba and Pakistan's ISI were identified as having trained, armed, and coordinated the attackers.[3] The attack was conceived and executed as an act of war against civilian targets.

It was India's 9/11 moment. When aeroplane missiles slammed into New York's World Trade Centre towers on 9 September 2001, many in the US tried to learn more about Muslims and to understand them empathetically. But a large chunk of Middle America turned xenophobic, filled with feelings of hate and vengeance. After the 26/11 attacks in Mumbai, the attitude and responses of a large part of the fast-growing Indian middle class hardened. They wanted terrorism to be given no quarter. Far more than before, they identified Pakistan as the seedbed of terrorism. And far more Indians came to view militancy in Kashmir without nuance as evil terrorism sponsored by Pakistan. Increasingly thereafter, any sort of rebellion in Kashmir was viewed as an unannounced act of war by Pakistan. Once again, hardliners in Pakistan's ISI had delivered a body blow to the interests of Indian Muslims, especially those many young Kashmiris, particularly women, who sought peace with dignity.

To many Indians, Hafiz Sayeed became the symbol of Pakistani enmity. Sayeed was a Pakistani cleric who ran a university-sized madrasa[4] which not only preached violent jihad but also ran an army of jihad soldiers called Lashkar-e-Taiba. He had lost 23 members of his family while they were trying to migrate from India to Pakistan during the Partition in 1947. He hated India with a vengeance. His Lashkar had been the most lethal of the militant groups that operated in Kashmir. Its men often undertook suicide missions. Since he repeatedly spoke of jihad for Kashmir and against India, and evidently had the support of the Pakistani government, many Indians came to view Kashmir's movement through the lens of Hafiz Sayeed's exhortations to violent jihad.

So shocked had Indians been by the Mumbai attacks that even unarmed protests and agitations in Kashmir were thereafter viewed with suspicion—as the undercover attempts of an evil Pakistan to destabilize India. So, when rage again erupted with stones on the streets of Kashmir in 2010, the response of analysts and journalists across India was less sympathetic than in 2008. Many analysts tried to downplay the numbers on the streets, and to explain the boys as paid agents of the opposition PDP, the Hurriyat, or other troublemakers funded by Pakistan.

By the time Kashmiri youth briefly protested again on the streets in mid-April 2015, attitudes of analysts had hardened much further. Those protests erupted after the army killed two young men associated with militants (including Burhan Wani's brother) with horrific brutality in Tral in western Kashmir.

For many Indian nationalists, particularly those who were ideologically committed to Hindutva, Kashmir was about anti-national Muslim terrorists attacking the Indian state on behalf of its enemy, Pakistan. They had to be combated robustly. Collateral damage was acceptable. To many who thought along these lines, human rights abuses were shibboleths of anti-national activists.

A narrative that portrayed Muslims as violent, misogynistic, illiberal, and anti-national had been vigorously pushed in different parts of India. This narrative portrayed Kashmiris as uniformly anti-Hindu.

Most Indians now saw the situation in Kashmir in starkly black-and-white, bad-guys-versus-good-guys terms. They held that the forces were doing a great national service, and that their morale and the security of the country were of foremost importance. This was extended to mean that those who protested on the streets of Kashmir were evil, pro-Pakistan anti-nationals. Some of the Indian media took the line that giving any political space to a 'separatist' was to promote Pakistani interests—and tantamount to treason.

OPPRESSION NARRATIVE

A similarly black-and-white, bad-guys-versus-good-guys image of the situation had developed in the minds of many Kashmiris in the same period. The two processes were separate, but they converged as mirror images of each other.

From around 2010 on, many Kashmiris viewed the police and paramilitary forces as repressive, brutal, and venal. In this light, they viewed protestors as victims of horrific repression. A slew of images, comments, and reports on social media platforms influenced them, strengthening this black-and-white view. Horrible abuses of human rights had taken place during the 1990s. Generally, the worst offenders were the SOGs of the police, mercenaries working with various forces, and the paramilitary BSF. Being hung naked from a ceiling by one's hands or legs, being whipped with sticks, being made to lie naked on ice, rectal insertions, and electric shocks to genitals were among torture methods, particularly of the BSF. The army apparently preferred waterboarding. Some men's beards were plucked, some had their nails pulled.

All this had largely ceased at the beginning of the new century. Yet, it was not until the middle of the first decade of the new century that the international focus on human rights abuse in Kashmir sharpened. Relatively little was said about it when it happened, but it was presented from 2008 onward as if it was an unremitting, continuous process. Not only did the focus sharpen, the production of a narrative of oppression was orchestrated. This narrative came to light from 2008. Ironically, human rights abuses were rare at this stage. Militancy was more or less over. What is more pertinent is that, in the middle of the decade, the governments of both Pakistan and India had together tried hard to negotiate an agreement over Kashmir. For a while in 2004, there was even talk of a larger south Asian confederation. Armies, security hawks, as well as Western diplomats in Islamabad and New Delhi watched these developments keenly. The promised changes may have caused some unease, not only in China and the West, but also in pockets of the deep state in both Pakistan and India. Thereafter, those who chose to vigorously publicize narratives of oppression and cruelty found patrons in several quarters.

Starting around 2007, several young Kashmiri journalists, budding academics, and other opinion-makers focused sharply on presenting what they called a 'narrative' about Kashmir. The narrative got immense traction during and after the agitations of 2008. That narrative consciously used terms such as occupation, colonization, and mass graves, calculated to evoke comparisons with Palestine and Sarajevo. Torture and rape, exclusively by Indian forces, were the chief staple of this narrative. Resistance was emphasized. It was a narrative that was bound to increase conflict.

The narrative had several strands. Much was made, for example, of the value of the state's water resources, which the 'colonizer' was said to be looting.[5] This part of the narrative consciously projected comparisons of Kashmir's water resources with the oil resources of West Asia. The 'resource' was said to be worth Rs 50,000 crore, and then Rs 70,000 crore (approximately USD 10 billion), according to the narrative. It ignored the facts that the water from which hydroelectric power was generated in Jammu and Kashmir on the Indian side of the LoC was of the Chenab river, and the large majority of people who lived along that river wanted at that stage to remain Indians. Narratives about Kashmir's ownership of the state's water resources also ignored the fact that the only viable consumers of the power that could be generated were India's northern states—or Pakistan, which believed that all the water of the state belonged to it in the first place. Of course, certain world powers, particularly China, had begun by then to prioritize water sources.

These narratives further deepened the divide in perceptions. It had an impact among Indian activists, intellectuals, and liberal mediapersons. And it had a huge impact on young Kashmiris who were just becoming aware of the world around them for the first time. Their reading was often dominated by social media sites, mainly Facebook, where these narratives were pushed vigorously.

HISTORICAL NARRATIVES

The black-and-white categories and narratives obscured the fact that, in 2010 and again in 2016, only poor persons outside the networks of power and influence were killed or blinded. The vigorous promoters of narratives remained safe, generally in large mansions in Kashmir or in places far from the turmoil. Their popularity, and sometimes their careers, hinged on the conflict. This book will be denounced by those with a stake in the continuation of conflict. But, if stable peace is to come, and if justice is ever to be done to the poor and vulnerable, one must accept the extent to which the apparatus of counterinsurgency was responsible for the new militancy, and that there were common interests across the wide spectrum from pro- to anti-state.

The narrative began to be vigorously generated during the India–Pakistan peace process, which lasted from 2004 to 2007, but it dovetailed easily with the narratives of illegitimacy that had been promoted within Kashmir for more than half a century. School history textbooks did not teach facts about how the state of Jammu and Kashmir became a part of India. Most young Kashmiris learnt about what happened in 1947 in their homes, from the narratives of their elders, and from the *kunji* short notes most of them studied just before examinations. These kunjis often presented essays which students could learn by rote.

One common version that many young Kashmiris picked up was that Sheikh Abdullah was the leader of Kashmir when tribesmen attacked the place in 1947. So, Abdullah requested his friend, India's Prime Minister Nehru, to send Indian troops to help him to expel the tribesmen. Having done that, the troops never went back. Nehru stabbed his friend in the back and took over the place, which was independent until then. This narrative ignored the Dogra Maharaja, his relationship with the British Raj, and his accession to India under the terms of the Indian Independence Act, 1947.[6] But the narrative dovetailed neatly with the overpowering, intimidating presence of army and other forces amid which this generation had grown up. It seemed to add up.

Beyond such narratives, the facts were generally left fuzzy. As Shah Faesal, a well-known young Kashmiri government officer, wrote at the end of 2016:

> Rather than being right here, India was somewhere out there. Even in school, when lessons on identity were given, they went well when they were about my village, district, state; the moment it came to my country, the teacher either got tongue-tied or the school bell would chime, class was over and we'd be left guessing. As the conflict intensified, we grew up as confused citizens of a country in the making.[7]

On the other hand, most Indians only knew that the state's maharaja had acceded it to India and it had become an integral part of India. (The term 'integral part of India' was used in the state's constitution, which was adopted in 1956 and came into force in 1957.)[8] The discourse among the new crop of Indian nationalists was that Kashmir was indisputably India's territory and that India's enemy, Pakistan, was encouraging and funding people there to rebel against their country—and funding and sponsoring militant terrorist jihadists too.

BLACK AND WHITE

These polarized perspectives on Kashmir led to a surreal situation in which what seemed black to some seemed clearly white to others. Both views were in fact mirror images. That applied to emergent contemporary events even more than to history. Thus, most Indians, as well as most proponents of 'azadi', perceived the various protests on the streets of Kashmir simply as being anti-India revolts, regardless of the differing focus of each of the uprisings discussed in Chapter 2, 'Mass Rage'. There was little awareness of the various nuances in the opinions and aspirations of young Kashmiris—or of differences across space and time—which the survey findings explained in Chapter 4, 'Varied Opinions', showed.

Some Indian analysts described 'stone-pelting' in 2010 as a new form of militancy. Many policymakers did not seem interested in the causes of the anger that stone-pelting demonstrated. Rather, they perceived it as a calibrated provocation to destabilize the state without giving the appearance of armed rebellion. Much like calling 'wolf', this became an awful fulfilled prophecy after 2010. By 2015–16, common people at places near an ongoing encounter took to pelting stones at the armed forces who were engaging militants in a firefight.[9] It appeared that, at times, organizers of the new militancy used the pelting of stones as a part of coordinated multi-pronged attacks. Most of the pelters were genuinely agitated, but a round of pelting sometimes appeared to be launched by coordinated agents provocateurs.

DIVERGENT VIEWS

While protests certainly were revolts against the state at one level, they were often layered. Many in Kashmir saw some of the protests as expressing frustration over corruption or high prices—or over the fact that protests over such mundane matters were put down with lethal force. Further, they often saw all such protests as an accumulated response to the brutality Kashmiris in general had experienced through two decades of counterinsurgency. Many of them perceived the pelting of stones as an expression of rage by unarmed civilians pushed to a wall. They were sometimes seen as letting off steam over accumulated traumas. In that light, most people in Kashmir viewed protests from the perspective of how strongly they were put down, seeing the state's action against protests as intolerant and brutal repression.

In keeping with their view of Kashmir as an integral part of India and the Kashmiri freedom movement as Pakistan-sponsored treason, many Indian nationalists took the statist view that Kashmiris deserved whatever human rights abuses they might have suffered. They had asked for it, in the view of these nationalists, by taking up arms against the state. Reports, discussions, and analyses in sections of the Indian media often focused on mobs attacking the police and other forces, which tried valiantly to control those mobs. On the other hand, descriptions by Kashmiri youth, mainly on social media platforms, often focused on the killing of a youth in police action, or in an encounter with counterinsurgency forces, as the cause for the protest demonstration. In that light, they described action by the forces to quell such protests as brutal repression.

Pakistani flags became highly emotional talking points in descriptions of protests, in 2010 and in 2015. Protestors sometimes waved these in processions or placed them at highly visible public spots. Many Indians viewed these as extremely provocative anti-national acts. They also saw these as proof that Kashmiris generally wanted to join Pakistan. On the other hand, many Kashmiris saw the waving of flags as a form of protest. Those flags did not represent the desire to actually join Pakistan among more than a few Kashmiris. Their comments on social media compared the enormity of shooting down protestors with the act of waving a flag, and critiqued media channels that seemed to treat flag-waving as worse than firing. When Indian nationalists called for those who waved Pakistani flags to be sent to Pakistan, many Kashmiris interpreted such comments as proof of their long-standing complaint that Indians wanted Kashmiri land and not Kashmiri people.

After the Mumbai attacks, Indians by and large celebrated those of the forces who died in action as martyrs. Kashmiris, on the other hand, often viewed the police and other forces as venal and exploitative—and counterinsurgency forces in general as repressive tormentors with benefits, privileges, and extraordinary powers. So, while mainstream Indian opinion viewed action taken against errant men within the forces as lowering morale, Kashmiris generally saw punitive action as just—and indicative of good faith regarding the government's stated commitment to uphold human rights. Since the army highly valued morale and its image, it did not make public any action it did take on a charge of rape or unauthorized killing. That secrecy was counterproductive if one wished to bridge the gap, but the image that punitive action was not taken suited those on both sides who promoted polarized narratives.

MEDIA BATTLES

The media became a major arena for the exposition and spread of black-and-white, us-versus-them narratives. The milieu of the age contributed. Singular, exclusivist ideas of self and community were gaining ground in different parts of the world. During that decade of change, a variety of media platforms had emerged to offer mass communication not only for the masses but also by the masses. These allowed just about anyone to put out a message, a narrative. This undid established media standards of veracity, balance, and responsibility for not hurting others, or excluding them. Almost anything was good enough to publish.

This led to an intense competition to catch the eye of potential readers and viewers, by putting out the most sensational narratives. This encouraged one-sided narratives that overtly disparaged not only counter-views, but also any attempt at balance.

Srinagar-based newspapers became the prime vehicle of narratives that posited 'the Kashmiri people' as a whole as victims of deliberate, malicious oppression by 'India' as a whole. Ironically, many of those who wrote trenchant columns to project that black-and-white discourse of colonization and oppression had worked for the government, or still worked for the government.

The most potent vehicle for the Indian nationalist narrative was news television channels. While celebrating the work and sacrifices of the forces, several of them rudely castigated any talk of human rights or dialogue as illegitimate anti-national activity. They generally made no distinction between street agitations, militancy, and Pakistan's anti-India activities—until they did converge.

Television and social media analysts who treated state authorities as haloed saints, and Muslims in general as the enemy, pushed further into a corner those conflicted Kashmiri adults who might have been uncomfortable about the discourses among teenagers. It forced them to back the anti-state narrative.

In early 2018, even Dineshwar Sharma, New Delhi's Representative for talks in Jammu and Kashmir, urged the Home Minister to restrain these TV channels, taking the view that such intolerant programmes were harmful to India's national interest. [10]

SUITING PAKISTAN

To try and counter simplistic or exaggerated narratives with hyper Indian neo-nationalism was to confirm the two-dimensional simplicity of those narratives. Similarly, to talk of all opponents of the state within Kashmir as Pakistan's agents was to strengthen Pakistan's hands. For, Pakistan had very smartly utilized the narratives that had been spun since about 2008. At a time when—for example, in 2015—there were almost no rapes or murders in Kashmir, other than a few terror attacks, sophisticated videos were manufactured and spread about 'the honour of the mothers and sisters of Kashmiris'. Some of these uploads were traced to Pakistan. They smartly bridged the two major influences of that decade, by presenting a general scenario of horrific repression against the backdrop of Islamist symbols, themes, terms, and references.

When hyper Indian neo-nationalists disparaged Islam, or painted all Kashmiris with the same brush, they served Pakistan's purpose. The sharp focus of several Indian television channels on 'leaders' of the Hurriyat suited Pakistan even more. For, as demonstrated in Chater 6, 'Disillusionment with Politics', young people on the ground within Kashmir generally had very little regard for these 'leaders'. It was well known in Kashmir that many of them took money from both sides and had established lucrative networks of influence.

Pakistan needed to prop up these sordid profiteers as 'leaders' so that they might promote its cause. That was a tall order, for many Kashmiris had become increasingly disillusioned with Pakistan. The turning point for the disillusionment of many of those who had been born during the 1980s and 1990s was the assassination of the charismatic former prime minister of Pakistan, Benazir Bhutto, at the end of that year of endings and beginnings. As Musa's popularity showed, the millennial generation was more prone to back post-nationalist Islamism in any case.

That complicated an already divergent movement. As late as 2016, a group of Kashmiri journalists told Pakistan's High Commissioner in New Delhi that they were distressed that Pakistan kept trying to take over for its own benefit what those journalists saw as their people's struggles for Kashmiri independence.[9] The envoy reassured them as best he could, but it was no more than sweet talk. By then, Pakistan had undertaken a multipronged operation to set the stage to push up violence to another quantum level. Hordes of Pakistani and other foreign militants would join forces with the demonstrations, stone-pelting, and militancy by young Kashmiris. Over-simplified black-and-white narratives suited the huge convergence that was in the works.

SOCIAL MEDIA

The other major vehicle for both sorts of black-and-white narratives was social media. Facebook had very few users in Kashmir in that year of quiet beginnings, 2007, but the number had grown rapidly quite soon thereafter. Twitter too became a major way to communicate and spread ideas. WhatsApp became a very effective, and less generally visible, medium of communication.

Photographs and videos of Kashmiri boys and others who were killed, injured, or maimed in 2010 and 2016 made a tremendous impact to consolidate an 'us-versus-them' narrative of victimhood and repression. Videos of Kashmiri boys being beaten or whipped by the police, or being tortured with rollers, or forced under assault to yell abuse of Pakistan, made a huge impact in Kashmir. For their part, nationalist Indians circulated photographs and videos of soldiers being stoned, abused, and attacked by demonstrators. These too reinforced a one-sided 'us-versus-them' narrative, for no nuances, causes, or counter-arguments were acknowledged on either side.

Both sorts of narratives, mirror images, were generally circulated among those who preferred that sort of narrative—and trolls who sought out the opposite to vent their spite. That polarization not only promoted exclusivist hate, it made any movement towards a solution that might be acceptable all round more difficult. In fact, it paved the way to increased conflict. By around October 2016, and again in 2017, it had contributed to bringing South Asia close to the brink of war.

SLIPPERY CATEGORIES

Those who were meant to uphold the established state tended to go along with black-and-white narratives. A large part of the political spectrum, the media, and other pillars of the state had nourished that black-and-white perception of the situation in Kashmir. Representatives of 'mainstream' political parties based in the state tended to couch their discourses in the presumption that the entire population of the place was uniformly ranged against India. The subtext of that presumption was that the Government of India should fund them lavishly, and without seeking accountability, to stave off this perennial crisis. Those who spoke on behalf of political parties that ruled at New Delhi tended to take the second line— that all was well within Kashmir except for Pakistani interference.

As shown in Chapter 8, 'Conflict Economy', the neat theme of oppression-and-victimhood suited a wide variety of influential forces with power of various sorts within Kashmir.

While shades of grey could undermine the continuation of conflict, the perception of Kashmir as a simplistic polarity, like a great wrestling match, suited the influential. Indeed, the 'mainstream' and 'secessionist' categories were remarkably flexible. If the survey described in Chapter 4, 'Varied Opinions', showed that the poor and geographically remote were most likely to seek peace and progress, it also indicated that the sons of officers and others in powerful positions in government—including the police—were often the most sharply focused on narratives of oppression and victimhood.

The underlying message in the local discourse of several 'mainstream' politicians was that they were actually against the establishment.[11] In subtle ways, it freed them of responsibility, since the blame for all that was wrong belonged to the 'colonizer.' They were 'insiders' held hostage to the 'outsider' who was projected as the real culprit in all that the government did wrong. Meanwhile, those who wielded power on either side of the 'mainstream'–'separatist' divide took care of each other.

To some extent, the actions and words of powerful persons on both sides were like a ritual dance. So much so that the more cynical among those whose power stemmed from the conflict—or whose power it multiplied—might have wanted to manufacture a conflict if the Kashmir conflict had not offered itself to their exploitative interests—the way the neocons in the US manufactured narratives about weapons of mass destruction in Iraq in order to create conditions for a war. Their Iraq war had suited the weapons industry and companies like Halliburton, in which the then US Vice President Dick Cheney had interests.

That Iraq's President Saddam Hussein was a dictator who tortured dissidents was true. The fact came in handy for those who wanted war; it was the narrative they projected to pave the way for the Iraq war. In fact, as long as his policies suited global powers, he was to suppress his people harshly.

The rumour mills in Srinagar were full of incredible anecdotes. According to one, a top functionary of the government once telephoned a journalist to warn him against writing trenchantly against the separatist leader Syed Ali Shah Geelani. 'He'll send his goons to stone your house,' the man was reported to have warned—oblivious to responsibility for law and order and for the constitutional set-up in the state. It emerged in early 2017 that, at the height of the uprising of 2016, Geelani's grandson had been given a job at a high-profile conference centre under the control of the government.[12] That created a huge controversy.[13]

That sort of surreal cynicism was not limited to any one administration or party. During one uprising, newspapers and television channels run by powerful men intimately connected with the higher echelons of the ruling party vigorously projected stone-pelting and the repression of the forces. With headlines like 'bloodbath' in red ink, they whipped up the emotions of young demonstrators even when enthusiasm for the agitations might have been flagging. Despite promoting conflict thus, the owners of influential newspapers based in Srinagar continued to wield amazing influence in the corridors of power.

While interviewing a minister in the secretariat later that year, the representatives of a television channel that had reported with sobriety were taken aback when the minister berated them for projecting stone-pelting. After listening quietly for a while, one of the team asked the minister to explain why a television programme which his nephew anchored highlighted even the slightest pebble chucked by the smallest boy.

The truth is that propagating the two-dimensional narrative suited the ruling class. People at large took the view that the channel his relatives ran supported their anti-state movement. Meanwhile, the channel that had been restrained in its reporting (and had gone to interview that minister) lost credibility among people at large. They were agents of intelligence agencies, the rumour mills whispered.

NOTES

1. http://timesofindia.indiatimes.com/sa-aiyar/swaminomics/Independence-Day-for-Kashmir/articleshow/3372132.cms, accessed on 9 March 2016.
2. http://www.hindustantimes.com/columns/think-the-unthinkable/article1-331689.aspx, http://www.hindustantimes.com/india/think-the-unthinkable/story-Cy0vbBC97lKTYKL8cLfjxH.html, accessed on 25 June 2017.
3. 'The Hidden Intelligence Breakdowns Behind the Mumbai Attacks', Frontline and ProPublica, http://www.pbs.org/wgbh/pages/frontline/foreign-affairs-defense/american-terrorist/the-hidden-intelligence-breakdowns-behind-the-mumbai-attacks/, accessed on 25 June 2017.
4. The Dawat ul-Irshad Markaz was built on 200 acres near Lahore in 1987, when Zia-ul Haq was the dictator of Pakistan.
5. A senior professor at Kashmir University, who at the time hoped to be appointed a vice-chancellor, estimated the value at Rs 40,000 crore.
6. http://www.legislation.gov.uk/ukpga/1947/30/pdfs/ukpga_19470030_en.pdf, accessed on 24 January 2017.
7. Shah Faesal, *Indian Express*, 28 December 2016.
8. Article 3 of the J&K Constitution states that 'The State of Jammu and Kashmir is and shall be an integral part of the Union of India.'
9. http://www.rediff.com/news/report/two-militants-1-civilian-killed-in-encounter-in-kashmir/20150622.htm, http://indianexpress.com/article/india/india-news-india/south-kashmir-civilian-killed-in-clash-with-police-army/, accessed on 25 June 2017.

10. http://www.thehindu.com/news/national/other-states/dineshwar-sharma-flags-propaganda-on-tv/article22413701.ece, accessed on 8 February 2018) Sharma took up the matter after conversations that he had with a wide range of common Kashmiris over a couple of months made him conscious of how much damage these programmes did to India's interests.

11. http://www.firstpost.com/india/politicians-like-akbar-lone-fuel-violence-in-kashmir-valley-has-history-of-leaders-playing-both-mainstream-separat-ist-4345527.html, accessed on 12 February 2018.

12. http://kashmirguardian.com/separatist-geelanis-grandson-given-out-of-turn-job/, accessed on 28 May 2017.

13. http://www.outlookindia.com/website/story/mehbooba-government-supports-geelanis-grandsons-for-govt-job-while-kashmir-debat/298134, accessed on 28 May 2017.

11

MISPLACED RESPONSES

The Government of India tried in several ways to respond to the youth of Kashmir during the decade after 2007. But most of its initiatives were ill-advised. Some responses were based on such a poor reading of the complex situation that they actually strengthened the trends, processes, and forces that excited the fury of young Kashmiris. Several of these initiatives sustained the conflict economy. Although many of the policymakers and decision-makers who designed and approved these policies were well-intentioned, they simply did not understand the conflict economy, or the extent to which it caused violence to spiral. A few of the more cynical schemers with high stakes in that evil cauldron of corruption, exploitation, and repression were in the corridors of power. Some of their inputs may have been calculated to deviously ensure that even the 'solutions' kept the pot boiling.

India's Ministry of Home Affairs tended to depend on its Intelligence Bureau and the state police force for inputs on what needed to be done in the state. For decades, those inputs had lacked insight, imagination, and even, for the most part, basic information. Most often, the inputs focused on justifying whatever those forces had done—or neglected to do—and on seeking more funds and powers for those forces. When things seemed obviously to have gone wrong, the mandarins who ran the ministry fell back on the argument that they could not interfere, since the state was autonomous.

At times when Kashmir was raging with protest, as during the summers of 2008 and 2010, the ministry tended to have two sorts of responses: it would send more CRPF (since the mandarins were quite blind to the sort of hate and rage that the force generated) and lots more money. Having no idea how to spend that money to build a functional and responsive system, they disbursed much of it to police and paramilitary forces, the very faces of the Indian state that generated the most rage. Or, they disbursed money to various busybodies (quite often Kashmiris) who assured them that they would bring peace.

So impressed by such activists were some of the mandarins that a man at the pinnacle of the pyramid of mandarins wept in appreciation when he went to visit one of the NGOs in a remote part of Kashmir. He seemed very impressed with the self-help work the NGO did with women in that remote area, dominated by non-Kashmiri ethnic groups that were least likely to get involved with uprisings, at least in 2008 or 2010.

As for paramilitary forces, much money was spent on re-training CRPF units after the 2010 uprising. Although that re-training appeared to have done some good, the improvement did not last. Halfway through the uprising of 2016, some CRPF units again broke window panes in entire areas from which some stones had been pelted—just as they had in some phases of the 2010 uprising. This was evidently not an approved response. For, when a senior police officer tried to physically stop some paramilitary men from destroying property during the uprising of 2010, some of those men pushed him, tearing his star-studded shoulder epaulettes. It was direct and clear insubordination, for paramilitary platoons were meant to function under the control of district police officers.

The upgradation of equipment did not seem to help. In fact, it only added to the problem. After strenuous protests over the almost daily killing of one or two youths during the summer of 2010, the mandarins and politicians in charge did not seem to feel the need to investigate how and why that had happened, even though it had kept demonstrative rage stoked for weeks on end. Instead, they approved the purchase of pellet guns as 'non-lethal weapons' to be used in future. When pellet guns were used in 2016, they caused some fatalities. They also caused blindness among a lot of Kashmiri youth, and terrible bodily injuries. So, they caused another wave of rage.

One reason for the blindings was that the police and paramilitary forces generally did not seem to aim for the legs of protestors. Protestors tended to be hit on the chest or head—even by tear-gas canisters, which also caused fatalities. The local police did not apparently take the practice sessions mandated for them seriously. According to a young man who occasionally went to a police firing range to practice shooting, policemen sometimes used medical or other excuses to avoid the mandated annual practice. It did not seem to strike any of the mandarins or politicians charged with supervision that just getting the mandated system to function properly was the key challenge. This includes training, discipline, the sanctity of records, being accountable, sticking to standard operating procedures, and simply following rules. All this was far more important than the fire-fighting and high-spend responses they seemed to prefer—responses which, often enough, only kept the conflict economy stoked.

Such was the logic of governance that seriousness of purpose tended to be measured by how large one's budget allocations were, rather than how seriously one studied, understood, and engaged with issues. To some extent, the sharp focus on enhancing budgetary allocations stemmed from the unstated competition between the various ministries and forces which regarded 'the Kashmir issue' as their responsibility. It did not help that, at times, all of these competing ministries, forces, and agencies seemed to view it through the international prism of Pakistan, and so viewed and projected their expenditure on it as an effort to secure India from external enemies.

For a few years after the uprisings of 2008 and 2010, the Ministry of Home Affairs spent a vast amount of money to try and 'modernize' the police and paramilitary forces. For some years, the budget for upgradation of equipment for the police in 'terrorism affected' states was a whopping Rs 1,000 crore (ten billion rupees) a year. Since corruption was par for the course in these years, this was a powerful incentive for the cynically self-seeking to keep the situation on edge.

EARNEST INITIATIVES

From the time his party got the chief ministership of Jammu and Kashmir in 2006, Prime Minister Manmohan Singh tried earnestly to engage with people from across the state at several round table conferences. Many of the invitees tended to be those who had participated in the development of the existing situation. Their thinking tended to continue in the rut of how things had been done before. The organizers did not seem to see that a new generation was coming of age, one that had little regard for established political or social leaders—a generation, moreover, that was little understood by these established political and social figures.

Efforts were made to reach out to established 'separatist leaders' too. But, having responded to Vajpayee's overtures when India and Pakistan were earnestly engaged in negotiations for visionary peace-making, they had turned chary after a point. The several world powers which did not want that process to reach fruition may have played influencing roles. Pakistan too seemed uneasy by 2006, less confident about the new Indian government's political will and ability to walk the talk than it had been about Vajpayee.

Manmohan Singh announced 'zero tolerance' for excesses by the security forces, but backed down when the army refused (publicly on one occasion) to decrease deployment. In the weeks preceding the first of the prime minister's round table meetings, the former chief minister of the state, Mufti Sayeed, had been rudely condemned as 'anti-national' after he had called for a reduction in troop deployment. The generation that had been born in violence was coming of age—tired of the conflict, immune to fear, and full of aspirations. Generally, they perceived the huge deployment of troops as repressive, humiliating, and unreasonable.

As pointed out in Chapter 1, 'Endings and Beginnings', the killing of the Amar Singh College student at Dalgate was a turning point. The young man's behaviour in the bus, and his college mates' response the next day, were graphic indications that this generation would no longer tolerate deployment in excess of the requirement, particularly checking and frisking which they saw as intrusive and humiliating. In general, Kashmiris began to focus for the first time on special powers, which seemed unreasonable in the context of the much reduced militancy. Until about 2006, most Kashmiris used to look confused if one spoke of the Armed Forces Special Powers Act (AFSPA); most of them had no idea what it was at that stage. During the subsequent decade, it became a major talking point.

LACUNA IN EDUCATION

To the prime minister and his advisors, dealing with Kashmir apparently involved tinkering with formal structural links between political and geopolitical units—states and regions. The people were apparently not in focus. The Indian state did not seem to have become aware yet that the established 'separatist leaders' had no clear idea, collectively, of the road ahead. Nor did the earnest and well-meaning among decision makers seem to realize the size or depth of the conflict economy, or the array of vested interests that were involved with it—including some of those who advised them.

The government should have focused sharply on education and the narratives that young people were receiving from television and other sources. Telephony was just picking up; and, along with it, access to the internet. It was just the time when narratives about the global oppression of Muslims were coalescing, and narratives about the situation in Kashmir were being vigorously generated. It was also just the time when the physical infrastructure for education—new or expanded schools, new colleges, and new universities—had increased rapidly, across the state. It was apparent that quality faculty and educational tools did not match the brick-and-mortar structures that had been built during Mufti's stint as chief minister. His successor, Ghulam Nabi Azad, turned his attention to other kinds of infrastructure—roads, bridges, administrative buildings—mainly in the Jammu region of the state, from which he hailed and where he hoped to gain political advantage.

Meanwhile, some of the new educational institutions which the state had established struggled for lack of funds. Politics appeared to be at play. So, for example, the new Islamic University of Science and Technology (IUST), which the state Waqf Board had set up at Awantipora in south Kashmir, was starved of funds. The University had been established through an act of the state assembly. Getting it started—in a school building—was among the last things Mufti Sayeed did during that stint as chief minister. Since the chief minister was also the chairman of the Waqf Board, it was up to Azad, who took over from Mufti as chief minister, to nurture the institution. He did not. He seemed to view IUST as a project of his predecessor. Indeed, it was in the heart of south Kashmir, the stronghold of the PDP, over which the Mufti family presided. It was precisely in south Kashmir that the new militancy came to be centred just a few years later.[1]

After the 2008 and 2010 uprisings, New Delhi sanctioned a world class Indian Institute of Management, and a Central University (run by the federal government) for the state. After a heated wrangle between 'leaders' of the Jammu region and of the Kashmir region, that was converted to a Central University for each region. Omar Abdullah, who was chief minister by then, arranged land for the Central University in the Valley on wetland at the edge of his constituency. Whereas the IUST was more than 40 km from the older Kashmir University, this site was less than 20 km from Kashmir University. Some Kashmiris said a site ought to have been identified further north, so that students from those areas could have had access to a university. But politics was in play again, they held. In response to such complaints, a 'north campus' of Kashmir University was established at Delina near Baramulla in the north, but it did not seem to be a very active hub of learning and education.

As the government increased the brick-and-mortar infrastructure of education while neglecting the crying need for educational aides, resources, and faculty enhancement programmes, things had come to such a pass after 2010 that the then chief minister, Omar Abdullah, said publicly that the state faced not only a problem of unemployment but also 'unemployability'.

THE MEANING OF EMPLOYMENT

After the uprising of 2008, unemployment was identified as a major reason for young people pelting stones. A number of schemes were initiated to provide livelihood to young men. The prime minister set up a committee chaired by the former governor of the Reserve Bank of India, C. Rangarajan, to explore ways to create jobs and develop skills among youth in the state. In 2011, a scheme called Udaan (flight) was established as a result of the committee's recommendations. The scheme was to train up to 100,000 young Kashmiris over the next five years, so that they might be placed in suitable jobs in different parts of India. The Committee also recommended scholarships for 25,000 students over the next five years.[2]

Five years later, the uprising that followed the killing of Burhan underlined the extent to which the schemes had failed. In fact, they had been misconceived from the start. Far from a hundred thousand, only a couple of hundred young men had actually remained employed in the placements that had been found for them under the scheme; most of those found the emoluments inadequate. The Udaan scheme had not reached nearly as many young men as it was meant to. Those who ran the scheme travelled all over the Valley in search of young men to recruit for training. After a lot of persuasion, some joined the training programme, and some even went for internships. But it was clear that the committee that came up with the scheme had misunderstood the meaning of unemployment in the context of Jammu and Kashmir. Nor had they taken on board the conflict economy from which many—particularly those who had grown up in it—wanted to gain benefits for themselves.

So a 'job' quite often meant a secure and pensionable government job, one that turned one into a part of the network of power and influence. When people spoke of a 'job', they often had in mind something that allowed them to do favours, disburse patronage, to be on the ladder of hierarchy that could command social respect, that could jump queues of all sorts. The word 'job' had less to do with work than the power to move or impede a file—for government functions had, in most minds, been reduced to bureaucratic red tape. For the most part, a 'job' was about a designation, so that one could feel important, be treated with servility, and treat others with contempt.

Of course, this was a large part of the lived reality of their society that so enraged those young people who were not a part of the network of power and influence. It did not, however, stop a large number of them from aspiring to become a part of that repressive yet alluring set-up, stultifying for others but satisfying for those who occupied its seats of power and influence—under whichever overarching state power.

For many, a large part of the attraction of a government 'job' was the opportunity it might offer for corruption. This meant that the salary a 'job' offered was a much smaller part of its allure than the potential for extra income. So, several instances were cited of persons who gave up a higher salary in the private sector for a lower paying job in government.

The Government of India appeared to have no idea of the ground situation, the meaning of expressed sentiments, and of words such as 'unemployed'—for at least some of those who used such words. Even six years after it had launched and tried to implement the Udaan scheme, the Government of India was still apparently blind to the reasons why the scheme was not taking off.

On the sidelines of a conference on economic issues facing the state, one of India's senior economic policymakers said that the government needed to figure out the optimal salary level at which Kashmiri youth would be happy to take up jobs in other parts of the country. He said this while talking informally at a lunch table during the conference at the end of October 2017. Inadequate pay, compared with the cost of living, was a reason that had been given by many of the young men who had returned to Kashmir after a short orientation or internship at a company in Delhi or some other part of the country. The reason had been given repeatedly by young men over the past five years. Even after several years, the government had apparently not figured out the patterns that lay behind the argument.

The Rangarajan Committee, which had recommended Udaan and related schemes, might have understood the meaning of 'job' and 'employment' if it had dug deeper. But it did not investigate sufficiently the discrepancies it noted between the figures of the employment bureaus in the state and of the National Sample Survey Office regarding the number of unemployed in the state. The committee certainly discovered the discrepancy, for the first chapter of its report reads like a long lament over its inability to make sense of the differing figures.

The committee ought to have applied the brakes when it discovered the discrepancy, and not moved ahead until it had resolved the contradiction. It needed to understand what the word meant to persons who registered themselves as 'unemployed'. It might have found that several of those who described themselves as 'unemployed' in fact had jobs in the private sector, or ran small businesses, or had substantial incomes from horticulture.

A young man who visited me in Srinagar around the time the Rangarajan Committee was engaged in its labours described himself as being in 'economic crisis'. It turned out, however, that he was a teacher in a private school, that his family ran a shop, and had annual income from their saffron crop. He was a bachelor, and lived in the family home near the farm. Despite all this, he repeated several times that he was in an 'economic crisis', almost as if he had no income or sustenance at all. To understand the meanings of words the way they were used was vital, more so in an age of discourse shaped by Derrida and then post-truth.

The primary purpose of the young visitor's meeting with me was to talk about his prospects. During our conversation, it turned out that one of the reasons why he craved a government 'job' was that it would hugely help his prospects of a 'good' match in marriage. That was one of the issues in Kashmiri society. The security and the pension of a government 'job' were much in demand, not only for the one seeking the job but also among those looking for a 'suitable' groom (and, in some cases, bride) for marriage.

ECONOMIC CHANGES

The Committee recommended a range of initiatives to expand agriculture, tourism, handicraft, horticulture, and animal husbandry. It seemed oblivious to the fact that all these sectors of production were in decline, except horticulture. In fact, large tracts of land were being converted in this phase from agriculture to either orchards or for the construction of concrete buildings. The effect was that Kashmir's traditional koshur bhatha rice was barely available in the market. Apples had become the major crop—and, in some years, almond and walnut production too flourished. Animal husbandry too had declined. Most consumers now depended on factory-packaged milk, yoghurt, and other dairy products. Hundreds of trucks carried chickens to Kashmir every day, mostly from Punjab.

The labour market had changed dramatically since the turn of the century. Wage rates for daily labour in Kashmir were higher than in other parts of India. Most of the labour working in Kashmir were now from other states. Labour from certain states were far more common as domestic workers than ever in the past. Most of the plumbers in Kashmir were from Odisha, carpenters from certain districts in Punjab, and barbers from Bijnor district in UP. So dependent had many become on migrant labour that one of the few times there was an uproar of protest against a statement from Syed Ali Shah Geelani during the decade after 2007 was when he publicly called for guest workers to leave Kashmir.

The Committee spoke of a long-term plan to promote Information Technology, including BPOs, in the state. That was a good idea but, as the Committee noted in the same report, this hinged on a peaceful environment and infrastructure. Lacking a grounded sense of the roots of rage among young Kashmiris, it was unlikely that the government could provide a peaceful environment. Indeed, a new militancy had already germinated when the Committee submitted its report to the chief minister of the state. In a couple of years thereafter, a new militancy had well and truly arrived.[3]

As for infrastructure, power supply remained a major problem for at least five years after the Rangarajan Committee completed its work—particularly in the winter months, when electricity was most acutely missed. Although internet connectivity was widely used, the government had taken to routinely shutting down net connectivity—or at least slowing speed—during times of unrest. At times, this could go on for several weeks on end.

ELUSIVE ENTREPRENEURSHIP

The government spent a vast amount of money on an Entrepreneurship Development Institute (EDI). It was housed in a huge building, with large adjacent residential blocks, on the main highway on the outskirts of Srinagar. The EDI ran courses for a few weeks, during which trainees were expected to submit a proposal for an enterprise. Chosen proposals were meant to get funding from the government-run J&K Bank and some incubation facilities. After it had functioned for several years, there was no sign that a spirit of enterprise had been sparked, or that new companies had come up in Kashmir. It was a white elephant that twice drew attacks from the new militants—who evidently did not see it as promoting opportunities for their generation.

Economist Haseeb Drabu, who was Jammu and Kashmir's Finance Minister from 2015 to 2018, had said in 2005 that the J&K Bank (of which he was at the time the chairman) had a number of schemes to not only finance entrepreneurs, but also incubation programmes to hold the hands of entrepreneurs who took loans, to walk them through the difficult start-up period.[4] But, he added that nobody wanted to invest and wait for returns; people wanted profits the next day.

BUREAUCRATIC ARROGANCE

Within Kashmir, the network of power and influence not only dominated the environment, it either sucked in or repressed those who lived under its enveloping shadowy shroud. The economic policymaker from New Delhi left after that informal chat at the lunch table during that conference, but he might have found the next session revealing. A senior bureaucrat rolled out an impressive array of statistics. Then, an entrepreneur who had returned to Kashmir from the US to invest in a high-yield crop described the road-blocks he had faced on his very bumpy journey of enterprise in Kashmir. He had been shown a large number of plots of land from which to choose one for his high-yield crops. He could buy any of those plots he liked at a competitive price, he was told. So he selected the best plot with great care. When he returned to that government office a few days later with his heart set on that plot, he was told that plot had already been reserved by someone. He could select another. It seemed that an extra price needed to be paid under the table to get a preferred plot.

The body language of the two panellists as they stood outside the conference centre after that discussion was telling. The civil servant stood expansively on the drive, exuding an air of entitlement—unlike the body language of the policymaker from New Delhi. The entrepreneur's posture seemed clenched; he held his arms tight against his chest.

OUTSIZED GOVERNMENT

Since the early 1990s, the Government of India had argued for less govern-ment and more governance. It would have done well to implement that slogan in Kashmir. Instead, it repeatedly provided funds for more and more employment within the vast spread of government activities, ranging from administration to engineering to medical facilities to gardening to tourism-related work to agricultural services to police work of one sort or another.

Meanwhile, instead of improving educational infrastructure, faculty, and methods, the government spent vast amounts to encourage students from Kashmir to study elsewhere. A large number of scholarships were announced, which the prime minister's office was to pay. The Rs 1,200 crore which the expert Committee had recommended for the scholarship programme was meant to cover not only full tuition fees, but also books. When students were admitted to various universities across India, some of them found that the scholarship amounts did not always reach them or those universities. That led to a certain amount of resentment.

In particular, the Rangarajan Committee recommended that prestigious institutions such as the Delhi Public School be encouraged to reserve a few seats for students from the state. While it was good for outstanding students from the state to be provided quality education, such moves did nothing to address larger concerns regarding the situation in Kashmir. Those students who might aspire to work for the private sector would prefer larger companies, including multinationals, rather than to return to work in Kashmir.

On the other hand, the home ministry of India spent a large amount of money to build a separate hostel for Kashmiri students at the Muslim-majority Jamia Millia Islamia university in Delhi. To place Kashmiri students in ghettos in different parts of India, even in broadly Muslim environments, seemed counter-intuitive. Somehow, the priorities and thrust concerns of government policies had become tangled up.

CONTINUING BLINDNESS

Even after the agitation of 2016, policymakers did not seem to realize that they had been on the wrong track after the agitations of 2008 and 2010. Nor did they seem to take on board that the three uprisings marked a progression. The 2008 agitations were in response to a perceived threat to Kashmiri identity, while 2010 was essentially a protest against the murder of persons not involved with militancy, and the misrepresentation of those murders as counterinsurgency operations. The agitations of 2016 were actually a little less intense than those of 2010, but they marked a huge progression. For, stone-pelting had become intertwined with a new militancy. Starting from 2015, people often used stones to attack soldiers engaged in battle with militants—to divert the focus of those soldiers, to allow those militants to escape, and to delegitimize the forces' operations by forcing them to fire on non-militants. So, while the 2010 agitation was essentially a scream of frustration that the rule of law was not upheld, many of those involved in the 2016 agitation had given up on the rule of law. They had discarded the system altogether.

It is important to understand this progression—and the failure of various initiatives ranging from Sadbhavana to Udaan—if one is to make sense of what happens ahead, and respond meaningfully. The tragic fact, however, is that it suits a range of analysts on various sides to view the agitations of this decade as repetitive events—with the same cause, representing the same aspiration, and calling for the same response. Those who wish to promote Kashmiri freedom have used an unchanging, un-nuanced, and inflexible narrative of victims and oppressors during this decade. In the view of most hardline Indian nationalists, on the other hand, Kashmir is a story of rebels challenging the state—ceaselessly, reflexively, without reason or context. Their narrative too is inflexible and without nuance. Both sorts of analysts see it as Muslims against Hindus. In addition, hardline Indian nationalists tend to see Kashmir through the prism of Pakistan.

To them, even the agitations of 2008 were whipped up by Pakistan. Spokespersons of the Congress party, which ruled India at that time, said so publicly at the time. That only angered Kashmiris further, provoking more furious demonstrations. For, in 2008, it was not true. Pakistan, which was in the throes of a wrenching domestic regime change, was probably taken by surprise by the uprising in Kashmir—as were various established leaders of the freedom movement even within Kashmir. But projecting it as 'Pakistan-sponsored terrorism' suited policymakers. It gave them temporary political relief by deflecting public attention from their blind and unresponsive governance to the machinations of an enemy country.

By 2016, Pakistani handlers were actually in the driver's—or navigator's—seat. That year's uprising was probably coordinated from there. This time, it was intertwined with the militancy which had grown afresh after 2008. This was a different militancy from the one that had petered out by 2007. Its patterns were different. So was its demographic. And its tactics. Although this militancy was intertwined to some extent with stone-pelting demonstrations, it would be a mistake to think that the entire population, or even all youth, supported it. As the survey described in Chapter 4, 'Varied Opinions', makes clear, aspirations as well as attitudes to militancy were different at different times—and differed across different people even at the same point in time.

Even though Pakistan may have been manipulating events in the Valley by 2016 and after, it was a mistake to continue to view the people of Kashmir solely through that prism. But so stuck in their simplistic black-and-white view of the situation were many statist analysts that they continued to interpret agitations in 2017 and 2018 too solely through the prism of Pakistan's war-like manoeuvres against India. Those who said that in 2008 were wrong. Those who said it in 2016 and after were right, but only partially. Agitations may be coordinated from Pakistan, but only the chief organizers within Kashmir would know that. Among most Kashmiris, there was relatively little support for the idea of merging Kashmir with Pakistan—however high-pitched protests might be, and whatever the rhetoric, symbols, and narratives of those protests. Cynical exploitation and repression had created a pool of rage that could be easily harnessed.

SHARPENED CONFLICT

Conflict increased sharply in Kashmir from 8 April 2017, when eight people were killed during clashes around polling booths for a parliamentary by-election.[5] On the surface, the stone-pelting and other acts of resistance that day were meant to tell the world that Kashmiris had rejected elections held under the aegis of India. However, the public statements of youth leaders such as Zakir Musa made it clear over the next few weeks that those acts of resistance were against democracy as a system, for Islam, and against 'kafirs'.[6] Some hard-line nationalists confused any sort of Islamism, indeed Muslims in general, with Pakistan. This was a mistake. Pan-Islamism of Musa's kind rejected Pakistan too.

Political activists at the grass-roots level were murdered in that period. Some of these had been extraordinarily responsive to common people without access to the network of power and influence.[7] Other targets included law officers who had prosecuted terrorists in the past;[8] the chief targets were Kashmiri policemen and politicians.[9] It was mainly Kashmiri militants who had showed their hand until the spring of 2018, but a very large number of Pakistani terror agents lurked in the vicinity of Hajin, Bandipora, Sopore, Baramulla, Rafiabad, Langate, and other parts of north Kashmir. The grapevine in Kashmir held that hundreds of fresh ones had crossed the LoC that year, even before the snow melted and passes opened in May. Large numbers had already crossed the LoC over the past three years. Most of them crossed the Shamsabari range, but some were said to have come via Dras and Tuleil. Their sheer numbers made for a nightmare scenario. The grapevine also spoke of more heavy duty weapons than had been common during the previous decade, even machine guns. But neither the sheer numbers nor the quality of weapons was the most potent aspect of the violence that seemed to lie ahead. The distress among youth was far more potent.

Most adults were not enthused, but the tragic effect of the cycle of killings was that the majority of Kashmiris—including most adults and women—were sidelined. Many of their elders were extremely uneasy about the radical world views that animated the millennial generation, who were the bulwark of the new militancy after 2016. But, faced by sharp extremes of the simplistic sort discussed in Chapter 10, 'Hateful Polarization', adult Kashmiri Muslims in general were left with no option but to go along with the boys. The nuanced truth about the earlier militancy needed to be acknowledged in order to give the silent majority a reasonable opportunity to contest radical Islamism while they still could. They had a very narrow window, and it was fast closing.

NOTES

1. The author had close interactions on a daily basis for a few months in the summer of 2007, during which he held charge of students' welfare at the University.
2. http://www.igovernment.in/articles/32698/panel-rolls-out-job-plan-for-kashmiri-youth, acessed on 29 January 2018.
3. https://www.hindustantimes.com/india/the-betrayal-of-hope/story-6WMX-q16zQlLQX2JT1WnSCO.html, accessed on 31 January 2018.
4. Author's interview with Haseeb Drabu in the office of the Chairman, J&K Bank, during the making of a documentary film in August 2005.
5. http://www.hindustantimes.com/india-news/bypolls-in-8-states-triggersviolence-in-2-clashes-in-srinagar-kill-7-as-voter-turnout-hits-less-than-10/story-V5tp2N7ISX4VoEIbsyBtQI.html, accessed on 14 June 2017.
6. https://www.youtube.com/watch?v=Qhb4cDCzQbM, accessed on 25 June 2017.
7. The celebrated government official Shah Faesal posted on Facebook on 13 March 2017:

    A few years back when I was posted in Pulwama, there were two Sarpanchs both named Fayaz, both young, both public spirited and both from the same locality of Kakapora. One was taller than the other and one was more hysterical than the other. I would often see them coming to DC Office with issues related to ordinary lives of ordinary people.

    Then last year the shorter Fayaz was suddenly shot dead. And today the taller Fayaz has been killed in cold blood. I had not talked to them since I got transferred from there. But their death has terrified me. ... (https://www.facebook.com/shah.faesal.3?ref=br_rs, accessed on 14 June 2017).

8. http://risingkashmir.com/news/lawyer-killed-in-shopian-, accessed on 14 June 2017.
9. http://indiatoday.intoday.in/story/pdp-abdul-gani-shot-in-pulwama-jammuand-kashmir-srinagar/1/936678.html, accessed on 14 June 2017.

Index

Abdullah, Farooq, 97–98, 154

Abdullah, Omar, 31–33, 35, 71, 100, 129, 158, 205

Abdullah, Sheikh, 31, 189,

Accountability Commission, 143

Advani, L.K., 108

Afghanistan, 17, 86, 93, 177

Ahle-Hadith movement, 15, 66, 72, 80,. 87–88, 91

Ahmad, Bashir, 162

Ahmad, Israr, 88

Aiyar, Swaminathan A., 184

Akhrani, Mohammed Maqbool, 87

Alam, Masarat, 96, 132

Al Badr group, 24

Al Baghdadi, Abu Bakar, 87

Al Qaeda, 83,

Ali, Mohsin Haider, 53

Amar Singh College, Kashmir, 7

Anantnag, 53, 56, 76, 87, 133, 154, 162–63

Andrabi, Jaleel, 119, 161

Antony, A.K., 171

APDP. *See* Association of the Parents of Disappeared Persons

Armed Forces Special Powers Act, 117, 204

Arms Act, 27

Army Goodwill School, 156

Association of the Parents of Disappeared Persons (APDP), 172

Azad, Ghulam Nabi, 204

'azadi' (freedom), 29, 61–62, 64, 70, 98, 111, 131, 147, 180

Baghdadi, Abu Bakar Al, 87

Baramulla, 22, 25, 205, 215, 64, 74, 76

Beijing Olympics, 17

Bharatiya Jana Sangh, 105

Bharatiya Janata Party (BJP), 36, 90, 103

Bhat, Abdul Ghani, 182

Bhat, Hilal, 163–64

Bhat, Muzaffar, 131–32

Bhat, Sabzar, 26, 82

Bhat, Zakir, 80

Bhutto, Benazir, 194; assassination of, 3

BJP. *See* Bharatiya Janata Party

black economy, 145

Bloeria, Sudhir, 144

Border Security Force (BSF), 27, 64, 73, 119–20, 173, 186–87

bureaucratic arrogance, 210–11

Business Line, 38

Business Standard, 124

caliphate law, 79

'Cargo', 126

Central Reserve Police Force (CRPF), 7, 113, 201

Cheeni Chowk, 162–65

Cheney, Dick, 197

Chidambaram, P., 13–14

Chinar Bagh, 134

CID intelligence, 147

CIK, 147

Civic Action Programme, 158

conflict zone, 105

corruption, 144, 150, 153–54, 202

counterinsurgency discourses, 89–91

counterproductive strategy, 110–12

crackdown, 42–45

CRPF. *See* Central Reserve Police Force

currency denomination, 139

cyber telephony, 14–16

cynicism in new generation, 166–67

Dalgate, 8–9, 52, 203

Dal Lake, 127

Delhi: atrocious event, 9

Delhi Public School, 212

Downtown, 38

drugs: abuse, 49; smuggling of, 163

Dulat, A.S., 100, 109

Dujana, Abu, 139

economic changes, 209–10

education system, 50–52; lacuna in 203–05

employment, 206–08

empowerment, 28, 47

'encounter death', 8–9

'Engineer', 126–27

Entrepreneurship Development Institute (EDI), 210

exclusionary binaries, 180

extortion, 135, 151,

Facebook, 14, 25, 28, 68

Faesal, Shah, 189

Farooq, Mirwaiz Umar, 96–97

floods, 102, 103, 104

Freedom Movement (Tehreek-e-Hurriyat), 181

free trade, 3

Frontline magazine, 168–71

fudged records, 126–28

Gandhi, Sonia, 13

Geelani, Syed Ali Shah, 7, 71, 81, 96, 111, 132, 209

generational change, 33–35

Governance Now, 54

Government Higher Secondary School, 74

government job, 208

Guru Nanak, 67

Hajam, Mohammed Sidiq, 122
Hanafi group, 67
Haq, Zia-ul, 176
hawala, 138
Hindus, 67–68; conflict between
  Muslims and, 16; Hindutva-based
  anti-Muslim forces, 61; Pandits, 68,
  117; Rashtriya Swayamsevak Sangh
  (RSS), 91
Hindustan Times, 184
historical narratives, 188–90
Hizb ul Mujahideen group, 26, 80, 84,
  91, 138
Hooda, D.S. (Lt General), 29, 145, 174
Hurriyat Conference, 59, 70, 81,
  96, 182
Hurriyat group 140, 143, 150
Hussein, Saddam, 197

Ikhwan groups, 122–23
incentives for deployment, 154–55
India: blindness of Indian state, 10–13;
  vs. Kashmir, 180–81
Indian Army, 15, 29, 43, 118,119, 168,
  173–74, 230
Indian Independence Act, 1947, 189
Indian Police Service, 150
In Search of a Future, 142
insurgency, 12, 20, 116–17
Intelligence Bureau, 200
intergenerational conflict, 49
ISI, 91
Islam, Nazar-ul, 45
Islami Jamiat-e-Tulaba, 104

Islamic State, 34
Islamic University of Science and
  Technology (IUST), 205
Islamist: exclusivism, 33; fashionable
  ideas, 65–67; Jamaat-e-Islami, 36;
  other faith, 67–68
Israel, 15

J&K Bank, 210
Jaish-e-Mohammed, 24, 83
Jamaat-e-Islami group, 53, 140, 156,
  66–67, 80, 87–88, 91, 101, 104,
  140, 153
Jamia mosque, 104
Jammu, 63
Jamwal, Anuradha Bhasin, 169
Jan, Omar, 39, 41
Jan, Waseem, 121
jihad—jihad-e-awwal, 65

Kashmir Images, 157
Kashmir Times, 169
Kashmir University, 42, 83, 134, 205
Kashmiris; new generation, 4–5,
  self-worth, 10
Kenwood tracker system, 120
Khaliq, Abdul, 124
Khan, Bashir Ahmed, 121
Khanday, Fardeen Ahmed, 84
Khanday, Imtiaz, 40–41
Khan, Naeem, 110
Khan, Shaukat, 169
Khan, Tanveer Hussain, 146–47, 154
Khrew, 145

Kokernag, 1, 167, 170

Kulgam, 76

Kumar, Ghulam Hasan, 126

Kupwara, 76

Ladakh, 63

language, 5, 49, 52, 62–63, 74, 82, 211

Lashkar-e-Taiba, 83, 138, 169–70, 173, 184

Line of Control (LoC), 23–24, 41, 137–38, 144, 215

linguistic-ethnic identity, 61

LoC. *See* Line of Control

Lolab, 1

madrasas, 59, 87

Maharaja Bazar, 109

Malik, Yasin, 96

Marwah, Naresh, 114

Masoodi, Maulana, 86–88, 91, 182

mass rage, formative factors, 32–33

Maududi, Maulana, 88, 91

media platforms, 25, 68, 191–92

Ministry for Human Resource Development, 172

Ministry of Home Affairs, 200

Ministry of Rural Development, 130

Mir, Manzoor Ahmed, 41

Mishra, Brajesh, 100

mobile telephony, 14–16

Modi, Narendra, 103

Mohammed, Khushi, 41

Mufti, Mehbooba, 35

mujahid, 44, 84, 91

mukhbir, 117

Mukhdoomi, Javid, 5–6, 115

Murtaza, Mohammed, 122

Musa, Zakir, 8, 81–88, 91–92, 194, 214–15

Musharraf, Parvez, 12, 92, 156

Muslims, 80, 85–86, 89; conflict between Hindus and, 18; Kashmiris as, 62; romanticization, 67

Naik, Zakir, 88

narratives 13, 32, 36, 41, 71, 80, 88–89, 114, 116, 161, 171, 175, 181, 187, 188–89, 192–97, 204

National Conference, 101

National Investigation Agency, India, 109, 142

National Law School, Bangalore, 172

National Rural Employment Guarantee Scheme, 131

National Rural Health Mission, 131

Nehru, Jawaharlal, 189

Nepal, 144

NGO. *See* non-governmental organizations

9/11 attacks, 184

Nisar, Qazi, 104, 229

non-governmental organizations (NGOs), 141, 201

Non-Involvement Certificate, 146

'occupation force', 16
Operation Eagle, 119, 126
'Operation Sadbhavana', 157
Operation Tiger, 119, 126
oppression narratives, 186–88

Paddar, Abdul Rehman, 168
Paddar, Saddam, 85
Pakistan: ISI of, 11, 184–85; Lashkar-e-Taiba, 83, 184; Nepal and, 144; peace process with India, 3, 30, 182–83, 213; salaries and loot, 140–42; self-fulfilling prophecy, 11, suiting, 193–95
Pampore, 145
Pandey, R., 169
Pandits, 48, 68, 117
Para, Waheed ur Rehman, 118–20
Parihar, H.R., 168
Parimpora, 126
Parray, Kuka, 131
PDP. *See* People's Democratic Party
PDP–BJP alliance, 36
peace process: Atal Behari Vaipayee, 3, 34, 203; India and Pakistan, 3, 30, 182–83, 203
People's Democratic Party (PDP), 36, 90
Pillai, G.K., 161
police: Indian Police Service, 150; nuanced view of forces, 75; perceptions about, 77–78; 'Ponda police', 33; Special Operations

Police, 33; Special Police Officers, 148; Special Task Force, 27
Police Academy, Sher-e-Kashmir, Udhampur, 150
Prophet of Islam, 51
Public Safety Act (PSA), 27, 31
Pulwama, 34, 53, 56, 70, 76, 84, 90, 97, 178

Qasim, Abu, 139
Qazigund, 76
Qureshi, Fazl Haq, 110

Rangarajan, C., 206, 208
Rangarajan Committee, 209, 212
Rashid, Abdul, 126
Rashtriya Rifles (RR), 120, 163, 168–69
Rashtriya Swayamsevak Sangh (RSS), 91
Rehbar-e-Sehat scheme, 131
Rehman, Haji Abdul, 118–19
Reshi, Marryam H., 38–40
risk, national security, 146–48
RSS. *See* Rashtriya Swayamsevak Sangh
rural–urban gap, 64

SAARC. *See* South Asian Association for Regional Cooperation
Sadbhavana, 157–59, 213
Safapora, 122–25, 157,
Salafi, Ashiq, 87
Salafism, 66, 87

Sanghvi, Vir, 184

Sayeed, Hafiz, 82, 185,

Sayeed, Mufti Mohammad, 5, 14, 71, 100, 102–03, 119, 183

'secessionists', 106, 108, 137

separatist movement, 95

Shah, Amit, 102

Shah, Shabir, 105, 109

Sharda University, Noida, 41

Shariat law, 79

Sharif, Nawaz, 103

Sheikh, Ali Mohammed, 123

Sheikh, Ghulam Mohammad, 7

Sheikh, Hamid, 109

Shia, 66

Shopian, south Kashmir, 1, 22, 27, 87, 99–100 137

Sikhs, 67

Singh, Avtar, 119

Singh, Manmohan, 100, 108, 126, 203

Singh, V.K., 171

social alienation, 47

social changes, 47

social cohesion, 47, 106

social media, 195

social norms, 80

social space, 52–53

social transformation, 47–49, 64

Sofi, Ghulam Mohammed, 165

SOG. *See* Special Operations Group

Sopore, 22, 25

South Asian Association for Regional Cooperation (SAARC), 3

Special Operations Group (SOG), 26, 98, 123, 164

Special Operations Police, 33

Special Police Officers (SPOs), 148

Special Task Force, 27

SPOs. *See* Special Police Officers

Srinagar, 38, 76

Srinagar Times, 165

State Human Rights Commission, Jammu and Kashmir, 172

'stone-pelters' treated as criminals, 11, 28, 182; in Newa, 34

stone-pelting, 34, 152, 212; responses, 71–73

Sunnis, 66

systemic distortions, 115–16

Tablighi Jamaat group, 15, 45, 86, 88

talashi party, 43

talashi wala, 43

Tehreek-e-Hurriyat, 81

televangelism, 80

Thakur, Khushal Singh, 124

Tiananmen Square, 102

timber-smuggling operations, 170

The Times of India, 165, 184

torture, xv–xvi, 9, 20, 22, 27, 44, 45, 64, 117, 118, 120, 124, 133, 187, 195

Tral, 22, 76, 185

Transparency International, 154

trauma: at birth, 53–58; extortion and, 122

Turey, Zubair Bashir, 27, 139–40
26/11 attacks, Mumbai, 184
Twitter, 195

Udaan scheme, 205, 208, 213
United States (US), 15, 17, 184, 197
University Grants Commission, 172
urban–rural differences, 64

Vaid, S.P., 90
Vaipayee, Atal Behari, 78, 93 100,
    104, 108, 132, 174–75, 203; peace
    process, 34, 203
Veeri, Maulana Mushtaq, 87–88
Vohra, N.N., 171
Wahab, Mohammed ibn Abdul, 86
wahadat, 67

Wani, Burhan, 25–26, 79, 84, 113,
    151, 185
Wani, Nazar-ul Islam, 42, 45
'War on Terror', 15
WhatsApp, 195
wazwan, 52, 143, 145
Winning Hearts and Minds (WHAM)
    programme, 156
women's rights, 68–69

youth alienation, 150–53

Zahid, Abu, 169
Zaki, M.A. (Lt General), 49,
    174
zero tolerance, 203
Zia-ul Haq, 176

About the Author

David Devadas is a Distinguished Fellow of the Institute of Social Sciences, New Delhi, India and Contributing Editor at the leading independent news portal Firstpost. He has been a Visiting Professor at Jamia Millia Islamia, Delhi, India; Senior Fellow at the Nehru Memorial Museum and Library, New Delhi, India; and Political Editor at *Business Standard*.

Devadas has reported and analysed Kashmir in depth, having lived there for long periods to undertake extensive research. He has edited Kashmir's largest English language daily, and participated in establishing the Islamic University of Science and Technology at Awantipora. His books, documentaries, columns, and articles have given new perspectives to understand both the history of Kashmir and the contemporary situation there. An authority on Kashmir, his predictions on the situation in the region have proven consistently true since 1988.

An expert on geopolitics and strategic affairs, Devadas has travelled to more than fifty countries. He has written incisive analyses of contemporary events, including trends in Syria, Turkey, the refugee crisis, Brexit, and German politics. He covered the first Reagan–Gorbachev summit in Geneva in 1985, the Conference on Disarmament which drafted the Comprehensive Test Ban Treaty in 1996, the United Nations General Assembly, and several summit meetings, including Prime Minister Atal Behari Vajpayee's historic visit to Lahore in 1999.